The rise and fall of the Orange Order during the Famine years

The rise and fall of the Orange Order during the Famine years

From reformation to Dolly's Brae

Daragh Curran

FOUR COURTS PRESS

Typeset in 10.5 pt on 13.5 pt AGaramondPro by
Carrigboy Typesetting Services for
FOUR COURTS PRESS LTD
7 Malpas Street, Dublin 8, Ireland
www.fourcourtspress.ie
and in North America for
FOUR COURTS PRESS
c/o IPG, 814 N Franklin St, Chicago, IL 60610.

A catalogue record for this title is available
from the British Library.

ISBN 978-1-84682-864-5

SPECIAL ACKNOWLEDGMENT

This publication has been made possible by financial assistance from the
Ulster Local History Trust.

Printed in England
CPI Antony Rowe Ltd, Chippenham, Wilts.

Contents

ABBREVIATIONS 6

ACKNOWLEDGMENTS 9

INTRODUCTION 11

1 The first forty years 16

2 Dissolution and reformation 72

3 Famine and unrest 114

4 Overtures from Young Ireland 147

5 Dolly's Brae and its fallout 175

CONCLUSION 204

BIBLIOGRAPHY 207

INDEX 217

Abbreviations

NAI: Outrage Reports	National Archives of Ireland: Chief Secretary's Office Registered Papers: Outrage Reports
PRONI	The Public Record Office of Northern Ireland
AC	*Anglo Celt*
AG	*Armagh Guardian*
BCC	*Belfast Commercial Chronicle*
BN	*Belfast Newsletter*
BOU	*Banner of Ulster*
BPJ	*Belfast Protestant Journal*
CC	*Coleraine Chronicle*
C Con	*Cork Constitution*
CCS	*Constitution and Church Sentinel*
CE	*Cork Examiner*
DCJ	*Drogheda Conservative Journal*
DD	*Dundalk Democrat*
DEM	*Dublin Evening Mail*
DEP	*Dublin Evening Packet*
ECEP	*Enniskillen Chronicle and Erne Packet*
FJ	*Freeman's Journal*
KI	*Kilkenny Independent*
LJ	*Londonderry Journal and Tyrone Advertiser*
L Sen	*Londonderry Sentinel*
LS	*Londonderry Standard*
NELA	*Newry Examiner and Louth Advertiser*
NG	*Nenagh Guardian*
NS	*Northern Standard*
NT	*Newry Telegraph*
NW	*Northern Whig*
PW	*The Protestant Watchman*
TC	*Tyrone Constitution*
UI	*United Irishman*
VIN	*The Vindicator*
WC	*Wexford Conservative*

PARLIAMENTARY PAPER ABBREVIATIONS

Select committee of Ireland report
Report from the select committee of Ireland, HC 1825 (129)

State of Ireland report
Minutes of evidence taken before the select committee of the House of Lords, appointed to inquire into the state of Ireland, more particularly with reference to the circumstances which may have led to disturbances in that part of the United Kingdom, 24 March–22 June 1825, HL 1825 (521)

First report on Orange lodges
[First] report from the select committee appointed to inquire into the nature, character, extent and tendency of Orange lodges, associations or societies in Ireland, HC 1835 (377), xv

Second report on Orange lodges
[Second] report from the select committee appointed to inquire into the nature, character, extent and tendency of Orange lodges, associations or societies in Ireland, HC 1835 (475) (476), xv, xvi

Third report on Orange lodges
[Third] report from the select committee appointed to inquire into the nature, character, extent and tendency of Orange lodges, associations or societies in Ireland, HC 1835

State of Ireland in respect to crime
Report from the select committee of the House of Lords, appointed to enquire into the state of Ireland in respect of crime, and to report thereupon to the House; with the minutes of evidence taken before the committee, and an appendix and index. Part 1. Report, and evidence, 22 April to 16 May 1839, HL 1839 (486), xi.1, xii.1

Hand-loom weavers report
Hand-loom weavers. Return to an address of the Honourable the House of Commons, dated 15 February 1839: – for, copies of certain reports of the assistant hand-loom weavers' commissioners, HC 1840 (43–11), xxiii.367

The Devon Commission, part I
Report of Her Majesty's commissioners of enquiry into the state of law and practice in respect to the occupation of land in Ireland, HC 1845 (606), xix

The Devon Commission, part II

Royal commission of inquiry into the state of law and practice in respect to occupation of land in Ireland, HL 1845 (672) (673), iv, v

Dolly's Brae enquiry

Papers relating to an investigation held at Castlewellan into the occurrences at Dolly's Brae, on the 12th July, 1849, HC 1850 (1143) LI331

Acknowledgments

THIS BOOK HAS BEEN A LONG TIME IN the making and a number of people deserve thanks for their assistance in its completion. Dr Jonathan Mattison of the Grand Orange Lodge of Ireland was extremely helpful, as was Jack Johnston with his suggestions. Archive research was made much easier due to the assistance provided by the staff at the National Library of Ireland, the National Archives of Ireland, the Public Records Office of Northern Ireland, and Queen's University Library.

I would like to thank Martin Fanning of Four Courts Press for his help, guidance and patience, while a special acknowledgement is due to the Ulster Local History Trust who have provided generous financial assistance for the publication of this book.

Most importantly, I would like to express my gratitude to my family for their support and encouragement, and to my partner Maggie for her understanding and patience throughout the entire process.

Introduction

In the early months of 1836 the Orange Order – the largest Protestant association in Ireland with a reported membership of 200,000 – wound itself up and officially ceased to exist. The decision to do so was prompted by severe government pressure. But it was a decision taken at a curious time, a time of intense social, religious and political transition for large numbers of Protestants in Ireland with an increasing fear of a Catholic rise to social dominance. The seeming Catholic rise coincided with the feeling that a priest-driven campaign to destroy Protestantism was already well underway.

Such religious apprehension and increased zeal were not a new phenomenon within the minority Protestant population of Ireland. Since the 1740s Methodists had led the way in successfully spreading evangelical thought throughout Ulster especially, and had provided something of a template and a stimulus to other Protestant Church denominations. Some within these various denominations had, in their own minds, faltered in their perceived duties to God. As a result, they were paying the price as Catholics roused themselves from a subjugated base. Whipped up by itinerant preachers, Ulster in particular had undergone a number of evangelical religious revivals throughout the previous decades. The 1820s and 30s was a time during which yet another spiritual re-awakening was underway. This awakening was added to by a vigorous anti-Catholic feeling not necessarily present in previous religious campaigns of this ilk. Running concurrent to this religious reawakening was widespread Protestant political mobilization, a mobilization in which the lower classes had not previously been involved. Both these well-publicized parallel crusades of the day had the effect of creating a groundswell of popular Protestant support for the Orange Order. The Order already had in its short existence provided a buttress of security to many Protestants throughout the country. In addition to the religious and political issues that were key in attracting membership, growing social change and economic recession attracted many 'ordinary' Protestants desperate to cling to what they considered the remnants of the Protestant ascendancy. This ascendancy had, in the preceding half century especially, fallen somewhat from its previous impenetrable position. The Protestant ascendency could now justifiably be termed, in the words of David Fitzpatrick, as being in a state of 'descendancy'. As flagged by Fitzpatrick, 'poorer Protestants gained little or no material benefit from supporting an "Ascendancy" to which they did not belong'.[1] Indeed, the

1 David Fitzpatrick, *Descendancy: Irish Protestant histories since 1795* (Dublin, 2013), p. 3.

relationship between the landed Protestant class and its tenantry had weakened substantially in the previous decades. Nonetheless, for many Protestants within the bottom rung of society, this ascendancy or indeed 'descendancy', from which they remained excluded, still shone like a beacon to guide them through what was becoming an increasingly murky and dangerous existence. For it could be claimed with some justification that the 1830s and 40s presented the period of greatest alarm to Irish Protestants since the bloody rebellion of 1798.

The 1836 dissolution of the Orange Order was not the first disbandment of this largely lower-class association but it could be argued that it occurred at a point when it was needed most by its membership. The 1829 granting of Catholic emancipation had come as an enormous shock to many within a community that had complacently almost stood by and allowed Daniel O'Connell and his Catholic droves to pressurise the government into what was, at least on paper, a seismic concession. Far from ending Catholic demands, the confidence gained throughout this campaign spurred O'Connell and the general Catholic community to further action, which was facilitated to a degree by the Whig government in London. Anxious to address the disturbed state of Ireland, the government carried out a policy of social reform within a wider domestic policy. This was designed to placate at least some Catholic grievances thereby ensuring (at least in theory) a more contented and peaceable majority population. Against this background and a determination to halt further government appeasement, Protestant mobilization, driven by many figures of influence within the elite classes, mushroomed. This mobilization was manifested through the hosting of mass political meetings and great processions. Additionally, increased support (often violently displayed) was provided for extreme Protestant candidates during election contests. Central to this mobilization and resistance was the Orange Order. This popular Protestant fraternity had, in terms of numbers and weaponry, the potential to become a serious destabilizing influence in the country. It was a formidable force that could and did physically oppose Catholics, and a force that could in theory, if driven far enough, physically oppose the government and its various state agencies. Under pressure from O'Connell, by now in alliance with a government desperately seeking to maintain its parliamentary majority, measures were taken to outlaw this potentially threatening body. Before this could formally happen, to avoid embarrassment, the upper-class leadership of the Order (without the mandate of its core membership it must be said) voted it out of existence.

An exodus of the better classes anxious not to displease the king's government resulted, although some extremists did remain. But more importantly, large numbers of the lower classes refused to turn their backs on a way of life that had become of essential importance to them in this period of economic recession, agrarian violence and increasing Catholic political demands. The importance of these issues was such that some nine years later in August 1845, from the embers of its self-imposed dissolution, the Order began a process of national reformation and embarked on a journey along a road that it hoped would lead to a return to its former popularity and political strength. This path turned out to be far from linear. Many obstacles were faced along the way including internal dispute, the national calamity of the Famine, and a rebellion that had the aim of toppling the establishment to which the vast majority of Protestants still pledged their alliance. That the Order overcame such dramatic events, and indeed grew in strength, is a testimony to its importance within the Protestant community. It also highlights the stress that this sizeable minority felt itself under. However, from the heights of government acceptance that followed the republican Young Ireland rebellion in 1848, this growth was severely arrested following a fatal clash with Catholic Ribbonmen at Dolly's Brae in County Down the following year. From the outrage that followed, the Orange Order, although not outlawed or feeling the necessity to disband, suffered a downturn in popularity from which it struggled to recover for decades. This stunted odyssey from 1836 to 1849 will provide the central thesis of this book.

To date, there has been little study of the Protestant community in Ireland, particularly its lower classes, in the period. Allan Blackstock and Jacqueline Hill, in particular, have provided a continuation from A.T.Q. Stewart's seminal *The narrow ground* and David W. Miller's *Queen's rebels*, while David Hempton and Myrtle Hill have provided invaluable insight into the effects of evangelicalism on Ulster society. G.R. Hall has traced Ulster liberalism to great effect but there is great scope for closer scrutiny of an increasingly ultra-conservative Orange Order during what was a time of grave crisis for its mainly plebeian membership. There have been numerous recent monographs specifically concentrating on the Order but these have tended to provide general histories of the Association and have been too broad to provide any real in-depth study of its short-lived 1840s revival. The tendency has been to jump from dissolution in 1836 straight to the battle of Dolly's Brae in 1849 without any real consideration of the importance of the years in between. Senior's much-referenced *Orangeism in Ireland and Britain* places too much emphasis on the unreliable accounts of Ogle Robert Gowan and loses a little credibility as a result.[2] In any case, it concludes with dissolution in 1836, leaving a gap in the literature that with the recent 225th anniversary of the

2 James Wilson, 'Orangeism in 1798' in Thomas Bartlett, David Dickson, Dáire Keogh and Kevin Whelan (eds), *1798: a bicentenary perspective* (Dublin, 2003), pp 45–62.

Order's foundation surely needs to be filled. On a wider scale of published work, it must be recognized that the seminal events of the period, namely the repeal campaign of Daniel O'Connell, the Famine with its resultant loss of life and emigration, and the failed rebellion of the Young Irelanders (to a lesser extent), deservedly have preoccupied the thoughts of most historians of this period and indeed of popular national memory. Yet these issues have predominantly dealt with the majority Catholic population of the country; little work has yet been carried out into what was a substantial minority – a minority of over two million people. The majority of these laboured under the same poverty as their Catholic counterparts, and were coming under increasing strain because of economic, political and social change. This group of people, principally located in Ulster but by no means exclusively so, deserve to be brought in from the margins of Irish history. In some ways this work is a continuation of this author's *The Protestant community in Ulster, 1825–45: a society in transition*, although in this case the overall focus is tighter. By concentrating on the revival of the Orange Order and how it developed during arguably the most dramatic decade of the nineteenth century, this book will attempt to help redress this imbalance. It will, through this popular fraternal association, examine the tribulations that the Protestants of Ireland faced during a time of recession, famine, disease and rebellion.

That said, it is not the intention of this book to delve into the Famine or the rebellion of 1848 in microscopic detail. There is little new that can be ascertained from an in-depth study of either event other than, perhaps, to further recognize that the Famine actually affected Ulster to a greater degree than previously acknowledged (this is currently being addressed by the work of Christine Kinealy among others). More beneficial in the context of this work is the study of this particular group of people and their reaction to the bewildering events occurring around them, although of course naturally an overall context will be provided. By default, this work focusses on Ulster because the largest concentration of Protestants and consequently members of the Orange Order were found there. But the Order did have a presence in most counties, particularly in Dublin and Cork, therefore where possible 'southern' Orangemen are included in this book.

This book is divided into five chapters and tends towards a chronological approach. The first chapter provides an overall background by examining the early history of the Orange Order and how it had proceeded despite early trials and tribulations to enjoy the huge popularity evident in 1835. How membership dealt with the blow of its disbandment and what prompted the need for a revival of this association is traced in the second chapter. Within this chapter, the difficult process of national re-organization forms the core of its second half. This somewhat sluggish revival coincided with the outbreak of the Famine, a catastrophe that was potentially devastatingly destabilizing for the newly reformed Order. How the Order and its mainstay lower-class membership dealt with the effects of the Famine provide the basis for chapter three. Chapter four examines the rise of republicanism and the threat posed first by the Repeal Association and subsequently by the radical Young Ireland group. The religiously mixed leadership of Young Ireland sought to entice Orangemen to align themselves with the non-sectarian doctrine it espoused as it moved towards rebellion. The fifth and final chapter pays attention to the fallout of this failed rebellion and the resulting gaining of credibility for the Order. It will show how this acceptance was then almost immediately lost following Dolly's Brae, thereby sending the Order back to a political wilderness and an overall state of some reclusion. Overall, this book, in using the Orange Order's journey throughout the 1840s as its central nucleus, aims to bring to light the key fears, threats and issues of importance to the Protestants of Ireland during this pivotal decade of the nineteenth century.

Source material has been found in newspaper reports in particular, and from documents and records contained in the National Library of Ireland, the National Archives of Ireland, the archives of the Grand Orange Lodge of Ireland, and the Public Records Office of Northern Ireland, as well as from parliamentary papers, reports and debates. It needs to be noted, however, that little source material relating to the Famine period can be found in the archives of the Grand Lodge, as few records survive prior to 1850.

The term 'Protestant' is used generally as an umbrella term to cover all denominations within the Protestant religion, be they Church of Ireland, Presbyterian, Methodist or other, as it is not within the realms of this work to cover the complexities of the various denominations of Protestantism during this time of religious fervour. But where possible the distinction will be made as during this period as, just as in the present time, Protestantism was by no means a homogenous entity.

Stylistically, italics are included in quotations as they appeared in the original primary source report.

CHAPTER ONE

The first forty years

THE VICTORY OF William of Orange at the Battle of the Boyne in 1690 signalled the final cementation of the Protestant position of ascendancy in Ireland. Since the first plantations had been established in the early 1500s, the Protestant situation in Ireland had been fraught with difficulty and danger, a danger bloodily exemplified in the Catholic Ulster rebellion of 1641. The subsequent implementation of Penal Laws was designed to safeguard this position. These laws anticipated that denying Catholics civil rights (although limited as this concept was at this time), would ensure that this overwhelming majority of the population of Ireland could never again muster the strength to threaten the Protestant minority. Yet within the space of 100 years the security felt by the Protestant community in Ireland had evaporated to such a degree that it was deemed necessary by some to establish a fraternal association to act as almost a physical defence force against apparent insatiable Catholic advance. The purpose of this chapter is to trace the early development of the Orange Order from its humble beginnings in County Armagh in 1795 through to its 1835 period of peak popularity. Such popularity was brought about because of increasing Catholic political mobilization, general economic downturn, evangelical zeal, and an apparent abandonment of Protestant principle by the Westminster government.

AN INTERNATIONAL OVERVIEW

In January 1793 the guillotine fell on King Louis XVI, the following October the same fate befell his wife Marie Antoinette – seismic events in a world that was already undergoing irreversible change during this Age of Enlightenment. These events in France were the continuation of the ideals of liberty, equality and fraternity that had taken root in America and which had resulted in the defeat of the British Empire and the gaining of independence by its colonial settlers. In Ireland similar ideals sparked a rebellion in 1798, which ended bloodily with the loss of possibly as many as 30,000 lives. In the midst of such international events, the seemingly petty squabbles of lower-class Protestant and Catholic neighbours in the microcosm of north Armagh hardly seemed to be of any great importance. Yet these squabbles, sectarian but also economic, spawned an association that was to play a pivotal role in the lives of many Protestants throughout Ireland for the next 225 years – the Orange Order.

SECRET SOCIETIES AND ASSOCIATIONAL CULTURE

Despite its eventual growth, the formation of the Order would have attracted scant initial attention outside of mid-Ulster, for associational organization was not a new phenomenon in Ireland in the eighteenth century. It was not merely indulged in by the better classes who patronized Masonic lodges and cigar-scented old boys' clubs. Lower-class Catholics and Protestants also organized themselves fraternally, although for very different reasons than those of their social betters. These lower classes faced more pressing issues, such as the matter of self-defence, the provision of some measure of security for their increasingly tenuous existence on the land, and the protection of their livelihoods. From the mid part of the century, Catholics, in particular, had throughout the country organized at local level in a variety of strangely named groups designed to address their perceived grievances. Agrarian issues of discontent were violently dealt with throughout the eighteenth and nineteenth centuries by groups with such imaginative titles as the Houghers, Carders, Terry Alts, Caravats, and Shanavests, to name but a few. Such was the difficulty for the authorities in distinguishing between these groups and their ultimate aims (which were, it must be said, localized, vague, and extremely limited) that most of them were eventually uniformly labelled under the umbrella titles of Rockites, Whiteboys or Whitefeet. Drawing heavily from Masonry, secret passwords and oaths gave an air of excitement, exclusivity, and belonging for the young men who predominated in the membership of these male-only associations. The excitement was arguably added to by the acts of extreme violence carried out at night by these groups against a variety of targets, most predominantly land agents (but seldom landlords), middlemen, tithe proctors, and tenants (even fellow religionists) brought in to replace evictees. In general, these groups located mostly in the mid and southern counties of Ireland did not indulge in concerted campaigns of a sectarian nature most probably because too few Protestants lived in these areas to be considered a feasible threat in local issues, and certainly they had no thoughts of a national overthrow of British rule in Ireland.

COMPLEXITIES OF ULSTER

The situation in Ulster was very different however. Taken as a whole, this was a province roughly divided in equal numbers between Catholics and various Protestant denominations. Counties Antrim and Down were dominated numerically by Presbyterians although the ever-expanding Belfast was party to increasing amounts of Catholics and Church of Ireland Protestants moving from the country in search of employment. The mid-Ulster counties of Tyrone and Armagh were divided almost equally between Catholics and a combination of Church of Irelanders and Presbyterians. Counties Cavan and Monaghan were home to a majority of Catholics but did contain around 20 per cent of mainly Church of Ireland Protestants. The Protestant population of Fermanagh belonged almost exclusively to the Established Church and existed almost numerically evenly alongside the county's Catholic population. County Derry was also divided relatively evenly but with a much greater Presbyterian influence within its Protestant population. Donegal, on the other hand, was dominated numerically by its Catholic population but Presbyterianism was strong in the east of the county especially. The important thing to recognize is the religious diversity of the province and that in mid-Ulster most notably, the Catholic and Protestant populations lived side by side both rurally and in the urban setting. While it is true that Belfast was beginning its ghettoization with the influx of country workers, the grouping together of people of a common religion or culture was not yet a common practice in the rest of Ulster. Catholics and Protestants lived in close proximity, often in increasingly overcrowded areas. This situation was facilitated by the vitally important linen industry.

The strength of the linen industry and its offshoots of flax preparation, spinning and weaving allowed for a slightly better standard of living for the rural lower classes, the majority of whom especially in mid- and east-Ulster were involved in these industries. Although a great degree of the independence enjoyed by weavers was declining rapidly because of industrialization, the fact that a viable living could be made without wholly resorting to crop growth enabled tenants to survive on ever-shrinking plots of land. This was key in facilitating a greatly increasing population. Although this industry had shown signs of decline, by the latter decades of the eighteenth century it was once more in a mode of expansion. Consequently, increasing numbers of Catholics, hitherto scarcely represented in the trade, chose this profession. This, naturally, had the effect of increasing competition for employment. Many Catholics could now afford to pay higher rents to landlords who had become less troubled in their preference to whom they rented in a religious sense. By the 1780s Allan Blackstock contends that Catholics, having long since abandoned ideas of an end to British rule, fitted into one of three categories of loyalists in Ireland, the others being Established Church loyalists and Presbyterian loyalists.[1] The shackles of the Penal Laws had been broken and Catholics were, albeit slowly, becoming an accepted part of the political and economic mainstream of the country. The crux of Senior's reasoning for the eventual formation of the Orange Order is that for many Protestants in the Lough Neagh 'linen triangle' this new competition was not at all welcomed.[2] Miller examines contemporary accounts and highlights that traditional deference towards the elites had broken down as the eighteenth century had progressed thereby allowing popular insubordination and subsequent violence against Catholics from among formerly law-abiding lower-class Protestants.[3] These reasons coupled with traditional alarmist suspicion of Catholics, who had of course violently rebelled in 1641, created a dangerous undercurrent atmosphere in such a densely populated interface countryside. Protestants in Ulster had their own tradition of secret society membership as Steelboys had emerged earlier in the century (further evidence of the breaking down of lower-class deference) to counter increasing rents and evictions. But while Steelboys and Oakboys had included Catholics within their ranks and were non-sectarian, gangs of Protestants known as Peep-o-Day Boys now began daybreak attacks on Catholic homes wrecking weaving equipment and seizing arms found on the property. The holding of arms was considered a badge of loyalty exclusive to Protestants. Catholics surely could not possess such loyalty given their past rebellious actions and supposed loyalty to Rome. Blackstock acknowledges that 'the right to bear arms had profound significance. It was taken to symbolize citizenship and gave poorer Protestants a status that they would have been otherwise denied by their lowly position in the social hierarchy'.[4] The Penal Laws had barred Catholics from possessing arms; these Protestants now sought to revive this prohibition and show that only they could be citizens loyal to the crown. The actions of the Peep-o-Day Boys had the effect of driving many Catholics from the area to the symbolic poverty-stricken west of Ireland as foretold by Cromwell. Catholics responded in kind by forming groups known as Defenders, who soon took the form of an inter-county organization organized at parish level and with a variety of oaths and passwords designed to ensure the loyalty and secrecy of members. Such advanced Catholic organization greatly heightened Protestant fear and suspicion, and ensured a formidable enemy was present throughout mid- and south-Ulster considered capable of striking at any moment.

1 Allan Blackstock, 'The trajectories of loyalty and loyalism in Ireland 1783–1849' in Allan Blackstock and Frank O'Gorman (eds), *Loyalism and the formation of the British world, 1775–1914* (Belfast, 2014), pp 103–24. 2 Hereward Senior, *Orangeism in Britain and Ireland* (London, 1966). 3 David W. Miller, 'The Armagh troubles, 1784–95' in Samuel Clark and James Donnelly, Jr (eds), *Irish peasants, violence and political unrest, 1780–1914* (Dublin, 1983), pp 155–91. 4 Allan Blackstock, *An ascendancy army* (Dublin, 1998), p. 27.

FORMATION AND EARLY EXPANSION

By 1795 the area of north Armagh and east Tyrone had become a hotbed of sectarian tension with clashes occurring on a regular basis. These clashes culminated in a Defender attack on Dan Winter's Inn at Loughgall, an attack that was beaten off by the heavily armed Protestants inside with the loss of possibly thirty Defender lives. Although considered a great Protestant victory, the 'battle of the Diamond' also served as a wake-up call for Protestants who were somewhat shocked by the organization and network of the Defenders for whom members had travelled from as far away as County Louth. It was decided at this point to form a Protestant association to serve as a defensive bulwark against the Defenders, and to protect the Protestant constitution of 1691 which was under attack from government concessions to Catholics. By the end of the eighteenth century most of the repressive Penal Laws that had been enacted in the early part of the century to keep Catholics subdued had been lifted. Moreover, Catholic relief acts had been passed, most notably the Catholic Relief bill of 1793 that allowed wealthier Catholics to vote. This met with the disapproval of many from within the Protestant elite whose position could have, at least in theory, been challenged by a small but up-and-coming Catholic middle class. The mainly middle-class Protestant Volunteers who had successfully pressurized the government into granting change following the 1782 Dungannon Convention had shown a degree of goodwill towards Catholics. Now, the unstable situation in France was reason enough for many to fall back upon traditional suspicion of 'disloyal' Catholics. Wilson argues that it was from within the middle classes of these by now disbanded Volunteers that the Orange Order had its foundation, rather than from the disorganized and sporadic Peep-o-Day Boys as had previously been suggested.[5] Also exhibiting discontent were Protestant weavers and tenant farmers existing at a social level beneath the average Volunteer. While national political matters may not have permeated the mindset of ordinary lower-class country or city Protestants, visible Catholic economic incursion at a local ground level certainly did, and had to be urgently countered.

This middle- and lower-class urgency manifested itself with the formation of the Orange Order at the home of James Sloan in Loughgall. The first membership warrant was issued to Dyan, County Tyrone, and the rapid issue of warrants followed throughout the area as local lodges sprang up at a swift rate. The structure of the Order was similar to that of Freemasonry with lodges soon organized at a local, district, and county level eventually overseen by the Grand Lodge of Ulster, which was formed in Portadown in 1797. Secret passwords were

5 Wilson, 'Orangeism in 1798' in Bartlett et al. (eds), *1798*, pp 45–62.

issued, and an oath of loyalty taken by what was almost exclusively a middle-to-lower-class membership. Parading became an essential part of Orange activity as a show of loyalty and strength, as well as a celebration of culture and past military victory. It also had the potential to antagonize Catholics as a constant reminder of the 'superiority' of Protestantism, to which its lower classes, especially, were clinging desperately. The first official parade of the Orange Order took place in Lurgan in 1796 with fourteen lodges taking part. Initial upper-class suspicion at the plebeian makeup of this organization somewhat subsided as the threat of republicanism loomed large. It could be contended that an overthrow of gentry privilege and position seemed a possibility as the 1790s progressed. Quite simply, as pointed out by Smyth, 'the numbers [of Orangemen] were too impressive for a government confronted by a serious revolutionary challenge to ignore'.[6] Under government instruction, Generals Lake and Nugent 'grudgingly harnessed the Orangemen as a counter-insurgency force'.[7] The revolutionary threat came from the United Irishmen, a group of middle-class radicals heavily influenced by events in France. Although this predominantly Presbyterian group sought to embrace members of the Church of Ireland as well as Catholics, they were considered a dangerous enemy by most Established Church members, by many Presbyterians of the Seceding variety especially, and by the Crown, which naturally had little desire to possibly fall in the manner of its French counterpart. Against the backdrop of a war with republican France, this Protestant loyalty became even more pronounced especially following the government suppression of the United Irishmen in the wake of Wolfe Tone's appeal for French military aid. Deeply alarmed by the French threat, the government (after some hesitation) sanctioned the yeomanry corps, the brainchild of Sir John Knox of Dungannon, as it considered that the regular Catholic-dominated militia, formed in 1793, could not be trusted in this critical period. In Ulster in particular, this part-time civilian military yeomanry force quickly became decidedly Orange as oaths of loyalty were introduced to ensure 'disloyal' Catholics and Presbyterians did not join. Armed and uniformed by the government, the yeomanry provided Protestants with a ready supply of guns and ammunition which, of course, could dually be used for Orange activity. During this period, 'the overlap between yeomanry and Orange membership grew, meaning that Protestant [Established Church] loyalism now meant armed loyalism', while also having the effect of embodying 'a militant Protestant loyalty which eventually marginalized the other varieties [Presbyterian Covenanters and Catholic]'.[8] These local units were patronized by

6 Jim Smyth, 'The men of no popery: the origins of the Orange Order', *History Ireland*, 3 (Autumn, 1995), pp 48–53. **7** Ibid. **8** J.H. Hill, 'Loyalty and the monarchy in Ireland' in Allan Blackstock and Frank O'Gorman (eds), *Loyalism and the formation of the British world, 1775–1914* (Belfast, 2014), pp 81–102.

the elites but were comprised of the lesser gentry and middle-to-lower classes, giving yeomanry a similar membership makeup as the Volunteers. This yeomanry force played a pivotal role in the government suppression of the United Irishmen (which had courted Catholic Defenders) in 1797 and again in the following year when rebellion did eventually break out by being party to many acts of brutality against republicans and those suspected of association with them. These acts, barbaric as they were, were generally accepted by a government thankful for civilian help in its ultimate defeat of the rebels. The fanatical Protestant Sir Richard Musgrave, MP for Lismore, claimed 'that the institution of Orange lodges was of infinite use, and that he would rest the safety of the North on the fidelity of the Orangemen, who were enrolled in the yeomanry corps'.[9] The inspection of the Orangemen in Belfast and Lurgan by Generals Lake and Nugent further seemed to indicate government approval. The activities of the United Irishmen and the general fear of French invasion allowed for what was quintessentially a local association dealing with local conflict to mushroom into a popular national organization. With this in mind, a national Grand Lodge was formed in Dublin in April 1798 with Thomas Verner as grand master as its central control body. As noted by Hill, 'the establishment of the Grand Lodge heralded the transformation of the Orange Order from a largely Ulster-based initiative into a national organization'.[10] Yet the driving force remained the middle class, few of the elite class had come on board. According to Wilson, the notion that the elite classes were involved from the outset was very much a fabrication concocted in later years by those such as Gowan pushing their own agenda.[11] Additionally, Wilson casts doubt on claims of rapid expansion throughout the country. While the southern counties of Carlow and Wexford had been badly affected by the rebellion and had therefore seen some lodge formation, it is unlikely that the widespread national expansion claimed by Gowan actually occurred. The Grand Lodge of Ireland was weak in the extreme, included few of the elites as yet, and was certainly not capable of sustaining a national organization. Ulster, naturally, provided the largest number of lodges, and Leinster lagged well behind. There was perhaps 20,000 Orangemen in Ireland in 1798, a sizeable number for what was still an infant organization.[12] This remained however a predominantly lower-class association with a middle-class leadership.

9 *The Anti-Jacobin Review, and True Churchman's Magazine*, Jan.–June 1815, vol. xlviii (London, 1815), p. 180. **10** Hill, 'Loyalty and the monarchy in Ireland', pp 81–102. **11** Wilson, 'Orangeism in 1798', pp 45–62. **12** Ibid.

THE ACT OF UNION

The government reaction to the rebellion saw the Act of Union being passed in 1801. Disquiet was voiced in some higher Orange circles over the transfer of parliament from Dublin to London as a loss of patronage was feared. More seriously, it was widely considered that the Union would become 'something of a constitutional wooden horse which would lead to the overthrow of the Protestant ascendancy in Ireland'.[13] However, although 17 of the 19 Orange MPs voted against the implementation of the act, no authorized opinion was offered by the Order as a body. This was indicative of an infant organization not as yet confident or strong enough to officially involve itself in such a grand matter. In any case, any apprehension was soon quelled by Westminster reneging on its promise of Catholic emancipation and by the increasing commercial opportunities afforded by the economic rise of Belfast. The Presbyterian Synod of Ulster publicly offered its loyalty to the state, helped by an increased *regium donum* from the government. Within a short number of years most Protestant opposition to the Act of Union had dissipated. In reality, little had changed regarding the position of Catholics in Ireland despite the move from the corrupt Protestant-only Dublin parliament of College Green. The Protestant monopoly on government jobs and departments remained tightly wound within the patronage system of the elites. The justice system, with its magisterial bias and packed juries, remained loaded in favour of Protestants; the civil service remained very much the preserve of Protestants while government favour and protection of the Church of Ireland persisted. Catholic emancipation, the main selling point of the Act of Union to the majority of the Irish people, was now a distant dream for the steadily increasing Catholic middle class. As the perceived Catholic threat had somewhat now subsided, the Orange Order shed to a degree its defensive ethos and took on an increasingly fraternal face. True, there was a slight increase in tension as the doomed Emmet appealed to Orangemen to join his ranks as he attempted to revive the spirit of the United Irishmen. This appeal however was met with derision by Orangemen who easily faced down Emmet's 1803 uprising. The early years of the 1800s had also seen renewed yeomanry mobilization as a new French threat loomed under Napoleon. This threat prompted the Armagh Grand Lodge to declare that it would 'use every assertion to assist the Government in opposing the common enemy; and should foreign treachery once more kindle the flame of treason and rebellion in our land, we are ready once more to venture our lives and properties to extinguish it'.[14] Such assistance was not needed as a Napoleonic invasion did not materialize, and in general over this

13 Gearóid Ó Tuathaigh, *Ireland before the Famine, 1798–1848* (Dublin, 1971), p. 15. **14** *BN*, 1 July 1803.

period the Order lost some of its importance as a defensive force. It would, in the long term, concentrate its attention at a national level against any possible granting of Catholic emancipation. Similarly, at local level, something of a lull existed for the first two decades of the new century. Nonetheless, an examination of the internal organization of the Order can provide insight into why this association continued to thrive despite the absence of a visible threat upon which to focus.

STRUCTURE OF THE ORDER

Organization was key in ensuring that the Orange Order did not become simply a rabble of uncoordinated local groups especially during periods of little confrontational activity. Like most other associational groups, the Order in terms of structure followed Masonic lines. Local lodges generally contained between 30 to 300 members (all male) and were headed by a lodge master who frequently came from the same lower class as his fellow members.[15] The necessity of wealth and social status was not a prerequisite for leadership at this basic level of organization. Lodge masters were often publicans and benefitted financially from the fact that lodges, lacking a meeting place or room, regularly met in taverns and inns. County Down Quaker James Christie explained how he employed a sawyer who was a local lodge master and another who was a mere occasional labourer.[16] This pattern was replicated throughout the country. Ballyshannon lodge master James Brown was a tailor and pawnbroker, fellow lodge master James Greer from Stranorlar was a woollen draper, while Drumholm's James Crawford was listed as being a tanner/chandler.[17] The trades of these lodge masters are indictive of those frequenting the lower rungs of society. Such people, however, were expected to keep within their social realm by the constraints of the time. Hence, a feeling of suspicion and contempt was often displayed by better class opponents of the Order who looked upon it as a gathering of rabble. James Christie described one lodge master as 'a very illiterate man' and explained that lodge masters in his locality were usually 'masons and labourers, professions of the lower classes'.[18] Tyrone magistrate Mr James Richardson poured scorn on one Richard Purvis warning, 'I take him to be a shady man [...] he is master of Mullinaho Orange lodge'.[19] Nevertheless, the position of lodge master allowed for a sense of leadership and importance – something not readily available to the lower classes. For those 'ordinary' members, participation was cheap, it allowed for social

15 *First report on Orange lodges*, p. 110. **16** *First report on Orange lodges*, pp 385–8. **17** *Pigot's Directory of Ireland* (Dublin, 1824). **18** *First report on Orange lodges*, pp 385–8. **19** NAI: Outrage Reports,

inclusivity and empowered a sense of belonging. As with many societies of the era, fear of being on the 'outside' played a part in attracting many young men to the various associational groups of this period. Lodge meetings were social occasions, a chance to meet with friends and briefly escape from the drudgery and often misery of everyday life. While the need for defence from Catholic hostility was a practical reason for joining the Order, for many people the social aspect provided an enticing attraction.

With some counties in Ulster containing over 200 lodges, districts were formed to deal with organization at a regional level within counties. These districts, encompassing often a handful of parishes, could contain anything from five to fifty lodges depending on population numbers. It is at this level of organization that social rank began to play its part. District Masters usually came from the middle classes – strong farmers, land agents, yeomanry captains and lesser landlords – but not always exclusively so. Donegal district master Acheson Holmes was a publican, similarly the infamous Sam Gray, district master of Ballybay, shared this profession, a profession looked down upon in many upper quarters. Gray, however, was a strong and forceful personality, well known in his locality; this probably explains how he transcended the norm and ascended to district master. Generally, however, district masters were 'gentlemen of fortune, others are a better class of farmers'.[20] The key point is that district masters were, through their professions, familiar with the people in their local vicinity and were closer to events at ground level than those from the real elite classes. This familiarity ensured that district masters played a key role in the discipline and control of the membership. Arguably, their role was more important within the Order than that of the upper classes who took it upon themselves to act as provincial and national leaders.

The district master class typified those people instrumental in the formation of the Orange Order. The upper classes and elites were slow in involving themselves in the Order but had by the beginning of the new century begun to position themselves within the organization. The higher organization of the Order had been quickly taken over by this grouping who possessed the wealth and mobility to meet and organize outside of the immediate local level. Naturally, less familiarity between the lower-class membership and leadership existed at levels such as at county or provincial governance. This position was reserved for the upper middle but most usually the elite land-owning classes. This meant that for the likes of Gray, district master was the very upper threshold of their leadership position. For those from among his social class it simply was not possible to climb to the next leadership step and become a county grand master. For these elites,

Co. Tyrone (1849), ?/28 (full reference not supplied). **20** *First report on Orange lodges*, p. 235.

reporting first to the provincial Grand Lodge and then to the highest body (the Grand Lodge of Ireland), leadership provided a continuation of mixing with their peers in the highest social circles. Meeting twice yearly, the Grand Lodge issued circulars of instruction to its members and considered matters of national importance. Its other duties included 'examining into business that has been done by the committee since the previous meeting of the Grand Lodge, attending to complaints, and issuing warrants and making any further rules that may be deemed necessary for the better governing of the institution'.[21] Based in Dublin, it was far removed from the lives of ordinary lower class members. But with heirs to the Throne such as the duke of Cumberland serving as overall grand master, a national governing body with apparent royal approval was in place to issue guidelines. It also sought to maintain, at least in theory, structure and discipline of what had become a countrywide organization. However, the Grand Lodge of Ireland struggled to impose its regulations on rank-and-file Orangemen, most of whom were concerned only with matters within their own locality. The level of notice taken of Grand Lodge instruction would prove an issue for decades to come.

RITUALS AND SYMBOLISM

It is clear that the vast majority of members could never be part of the higher levels of leadership. In any case, the everyday mechanics of associational activity were of much more importance than procedural meetings and central instruction. Part of the attraction of belonging to a fraternity is the secrecy and exclusivity that underpins the feeling of belonging. This secrecy was evident in the Order's secret article number eight, which demanded that 'an Orangeman is to keep a brother's secrets as his own, unless in case of murder, treason, and perjury, and that of his own free will'.[22] To maintain such secrecy, in addition to keeping the workings of any association from becoming public knowledge, the issuing of passwords known only to members was essential. The Revd Holt Waring later explained that, 'in order that they should know each other for the future protection, they instituted a sort of catechism, question and answer, signs, by which they might know each other'.[23] Once again following the lead of Freemasonry, the Orange Order issued passwords to its members, which were renewed at regular intervals. These passwords were usually Biblical, and related mainly to the exodus from Egypt. Failure to remember these passwords, or more

21 *First report on Orange lodges*, p. 84. **22** *BN*, 22 June 1813. **23** *BCC*, 18 May 1825. Holt Waring was the dean of Dromore. He joined the Order in 1798 and held the position of Chaplain.

seriously the leaking of these, could lead to non-admittance or even expulsion from the Order.

In an era where few people held little in the way of material possessions, word of honour and the upholding of one's name was of paramount importance. The taking of an oath was therefore considered a serious matter, the breaking of which could lead to actual exclusion from wider society as a whole. Hence, the taking of an oath of loyalty was regular practice within secret societies. The Orange Order was not a secret society but it still felt the need for its members to pledge their loyalty to Church and king. An early oath read, 'I, A.B., do solemnly and sincerely swear, of my own free will and accord, that I will, to the utmost of my power, support and defend the present king, George the Third, and all the heirs to the Crown, so long as they support the Protestant ascendancy, the constitution and laws of these kingdoms'.[24] Through time this would become problematic as successive governments grew to view oath taking with extreme suspicion as the practice called loyalty to the state into question. Additionally, the final line of this oath did not promise unconditional loyalty by any means. Secret society oaths also took precedence over oaths taken in the court of law, which naturally posed difficulties in the administration of justice. Judge William Fletcher explained that 'the sanctuary of oaths has ceased to be binding, save where they administer to the passion of parties. The oaths of the Orange Associations, or of the Ribbonmen, have, indeed, continued to be obligatory. As for oaths administered in a Court of Justice, they have been set at nought'.[25] The oaths taken by Catholic Ribbon societies were considered much more of a threat to national security than Orange oaths but suspicion fell on all such societies. As a result, Order hierarchy regularly reworded the Orange oath for fear of attracting state sanction, and the oath prevailed until eventual government suppression in 1823 with the passing of the Unlawful Oaths Act.

EARLY PARADING

The act of parading is a key component in the life of any association. While members value the aspect of secrecy and the mystery of rituals carried out behind closed doors, there lies an aspect within human nature that craves public attention. Parading in a semi-military fashion allows the public to see the power, strength and organization of any particular body. This strength and organization of the Order was facilitated by Yeomanry connections with the British military.

24 *First report on Orange lodges*, p. 2. **25** *The charge of the Hon. William Fletcher to the grand jury of the county of Wexford at the summer assizes in 1814* (Dublin, 1814), p. 5.

As well as using yeomanry weaponry during parades, military bands were allowed to march thereby adding to the spectacle. In 1802, Brother Major Fox of the Belfast district resolved 'thanks to Lieutenant Colonel Walker of His Majesty's 50th Regiment, quartered in Belfast, for allowing his band to be used in the [12th] procession'.[26] Similar expressions of gratitude were offered to Lieutenant Colonel Bagot of the Kildare Regiment for the use of his military band in 1806 and 1807.[27] The use of the king's bands provided an air of official legitimacy that Orangemen were glad to embrace. This added to the public recognition of the ordinary individual member, which was usually not forthcoming in everyday life.

The use of colour (also a sign of recognition) at this early period was relatively limited, the cost of obtaining orange or purple material in large quantities was beyond most members. However, in a similar manner to the future use of tree branches to signify the colour green by O'Connell's Catholic followers, Orangemen decorated arches with orange lilies and also wore lilies on their person during this early era. Parades were carried out in a carnival atmosphere with music and such colour prevalent. As pointed out by Bryan, 'the carrying of flags and banners, and the accompaniment of a band, or bands, and large drums seems universal', and the Orange Order fitted this stereotype perfectly as the early years of the century passed.[28] The choice of music played by Orange bands could be problematic as tunes with sectarian connotations such as 'The Boyne Water' and 'Croppies Lie Down' were offensive to the Catholic community and would provoke confrontation as the century progressed. The very act of parading is a public spectacle usually enjoyed by participant and spectator alike provided they share the same culture and tradition. This has not always been the case with Orange parades but it must be recognized, in the context of the Order's early years, that in comparison to the amount of processions that took place trouble was more irregular than concerted. Armagh grand master Colonel William Verner recalled that for the early part of the 1800s 'they assembled with flags and colours and music, and played party tunes, at which period no offense was taken'.[29] Stewart Blacker observed that Catholics first took offence only at processions in the years 1819–20 due to 'irritating speeches delivered about that period, and their being put in a new and offensive light before them whose interest it was to do so'.[30] But the recollections of Blacker and Verner need to be viewed through an Orange light as both men were high Order members with an agenda to forward. Farrell, nonetheless, agrees that the years 1804–10 were 'relatively quiet', but does highlight a serious clash in 1806 between Armagh

26 *BN*, 16 July 1802. **27** *BN*, 24 July 1807. **28** Dominic Bryan, *Orange parades, the politics of ritual, tradition and control* (Belfast, 2000), p. 36. **29** *First report on Orange lodges*, p. 22. Stewart Blacker was a barrister by profession; he was also grand secretary to the Grand Lodge of Ireland. **30** *First report on*

Orangemen and militia members from Limerick that resulted in fatalities.[31] This clash, however, was exceptional during this period and was probably magnified by the fact that the militiamen were from outside the local area. As such, they were not privy to the local conventions that governed and maintained a degree of civility between Orangemen and Catholics. The dynamics of sectarian conflict and the importance of localism will be discussed in detail presently within this work; for now, it is sufficient to say that these key features were not present in the Armagh clash of 1806. The absence of the 'local' rendered this clash as being abnormal in the years prior to 1810. At this point, following 'defeat' in 1798 and the subsequent government reneging on the granting of Catholic emancipation, Catholics were in a relatively cowed position and lacking in national leadership. Therefore, few were prepared to physically oppose Orange parades. As a result, with no visible enemy upon which to focus, 'the [Orange] movement had clearly lost much of its spirit and momentum'.[32]

BENEFITS OF MEMBERSHIP

Despite the Order losing some of its political and defensive importance it continued to grow. This was due in no small measure to the support mechanism of togetherness and friendship that members could avail of. Stewart Blacker later acknowledged the fees that members paid (although paltry) were:

> generally appropriated as a benefit fund to relieve brethren in sick or in indigent circumstances; applied also in various acts of charity to various institutions; for instance, my own lodge lately voted a sum of money to the building of a church and old men's asylum; they voted another small sum of money to assist a brother's wife to America to join her husband, also sums to orphan societies, and things of this nature.[33]

Deputy Treasurer H.R. Baker later explained that 'half their subscriptions are placed in a separate fund for the support of brethren who may be ill from the visitation of God and not brought on by any ill conduct of their own [...] these are the words of the rule: to relieve widows and orphans of brethren; and to bury the brethren who die poor'.[34] Lodges also donated to local causes. Funds were locally raised 'to relieve widows and orphans of the brethren' as demonstrated by the 2*s.* allocated 'as a charity to a widow of an Orangeman' by the Orange lodge

Orange lodges, p. 111. **31** Sean Farrell, *Rituals and riots: sectarian violence and political culture in Ulster, 1784–1886* (Lexington, KY, 2000), p. 55. **32** Farrell, *Rituals and riots*, p. 63. **33** *First report on Orange lodges*, p. 112. **34** *First report on Orange lodges*, p. 20.

of Glenawley, County Fermanagh, and 'to bury the brethren who die poor',[35] while a collection was held by Clones Orangemen in July 1844 'for the purpose of forming a fund for the relief of poor Protestants in the neighbourhood'.[36] The inevitable economic downturn that followed the ending of the Napoleonic Wars in 1815 led to a dire situation for many of the core weaving membership of the Order; therefore the support offered financially by the Order was most welcome.

But arguably more important than financial support was the sense of escapism that membership provided. As explained by Clark, 'lodges offered the same or similar attractions and opportunities for members as other voluntary associations, in particular, conviviality, entertainment, processions, fashionable patronage, employment, and help to migrants'.[37] Such an array of attractions surely made it very difficult for Protestant males not to join. McDonagh summarizes that, 'in one light, the Order represented a gargantuan, though exclusive, social security system; in another, it was an expression of mutuality; and yet in a third, it acted as an emollient, both in reducing class friction among Protestants and in satisfying men's appetites for display, mystery, and conviviality'.[38] From the lowest landless labourer to the highest of the elites, the Order appeared to offer something in an era of increasing instability for all classes in Ireland.

THE BENEFITS OF SOCIAL CHANGE

The growing strength of the Orange Order was greatly facilitated by the wider social changes that occurred during the first half of the nineteenth century. An increased capacity for travel, for instance, helped strengthen links among Orangemen as mobility was much improved by an ever-expanding transport network. Although canals were not the commercial success that had been hoped for, roads continually improved in the first half of the century. Mail coaches had provided a somewhat slow and expensive means of travel but as roads gradually improved, journey times were cut and most towns became linked.[39] Subsequent cheaper travel allowed the middle- and lower-middle classes greater travel access, which facilitated increased movement to and from urban centres of importance. Although rural roads remained rudimentary, transport links between bigger towns would prove important in the growth of the Orange Order. Commenting on Lisburn, a key centre for Orange processions, travelling commentator Samuel Lewis was impressed by the entrances to the town – 'A new line of road has been

35 *First report on Orange lodges*, p. 201. Account book of Glenawley Orange Lodge, Co. Fermanagh (PRONI D1433/1). **36** *ECEP*, 18 July 1844. **37** Peter Clark, *British clubs and societies, 1580–1800* (Oxford, 2000), p. 325. **38** Oliver MacDonagh, 'Ideas and institutions, 1830–45' in William Vaughan (ed.), *A new history of Ireland*, v: *Ireland, 1801–70*, pp 193–217. **39** Cormac Ó Gráda, *Ireland before and*

made at great expense at the entrance from Dublin on the south-west, and also at the entrances from Belfast and Armagh, by which the town has been much improved'.[40] Lisburn became scene to some of the largest Orange processions and protests in pre-Famine Ulster; its close proximity to Belfast and modern access routes (which would soon be supplemented by trains) ensured greater fluidity for Orangemen in terms of access and travel. Railways would develop in the pre-Famine period albeit at a slow rate but, as will be discussed later, also played a pivotal role in the expansion of the Order.

Of key importance in the spread of Orangeism was the supply of printed literature. Overcoming the poor road conditions in rural areas, travelling chapmen had sold books and ballads cheaply to a receptive public throughout the eighteenth century. Popular memory played an important role in both Catholic and Protestant culture. Thus, the medium of printed literature played a large part in keeping alive Protestant memory of 1641 and the later Williamite wars. For instance, Ashton's 1728 *Battle of Aughrim* went through twenty editions between 1750 and 1850 ensuring that 'it remained a staple text in the cheap book market' well into the new century.[41] The popularity of such texts overcame the hurdle of low levels of rural literacy. Blackstock asserts 'that "popular" printed literature had a substantial audience, even amongst the lowest social classes to whom it was mediated by readers like clerics and schoolmasters'.[42] This situation did change to some extent with the rise of Belfast and provincial towns but the market remained buoyant in rural areas.[43] A steady flow of printed literature was readily distributed through rural Ireland to an eager audience keen to recollect its heritage and cultural history. The increase in the number of printing presses and the growth of the newspaper industry, which was greatly assisted by the reduction of government duty in 1836, allowed the general public to stay abreast with developments in politics and the actions of political leaders while recalling a turbulent past. New ultra-conservative newspapers laced with militant opinion, such as *The Warder* (established in 1821) and the *Dublin Evening Mail* (1823), warned the Protestant public of the increasing dangers posed by Daniel O'Connell. This combination of pedlar-distributed literature and newspaper articles provided Orangeism with a huge platform to inform, influence and instruct its membership. Improved travel opportunity coupled with the increased distribution of cheap literature can be viewed as positive developments in the popularity of the Orange Order. Yet, adverse social change would also play a role in creating the need for such a society to exist.

after the Famine: explorations in economic history, 1800–1925 (Manchester, 1993), pp 35–7. **40** Samuel Lewis, *A topographical dictionary of Ireland* (Dublin, 1837), p. 278. **41** Niall Ó Ciosáin, *Print and popular culture in Ireland, 1750–1850* (Hampshire, 1997), p. 101. **42** Allan Blackstock, *Loyalism in Ireland, 1789–1829* (Woodbridge, 2007), p. 135. **43** Ó Ciosáin, *Print and popular culture in Ireland, 1750–1850*, p. 57.

ECONOMIC CHANGE

The need for escapism, belonging and commonality was greatly accelerated by the negative changes occurring in everyday life. The early decades of the nineteenth century were a time of great transition and instability particularly for the lower classes. This transition was forced especially by changes in the linen industry. As explained earlier, the domestic linen industry was the main employer in Ulster. The period from the 1780s until 1815 is described as the 'golden age of the handloom weaver'.[44] This golden age was drawing to a close however. It is true that competition from cotton had impacted on the price of linen but weavers in the greater Belfast area were able to switch from linen to cotton weaving.[45] This maintained demand for linen weavers, who were therefore able to sustain rural household incomes until around 1815.[46] The ending of the Napoleonic Wars, however, led to a severe economic depression. Linen exports were badly affected, while cotton production suffered badly also resulting in tumbling wages. Although some growth did occur in the early 1820s, this was due to the mechanization of the spinning process. Offsetting this was the fact that such mechanization decimated the household spinning industry. Machine-spun yarn was simply cheaper than hand-spun yarn. This home spinning had been mainly carried out by women; now, this key income was lost. To compound the issue, weavers now had to travel long distances to access their raw material. In any case, the linen industry could not withstand the influx of cotton imports from Lancashire, where it was cheaply produced. Such importation had the effect of destroying the cotton industry in Ulster. It also drastically affected the domestic linen industry which, by the late 1830s, 'was in a state of near collapse'.[47] The many weavers with little option but to continue in its employment worked long hours for paltry wages in the mills of Belfast. Thus, a situation of near destitution prevailed for many weavers who previously had been able to survive on minute plots of land mainly due to domestic spinning and weaving.

Overall, the period of peace post-Waterloo, together with increased mechanization, had drastically decreased employment previously available in what had been a largely domestic family industry. Kennedy and Solar conclude that 'the decline of rural textile production brought into question the viability of very small holdings'.[48] For many who had worked in this industry, finding labouring work was now their only option. This employment sector had now,

44 Liam Kennedy and Peter M. Solar, 'The rural economy, 1780–1914' in Liam Kennedy and Phillip Ollerenshaw (eds), *Ulster since 1600, politics, economy, and society* (Oxford, 2013), pp 160–76. **45** Kennedy and Solar, 'The rural economy, 1780–1914', pp 160–76. **46** Ibid. **47** Jonathan Bardon, *A history of Ulster* (Belfast, 1992), p. 268. **48** Kennedy and Solar, 'The rural economy, 1780–1914', pp 160–76.

however, become saturated with former weavers often travelling long distances seeking casual work. Such an increased labouring work force naturally increased competition and drove wages downwards, pushing large numbers of former weavers to near destitution and starvation. For many, emigration was the only option.

This uncertain situation for weavers and labourers alike was compounded by the tenuous existence on the land. This was brought about by changes applied by landlords seeking to modernize their estates, many of which were unprofitable or simply had been neglected through the years. Estates owned by absentee landlords or those in financial debt were frequently left in poor condition. Other landlords attempted to maximize profits. Agricultural prices were used as an estimate in the setting of rent prices. But Solar and Hens explain that agriculture 'prices could fluctuate wildly from year to year so expectations were likely to have been shaped by the experience of the previous five to ten years'.[49] This created a major problem as high rents were set in times of wartime prosperity. Such high rent saw the need for renegotiation of many leases post-1815 as income from agricultural produce slumped.[50] Few rent reductions matched the increases levied during the war boom period.[51] In response to this loss of rental income, landlords turned to the tighter running of their estates to compensate. Many actions carried out by such landlords or their agents such as enclosure, the eradication of middlemen, drainage, the ending of the system of rundale, and the attempts to end subdivision, were progressive in the sense of improving the land and overall productivity. But on numerous estates, few of the tenants enjoyed any real benefits and such improvements were not always welcome. Tenants-at-will had little security on the land and therefore little incentive to improve their holdings, while tenants holding leases found the length of their agreements becoming ever shorter. In the 1780s a standard land lease spanned three lives of typically 21 years, by the 1820s and 30s the length of leases had been reduced to one life or as little as seven years in some instances. In other cases, leases were not renewed by landlords at all, leaving tenants who previously had some security on the land now mere tenants-at-will and vulnerable to ejection at any time.

LOWER-CLASS REACTION

This deteriorating situation prompted some tenants to recall the activities of the Oakboys and Steelboys in the previous century, successful actions that had forced

49 Peter M. Solar and Luc Hens, 'Land under pressure: the value of Irish land in a period of rapid population growth, 1730–1844', *The Agricultural History Review*, 61:1 (2013), pp 40–62. **50** Ibid. **51** Bardon, *A history of Ulster*, p. 272.

some landlords to reduce rents. The importance of popular social memory cannot be underestimated, and it was by no means a given that landlords could expect unquestioning obedience from their tenants. This was borne out by the coming together of Protestants and Catholics in 1829 to disrupt the export of much-needed potatoes from County Down. This group known as the 'Tommy Downshire's' continued its activity throughout the 1830s and 40s and succeeded in pressurising landlords into reducing rents in some areas.[52] This tactic was also used by 100 of the tenantry of Hugh Gore Edwards who assembled at his residence in Tyrone and demanded that the rent be lowered.[53] Assisted by around 200 tenants from outside areas, they 'threatened to pull down his house, burn his stocks, etc. if their demands were not complied with – they also threatened his workmen, who left his work in consequence'.[54] Yet, despite the fact that Edwards himself was a magistrate, only one of the party was convicted for the assemblage; the other twenty accused were released by a seemingly sympathetic jury. Another coming together of armed men demanding rent reductions occurred at Aughnacloy a short time later. One of those arrested, Robert Wigans, was given a glowing character reference by magistrate Crossley who 'had known Wigans for thirty years; he was a yeoman, and was sixteen years under his command; no man in the country had a better character'.[55] These court cases did not halt the action against Edwards; he was later awarded £18 17*s.* 6*d.* by the Tyrone grand jury 'for a malicious burning' carried out on his property.[56] Lower-class artisans also were capable of disobedience. In the town of Rostrevor, it was reported that 'strikes sometimes take place among workmen', while 'stone-cutters from Newry, who are all members of the trade's union and being by that society supported when out of employment will not work for what they consider under-wages. They struck this summer when receiving 18*s.* a week, remained three weeks idle and did not return [to] their work until their wages were raised to 20*s.* a week'.[57] Thus, it is evident that while large numbers of tenants and skilled workers were Orangemen, they were not averse to taking action against their landlords and agents – fellow Order members or not. It also demonstrates the difficulties faced by landlords seeking a return to the relationship of deference that had previously existed. Miller contends that, 'by heading the Orange Order, Protestant landlords and magistrates reassumed the social leadership they had partially forfeited during the Oak and Steelboy agitations, and helped ensure that in spite of the economic distress of the post-war decades such *class*-based violence

52 Allan Blackstock, 'Tommy Downshire's Boys: popular protest, social change and political manipulation in mid-Ulster 1829–47', *Past and Present*, 196 (August, 2007), pp 125–72. **53** *LJ*, 25 March 1833. **54** *BN*, 26 March 1833. **55** Ibid. **56** County of Tyrone grand warrant for Lent assizes 1836 (Omagh, 1836), p. 228 (PRONI TYR 4/1/48). **57** Angelique Day and Patrick McWilliams (eds), *Ordnance Survey memoirs, parishes of County Down I, 1834–6 south Down* (Belfast, 1990), p. 30, p. 37.

among Protestants virtually disappeared'.[58] But for this deference to be regained, something had to be provided to tenants in return. Due in no small measure to Crossley's reference, Wigans was 'recommended to mercy' and was jailed for a mere six months, surely less than could have been expected. Although William Blacker called the Downshire's 'the lowest grade of all religions [...] a species of mob legislation', as a high Orangeman he depended on the likes of this 'mob'.[59] In many cases, the respect of tenants could only be gained by landlords engaging in a type of two-way relationship – one condition of many being that Orange tenants expected favouritism in matters of law and order.

LAW AND ORDER

By the beginning of the new century most local power regarding law and order remained in the hands of local magistrates. No legal qualifications were necessary for this position; a knowledge and familiarity of local matters was sufficient. While elite landowners did serve as magistrates, more commonly land agents, bigger farmers, or small landowners carried out the required everyday duties. This ensured that most magistrates remained bound by the wishes of large landowners and within a tight circle of patronage. In the context of the relationship that existed between landlord and tenant, a certain leeway had to be provided by magistrates towards Orange breaches of the law. A large number of magistrates were members of the Order in any case, district masters in many instances. This combination, together with loaded juries chosen by high sheriffs and a biased police force, ensured that crimes of a party nature carried out by Protestants seldom drew convictions. This, of course, left the Catholic community cynical in the extreme towards the justice system. Orange colours were frequently worn in court by court defendants, jury members and magistrates. In more serious cases, funding for the defence of Orangemen was provided by senior Orangemen. Character references continued to be widely provided as further evidenced in July 1834 at Tyrone assize court. Nine Orangemen arraigned for being in procession at Coagh were referred to as 'respectable and peaceful men' by the influential William Lennox Conygham, esq. of Moneymore. Because of this character reference, the judge jailed the men for a mere two weeks despite them blatantly breaking the law.[60] The monopoly enjoyed by magistrates would slowly be altered

58 Kerby Miller, *Emigrants and exiles* (New York, 1985), p. 87. **59** *First report on Orange lodges*, pp 235–6. William Blacker, from the Carrickblacker estate, joined the Order following the Battle of the Diamond. Composer of many Orange ballads, he served as high sheriff for Armagh and as a magistrate. **60** *NW*, 31 July 1834.

by the judicial reforms carried out by Robert Peel but for the first three decades of the nineteenth century the final say in the dispensation of justice remained mainly the preserve of local magistrates. This surely allowed Orangemen to feel as if the law, and more importantly the sanction of local magistrates, was with them. Given that the magistracy was part of the circle of patronage coming from elite quarters, it surely was felt that elite sanction was being given to Orange activity whether it be law breaking or not. This was clearly an example of the two-way landlord–tenant relationship in action.

In cases of the landlord not fulfilling the 'contract', the deference of the lower classes could quickly unravel. When prosecuting Orangemen for marching in 1834, Lord Downshire was addressed in court by a Dromore Orangeman named Leggett who stated 'he considered it rather strange, that his Lordship had abandoned those old friends, of whose assistance he was formerly glad to avail himself'. Leggett continued by pointing out that 'they had proved his best support at the elections for the county; and that but for them, his brother would not have been returned for Newry; and that, if his Lordship should look for their assistance again, on any similar occasion, he would find himself disappointed'.[61] The sentiments of Leggett were boisterously echoed by the large group of Orangemen who had assembled, and left Downshire in no doubt that loyalty could not be taken for granted. This was borne out as the Orangemen left the courthouse and attempted an impromptu march. In the ensuing melee, Downshire 'was jostled, and dragged down on his knees'. The Orangemen told Downshire 'that they considered their warrants as of higher authority than any he could produce'.[62] To ensure loyalty, something had to be returned to the lower classes – in this case turning a blind eye to a breach of the law. For a landlord, especially of a liberal disposition such as Downshire was at this stage, disobedience could quickly surface if they attempted to supress the desires of Orangemen.

ORANGE INFILTRATION OF THE STATE?

For the elites who were far removed from the dire economic situation that the lower classes found themselves in, political issues remained of paramount importance. Their influence steadily increased within Dublin Castle especially when the Orange-disposed viceroy earl of Richmond arrived. This coincided with the general election of 1807, which brought an anti-Catholic majority to Westminster and was best exemplified with the appointment of William Saurin as attorney general, a position he held until 1822. The appointment of the

61 *NW*, 31 July 1834. **62** Ibid. **63** Senior, *Orangeism in Britain and Ireland*, p. 181.

vehemently Orange Saurin, who ironically had vigorously opposed the Act of Union, as the government's legal voice personified the increasing grip of Orangeism within the circles of Dublin Castle. The appointment also continued to allow Orangemen something of a safety net when it came to breaking the law. As highlighted by Senior, 'it is not surprising, then with a viceroy sent by an anti-Catholic cabinet, and Saurin as attorney-general, the Orangemen took liberties they would not have taken under less favourable circumstances'.[63] The yeomanry continued to act almost as an independent military force and regularly re-acted very forcibly to Catholic activity. Those convictions of Protestants that did occur such as that of Saunders Bell, a yeoman executed for the murder of a Catholic James Birmingham in Portadown in 1809, were met with much condemnation and criticism of the government from the more indignant of those within the Protestant community.

Such Orange infiltration of state mechanisms was common. Still in its early stages of reform, the police force was considered to be rife with Orangemen, especially as magistrates retained a say in the selection of recruits. This view was no doubt heightened by the actions of Limerick chief constable Richard Going who encouraged Orange lodges to exist within his county constabulary. The fact that the constabulary of Going killed three Catholic Whiteboys in an ambush at Askeaton, County Limerick, in 1821 fed local perceptions that supposed reforms within the police force were actually meaningless.[64] Such a connection with Orangeism was not the sole preserve of the constabulary. Speaking to a government commission in 1825, future MP Richard Shiel cited the Custom House as a prime example of the rotten core that was present within the civil service. Shiel explained that:

> the Custom House was an object of patronage with the Government; members of parliament constantly exercised their influence for the purpose of obtaining small places connected with the Custom House; in consequence, very unworthy persons were appointed; those persons were generally Protestants; being brought together into one office, their feelings were strengthened by cohesion; they valued themselves on their religion; men assumed the pretensions of high gentlemen, who had only one qualification of a gentleman in Ireland, namely, the Protestant religion.[65]

This situation within the Custom House was replicated throughout the state apparatus and ensured a heavy tinge of Orangeism ran through the municipal

64 James S. Donnelly, Jr, 'Pastorini and Captain Rock: millenarianism and sectarianism in the Rockite movement of 1821–24' in Samuel Clark and James S. Donnelly, Jr (eds), *Irish peasants, violence and political unrest, 1780–1914* (Dublin, 1983), pp 102–39. **65** *Select committee of Ireland report*, p. 99.

veins of the country. This position had been briefly threatened by the short-lived 'Ministry of all the Talents' government of 1806, which included 'several whig ministers who were committed to Catholic emancipation'.[66] This particular administration took the step of not renewing the annual state procession on William's birthday, 4 November, but attempts to move towards emancipation were cut short as the government fell the following March. Other than this brief interlude, as correctly pointed out by Farrell, 'from 1800 to 1820 few Orangemen could complain about the general nature of British governance in Ireland'.[67] Although there was no formal or coherent alliance between the government and the Order many similar convictions were shared; this, of course, could only be beneficial to the Orange Order.

INTER-RELIGIOUS RELATIONS

While sectarian conflict certainly did occur, it was by no means always present. This was most evident in rural areas. At a higher social level, Oliver Rafferty correctly acknowledges the donations provided by wealthy Protestants for Catholic church building and charitable causes.[68] At a more grounded level, the success of the Tommy Downshire's was partly facilitated by the fact that rurally Catholics and Protestants lived side by side and co-existed in a generally peaceful manner, unlike some cities which were by this stage taking on the beginnings of a ghettoized appearance. While Presbyterians predominated in eastern Ulster and Catholics in the far west and south of the province, much of mid-Ulster was evenly mixed along religious lines. This is not to say that the east and west were exclusively Presbyterian and Catholic respectively; there were in fact large communities of other religious denominations spread throughout these areas. Given that few landlords discriminated against Catholics in terms of allocating plots of land, estates and villages were generally religiously mixed. Children were frequently schooled together, which helped create a familiarity at a local level. Such familiarity was evident following a sectarian clash at Carland, County Tyrone, in 1843. Protestant witness James Morrow 'had no idea whatever there would be a row, because I was acquainted with a great many of them [Catholics], living amongst neighbours'.[69] As pointed out by Rafferty, 'where individual Catholics had close contact with Protestants at an early age, often because of being educated by Protestant clergymen, they tended to remain friendly for the

66 J.H. Hill, 'National festivals, the state and "Protestant Ascendancy" in Ireland, 1790–1829', *Irish Historical Studies*, 24:93 (May, 1984), pp 30–51. **67** Farrell, *Rituals and riots: sectarian violence and political culture in Ireland, 1784–1886*, p. 65. **68** Oliver P. Rafferty, *Catholicism in Ulster, 1603–1983* (Dublin, 1994), pp 112–13. **69** *BN*, 13 June 1843.

rest of their lives'.[70] In general, the hardship endured by the lower classes did not differentiate between religious denominations. While tensions naturally increased in some areas during periods of marching, much of this was caused by the abuse of alcohol, which was also the cause of much trouble at the fairs and markets that littered the calendar. A prime example of this can be seen in the 1830 wrecking of Maghery, a Catholic village in the over-populated and religiously mixed area of north Armagh. Familiarity was obvious as a party of Orangemen passed through the village on their way to a lodge meeting in nearby Derryinver. The party played several non-sectarian tunes to the appreciative Catholic villagers before leaving for their meeting. On their return the following day, the Orangemen were requested to play again; this time, they launched into a rendition of the sectarian 'Protestant Boys'. The infuriated villagers smashed the Orange drums and broke the hats of the offending party. The Orangemen swore revenge; two days later they returned and wrecked the village.[71] This case shows how relations between the parties were not automatically hostile. The Catholic villagers were initially glad of the band entertainment and the Orange party glad to provide it. This would dismiss the notion of in-built hatred and hostility towards the other. It took the spark of probable drunkenness on the part of the Orangemen the following morning for matters to turn sour.

Relations were generally cordial, especially in rural Ulster, where Catholics often joined in with Orange processions. William Blacker described a sham fight outside Lurgan in 1834 at which 'the whole country was assembled. I suppose I rode through four miles of people, a large majority of them women; and I saw a number of Roman Catholics in the crowd, appearing to enjoy the fun just as much as anybody else, and that was the way they used to enjoy the fun in former days'.[72] At the coming of age of Charles Eccles, heir to the Eccles estate in Fintona, County Tyrone, it was reported that 'though those assembled consisted of different creeds and politics, no manifestation to riot occurred among them, nor did the slightest accident take place to interrupt the harmony of an evening which will long be remembered' even though the family had strong Orange connections. Daniel Eccles gave a toast to 'the clergymen of the parish of Fintona of all denominations' which was acknowledged by the parish priest, the Revd Mr Tierney, who 'returned thanks in a luminous speech, laudatory of the good feeling that existed between Roman Catholics and Protestants in that quarter'.[73] Such feeling was also evident at the funeral of Fr Patrick O'Kane in Coleraine which saw:

70 Rafferty, *Catholicism in Ulster, 1603–1983*, p. 119. **71** Farrell, *Rituals and riots: sectarian violence and political culture in Ireland, 1784–1886*, pp 102–3. **72** *Second report on Orange lodges*, p. 216. **73** *ECEP*, 29 May 1834.

> the most numerous assembly of persons that ever was seen to follow a funeral in Coleraine, and these principally Protestants; all our clergymen of the Establishment, and the Presbyterians, Seceders, and Methodists – all attended in scarfs and hatbands – all denominations of church and party; – one person, who is considered the leading man of the Orange Party here, actually closed his shop for the day, in token of respect to the interment of the priest.[74]

In areas of Catholic population dominance, Orange parades and activities often were ignored by Catholics who felt no threat given their numerical superiority. This was evident in Inishowen, County Donegal. Although the setting up of Brunswick Clubs in the peninsula had caused tensions, and tithe agitation had reared its head in Carndonagh, there was no trouble reported regarding Orange activity. Only one Orange lodge existed, that of Malin in the outer reaches of the extreme north. While it is likely that most Inishowen Orangemen made the short journey to lodges in Derry, those living in the Malin area would logistically have struggled to travel through what is a mountainous area, hence the probable existence of a lodge in this remote, predominantly Catholic area. Because of this isolation, little Catholic attention centred on its one Orange lodge. Police reported a quiet Twelfth in 1833 as Orangemen met at 9 o'clock in the evening in the house of Robert Gallagher, played some tunes for around two hours before dispersing in a peaceful manner unmolested by Catholics.[75] Conversely, the Coleraine funeral of Fr O'Kane took place in a parish of over 6,000 people, a mere 877 of whom were Catholic.[76] Such instances of tolerance were regular occurrences, especially in areas of religious numerical dominance. It is incorrect to think that this was a society at loggerheads with itself. Sporadic cases could, of course, occur; for instance, in the Protestant heartland of Castledawson, Catholic medical doctor John Smyth was moved to petition Dublin Castle following sustained sectarian harassment culminating in stones being thrown through his window.[77] But such instances would appear to be the exception rather than the rule. On the whole, such examples support Richard McMahon's opinion, which questions the traditional notion that sectarian violence was commonplace in Ulster in the first half of the century. McMahon agrees with the work of Akenson that claims that Catholics and Protestants drew from each other and 'provided a clear and uncomplicated world view that offered both comfort and stability to each community thereby lessening the need for violent conflict between them'.[78]

74 *BCC*, 26 April 1828. **75** *Second report on Orange lodges*, appendix c.5.a. **76** *Royal commission of state of religious and other public instruction in Ireland. First report, appendix, second report*, HC 1835 (45) (46) (47) xxxiii.1, p. 829, xxxiv.1, p. 218a. **77** NAI: Outrage Reports, Co. Londonderry (1848) 64/18. **78** Richard McMahon, 'The madness of party: sectarian homicide in Ireland, 1801–1850', *Crime, History*

This relationship was only threatened by outside forces and events that emerged particularly from the 1820s onwards. As explained by d'Alton, 'it seems that while the sectarian *climate* was set by reference to the national (and international, even), the sectarian *weather* is very much a product of local factors'.[79] The campaign for Catholic emancipation, the Second Reformation, government reform, and repeal agitation would indeed sharpen the sectarian *climate*, but the sectarian *weather* remained localized.

Some areas would take greater notice of matters at a national level than others. If d'Alton's sectarian *weather* was already clouded, then his sectarian *climate* could permeate local matters. It is apparent, for instance, that the Second Reformation was having a negative effect on the people of north Fermanagh. The theological debate between Fr Tom Maguire and Tresham Gregg captured the public imagination and permeated the minds of ordinary Orangemen if the following notice found nailed to a chapel gate in Pettigo is indicative of general feeling.[80]

Despite the remoteness of Pettigo, a small village on the Fermanagh/Donegal border, well removed from any urban centre, it would appear that evangelicalism had soured relations between Protestants and Catholics in this particular rural area. The previous summer in the neighbouring village of Kesh, an effigy of Maguire was burned.[81] The notice is explicit in its call for Catholics to turn from perceived heathenish practices and superstitious acts – key doctrines of evangelical zeal. The fact that this notice used official headed lodge paper shows some level of higher authority although the spelling errors would suggest a less-educated author. This is typical of printed notices of the era – threatening notices sent by Ribbonmen, for instance, displayed a limited grasp of literacy, contained crude drawings, and were usually written by someone of a basic educational standard. This notice suggests lower-class involvement, yet a knowledge of a national event being played out in Dublin seems obvious. It is difficult however to quantify the impact of national events on rural areas as the local dynamic could vary considerably. The conditions needed for conflict were present in northern Fermanagh, which appears to have been an area of considerable tension. It was reported that 'Orangeism and Romanism seem high throughout the district' of Devenish, which was almost equally divided in a religious sense.[82] In the parish of Enniskillen, 'among themselves there is great dissension and jealously with regard to their religious views [...] their ardour seems unabated [...] the same feeling seems to pervade the breast of the nobleman and the peasant'.[83] The parish

and Societies, 11:1 (2007), pp 83–112. **79** Ian d'Alton, 'From Bandon to ... Bandon: sectarian violence in Cork during the nineteenth century' in Kyle Hughes and Donald MacRaild (eds), *Crime, violence, and the Irish in the nineteenth century* (Liverpool, 2017), pp 175–92. **80** NAI: Outrage Reports, Co. Donegal (1839) 5421/7. **81** *ECEP*, 19 July 1838. **82** Angelique Day and Patrick McWilliams (eds), *Ordnance Survey memoirs, parishes of Fermanagh II, Lower Lough Erne* (Belfast, 1992), p. 49. **83** Angelique Day and

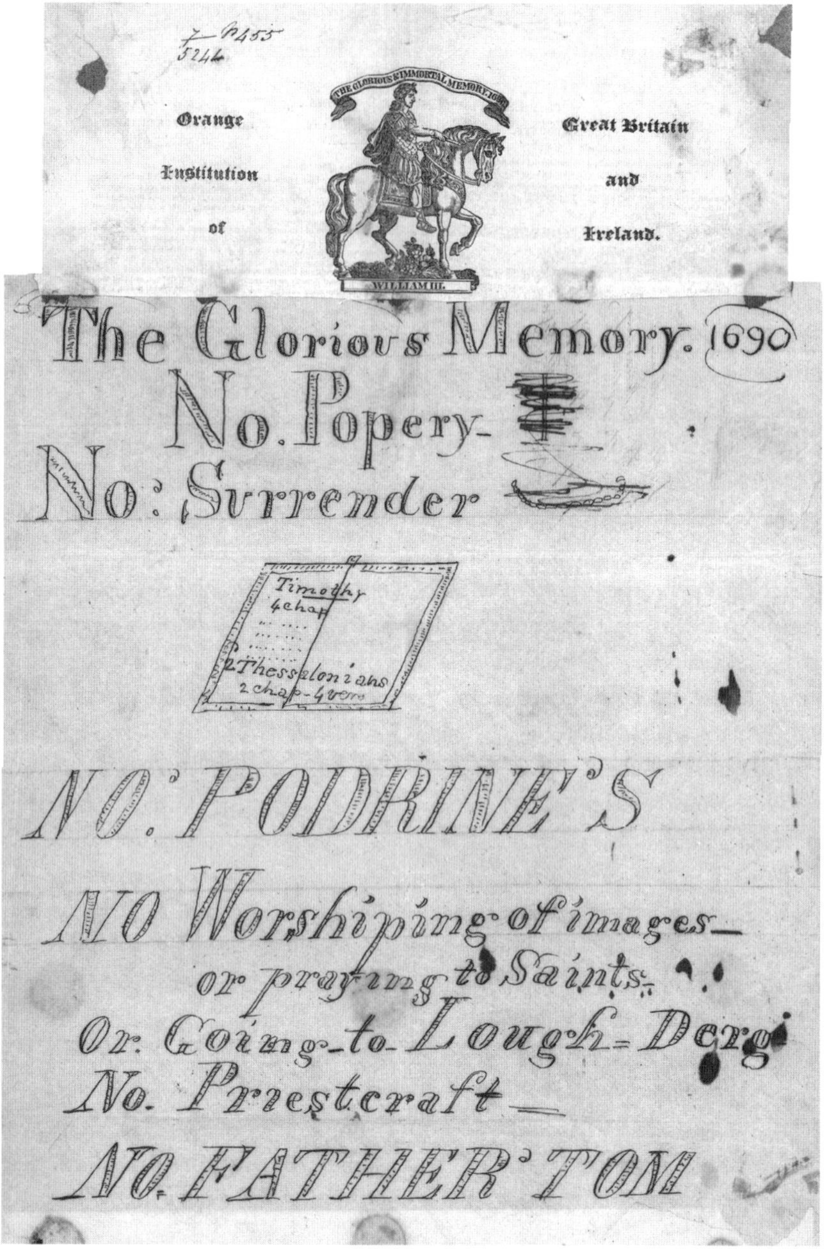

1 Threatening notice posted by Orangemen in Pettigo, Co. Donegal, NAI: Outrage Reports, Co. Donegal (1839), 542/7.

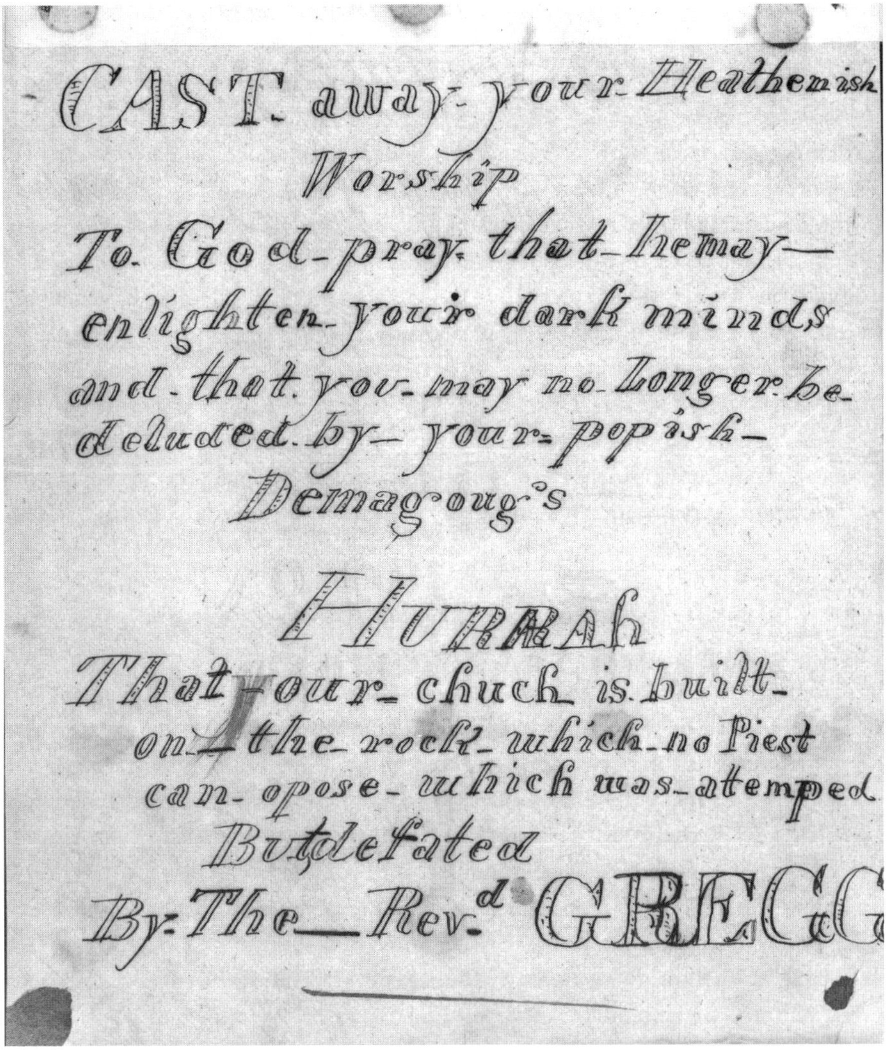
CAST. away your Heathenish
Worship
To. God pray. that he may
enlighten your dark minds
and that you may no Longer be
deluded by your popish
Demagoug's
HURRAh
That your chuch is built
on the rock which no Piest
can opose which was atemped
But defated
By The Revd GREGG

of Templecarne in which Pettigo is located was also evenly split along religious lines, as was Magheraculmoney in which Kesh is situated.[84] In addition to this, nearby Lough Derg was a popular site of Catholic pilgrimage. It was areas such as these where tensions could prevail on an ongoing basis. As noted earlier in Coleraine, areas dominated by one group were generally more settled as the 'enemy' was too few in numbers to be considered a threat. The opposite was true in north Fermanagh. The town of Enniskillen occupied a place in popular Protestant memory due to its withstanding of the siege of 1689, the Twelfth being celebrated with great gusto as a result. The earl of Enniskillen, the marquis of Ely, Sir Arthur Brooke and the Archdall family were all high Fermanagh Orangemen whose influence permeated the lower classes. The Protestant population was exclusively adhered to the Church of Ireland, and therefore much more likely to frequent the Order than their Presbyterian counterparts who held a more complicated view in their support of Orangeism. Thus, perfect conditions existed in northern Fermanagh for sectarian tension. The Pettigo notice points to a Protestant population, even in certain remote rural areas, that found itself increasingly nationally aware and rallying to the political and religious causes of the day.

It must be noted, however, that these conditions and their resulting tensions were not by any means indicative of Ulster as a whole. The case study of north Fermanagh provides a glimpse of the complexities of a province that was not in any way a single homogenous unit. In fact, responses to the 'other' varied greatly. Sectarian homicide rates remained low even in the 1830s and 40s, indicating that sectarian violence was seldom premeditated.[85] Sectarian violence generally occurred in a controlled, organized and frequently alcohol-fuelled situation, or was driven on by outside events. In microcosmic rural Ireland, 'ordinary' crime of a non-sectarian nature dominated the police reports sent to Dublin Castle. Examining the 167 outrage reports compiled by police in County Tyrone (a county evenly divided between Catholics and Protestants) in 1836, it emerges that only thirteen of these can be genuinely considered crimes of a sectarian nature.[86] Most crime was related to family dispute, theft, infanticide, land issues, and commonly waylaying and assault. Sectarian crime provided a small fraction of the outrages investigated by police. This would suggest that it simply did not permeate the lives of Protestants and Catholics on a regular basis, and allowed for a relatively cordial relationship to exist for at least the most part of the year outside of marching season.

Patrick McWilliams (eds), *Ordnance Survey memoirs, parishes of Fermanagh I, Enniskillen and Upper Lough Erne* (Belfast, 1990), pp 57–63. **84** Day and McWilliams (eds), *Ordnance Survey memoirs, parishes of Fermanagh II, Lower Lough Erne*, p. 49. **85** McMahon, 'The madness of party: sectarian homicide in Ireland, 1801–1850', pp 83–112. **86** NAI: Outrage Reports, Co. Tyrone 1836. Reports for the entire

OPPOSITION AND LETHARGY

It cannot be ignored however that an undercurrent of local sectarian tension played some part in the lives of the lower classes. This tension became more pronounced as the century entered its second decade. A new Catholic association, the Ribbon Society, had emerged as a natural successor to the Defenders and was determined to stand up to what they saw as Orange provocation and insult. From 1810 onwards clashes between Orange and Green became more frequent. Serious clashes took place in Belfast, Letterkenny, Ballinahinch, Killeter, Maghera and Kilkeel. One of the most notorious collisions took place in Garvagh in County Derry. In an almost carbon copy of the battle of the Diamond, the Catholic party was beaten off with loss of life by the superior firepower of the Orangemen stationed in the local tavern. The increasing frequency and violence of such clashes saw the erosion of much government acceptance of the Order, as it was recognized that the peace and stability of the country was being compromised by such continual friction. The report of Judge William Fletcher to the Wexford grand jury was indicative of the feelings of many government officials. Fletcher decreed that, 'with these Orange Associations I connect all commemorations and processions producing embittering recollections, and inflicting wounds upon the feelings of others; and I do emphatically state, it as my settled opinion, that until those Associations are effectively put down, and the arms taken from their hands, in vain will the north of Ireland expect tranquillity or peace'.[87] It needs to be stated that Fletcher came from a class 'of liberal dissenters' and therefore was inclined to be naturally opposed to Orangeism.[88] Nonetheless, the Order was increasingly becoming considered a nuisance by such like-minded members of successive governments. Although the 1806 coalition government had ceased official state Williamite celebrations in Dublin, official celebration was not renewed by the Tory governments that followed. Now the value of the yeomanry, ill-disciplined and a source of Orange firepower, was being debated. Already Robert Peel, as under secretary, was implementing a change in the policing of the country, change which would eventually render the yeomanry redundant. In addition to this, as the French threat came to an end, upper-class Protestants were becoming more secure in their positions. This security was added to with the defeat in parliament of Henry Grattan's Catholic emancipation bill of 1813. Thus, a distance began to emerge between the government and the Order during this period, a distance that would become ever wider over the course of the next three decades.

year are examined. **87** *The charge of the Hon. William Fletcher to the grand jury of the County of Wexford at the summer assizes in 1814*, p. 4. **88** Ibid., p. 21.

Respectability became the problem for many Orangemen from the higher social orders. The complexity of remaining within the law, while remaining within the Order, was one of delicacy for the upper classes. As a result, 1810 had seen the contentious secret articles of the Orange constitution omitted, while in 1814 the secret oath was amended in order to maintain the legality of the organization. Pleas were made to live in peace with Catholics but while localized sporadic clashes with Ribbonmen persisted, by the middle of the decade there was little overall Catholic threat to fear. For instance, in July 1815, it had been feared that the local Castledawson procession would be attacked by Ribbonmen. This did not happen however as, 'awed into silence and despondency by the torrent of our national successes, and well aware of the determined spirit of these true friends of their king and country, the crest-fallen mountaineers remained at home'.[89] The lessening of the perceived Catholic threat coincided with the defeat of Napoleon ensuring, 'as a consequence, Irish Protestants were able finally to contemplate an existence free of the threat of foreign invasion'.[90] It was widely considered that a French invasion would have resulted in a huge Catholic mobilization on the side of the invader. In addition to this was the fact that the government did not now need Catholic recruits to bolster its armed forces, which could be scaled back in the aftermath of Waterloo. This allowed it to conveniently drop the carrot of Catholic emancipation that had been dangled to ensure Catholic loyalty and recruitment. So ensued a period of Protestant comfort coinciding with somewhat of a drop in confrontational Orange activity. By 1816, the Waringstown parade passed 'without one instance of impropriety of conduct, or even a shadow of religious animosity [...] several Roman Catholics accompanying their Protestant neighbours in the procession'.[91] The following year, Belfast district went so far as agreeing that no parade would take place.[92] Indeed, it was later explained by Verner that, 'as the danger ceased, I conceive that the Orange Societies in a great degree ceased also [...] about the year 1814, the Society had in a great measure died away'.[93] This may have been greatly overstating the situation but without an external enemy (the threat from Catholicism) upon which to focus, the Order descended into a rather stale period that was punctuated by internal bickering. Without an external target upon which to focus, Orangemen could occasionally turn on each other. Following a parade in Kilrea, a band of Orangemen 'having continued at their rendezvous 'til a late hour at night' began to quarrel among themselves. The resulting fracas saw one man being stabbed, another receiving a fractured skull, while an elderly man

89 *Dublin Journal*, 20 July 1815. **90** James Kelly, '"Disappointing the boundless ambition of France": Irish Protestants and the fear of invasion, 1661–1815', *Studia Hibernica*, 37 (2011), pp 27–105. **91** *BN*, 16 July 1816. **92** *BN*, 4 July 1817. **93** *State of Ireland report*, p. 327.

was left 'in a dangerous situation'.[94] General inactivity also brought the problem of unsanctioned rogue Degrees to the surface. For instance, the legal status of the Order, so preciously guarded, came under threat from 'heathenish' degrees such as the Scarlet, Black and Royal Arch Purple, which sought to co-exist within the Order structure. These degrees allegedly sought to introduce 'ritualistic degrees into the Orange Institution and as a consequence make it a mirror of Freemasonry'.[95] Mattison explains that upon foundation in 1795 the Orange Order had two main degrees – the Orange and the Plain Purple. However, another degree operated in many rural lodges, the Royal Arch Purple, which traced its lineage from previous Protestant groups such as the Boyne Society and the Society of Aldermen of Skinners' Alley.[96] Stewart Blacker was of the opinion that such lodges, 'arose from the desire of the lower orders to have something more exciting or alarming in the initiation of members; I think it may be a mixture of freemasonry with that of the old Orange system, a species of mummery innocent in itself, and originating in the strong desire that vulgar minds in general manifest for awful mysteries and ridiculous pageantry'.[97] Such thought was prominent in Armagh especially and proved difficult for the Grand Lodge to eradicate. These degrees were much more mysterious and ritualistic than the Orange and Plain Purple Orders allowed by the Grand Lodge of Ireland. The Grand Lodge certainly had no place for bizarre initiation rituals or a plethora of different degrees under its umbrella. Possibly more important was the fact that upper-class authority could be undermined by such renegade Orders.[98] There was little or no gentry involvement in these degrees thus little control could be exerted by the upper classes. This posed a problem for the upper rung of society, which was eager to return to the system of deference and obedience that had come undone over the previous century. Countless steps were taken including purges and the expulsion of those who indulged in such activity but eradication proved difficult and the issue was never fully resolved satisfactorily. Potentially more damaging was the alleged leaking of signs and passwords to Ribbonmen, which although unproven, rocked the stability of the Order and summed up a period leading into the 1820s during which general inactivity bred internal dispute and mistrust.

94 *BN*, 21 July 1818. **95** Paul Malcomson, *The forgotten history of the Orange Order – the institution's historic struggle against the Royal Arch Purple and Black degrees (1798–1925)* (Banbridge, ?), p. 5. **96** Jonathan Mattison, '"From Dolly's Brae to Westminster", the loyal Orange Institution in Ireland *c.*1849–1886' (PhD, Queen's University Belfast, 2005), pp 94–5. **97** *First report on Orange lodges*, p. 122. **98** Mattison, '"From Dolly's Brae to Westminster"', p. 100.

CATHOLIC REVIVAL

This general lull however was to be broken by the onset of two important factors. The first of these was the rise of Daniel O'Connell as a political force and the re-invigoration of the campaign for Catholic emancipation that had again been denied by parliament in 1820. In creating the Catholic Association in 1823, O'Connell succeeded in creating a mass movement drawn from the lower classes and driven by the clergy – a dangerous combination in the eyes of many – to further his crusade for Catholic emancipation. Buoyed by the rising hysteria of the arrival of a Catholic champion, Ribbonism, which had been in decline, underwent a revival. Although O'Connell had absolutely no interest in such a violent society, many of its members saw his coming as a prelude to a day of reckoning that would culminate in the extermination of Protestantism in Ireland. Millenarian thought had become widespread on both sides of the religious divide especially after the turbulence of 1798; evangelical Presbyterians particularly eagerly awaited the Second Coming of Christ. Widely distributed pamphlets and the rantings of itinerant preachers had contributed to commonly held beliefs on both sides that final victory for their chosen religion was imminent. The popularized prophecies of Signor Pastorini, the pseudonym used by an English cleric, predicted that the absolute destruction of Protestantism would occur in 1825. In the early years of the decade, against a backdrop of such promise, Ribbon activity in the north of the country substantially increased. Additionally, support for the Rockite movement in Munster greatly intensified. Citing Benburb, Verner alarmingly described a typical Ribbon scene:

> where they assembled in very great numbers, dressed with white ribbons around their arms, and white bands upon their hats, having come in different directions into the town between one and two o'clock in the morning [...] from that period we may date the disturbances that have latterly occurred in that part of the country. After that period, for a length of time, they attacked the Protestants returning from the fairs and markets, whom they waylaid, knocked down and beat indiscriminately and unprovoked.[99]

There is, of course, a difficulty in separating the actions of individuals and Ribbon or indeed any secret society activity. Waylaying and assault were notorious occurrences throughout the country especially after fairs and markets where large amounts of alcohol were usually consumed and old scores settled. Therefore, it is difficult to pinpoint these crimes specifically to any sectarian

99 *State of Ireland report*, p. 329.

motive. Also problematic is the fact that many of the better classes (to which Verner belonged) had difficulty in separating more general Catholic activity and frequently included O'Connell, Ribbonism and sporadic unconnected acts of individuals as being part of a concerted Catholic campaign against Protestants. Verner nevertheless explained how the Order was reinvigorated as a result of this apparent pan-Catholic front:

> I think about four years ago [1821] the Orange societies had again ceased to meet in great measure, until the formation of the Catholic Association, when from the violent publications and denunciations of that body, and also from the meetings of the Ribbonmen, which about the same period spread a vast deal of alarm throughout the country, the Orange societies again met, and continued to do so.[100]

Verner, faced with defending Orange confrontational activity, felt a need to justify the Order's revival and play a blame game. Nonetheless, this revival was not to go unchecked by government authority.

RELIGIOUS REVIVAL

It might be thought that the campaign for Catholic emancipation triggered what became known as the Second Reformation. However, this is not the case. A tradition of Protestant religious revival was already firmly in place stretching back to the mid-1600s and had been especially active in the 1740s when John Wesley arrived in the country. Wesley built up a considerable following with his emphasis on 'faith, the literal truth of the Bible, personal conversion, and a new enthusiasm'.[101] Such teachings fell on fertile ground, especially with the shock and uncertainty that followed the 1798 rebellion. The economic downturn had left many Protestants bewildered and with little to cling to other than their faith. Yet, it seemed evident that the main Church groups were not equipped to deal with the uncertainty of the times. The stagnant state of the state-protected Established Church provided its more ardent followers with grounds to seek reform; indeed, Wesley's Methodists saw fit to split from Anglicanism in 1817. Many orthodox Seceding Presbyterians, uncomfortable with the liberalism of 'New Light' Arians, sought a return to an unquestioned civil authority. Also opposing 'New Light' Presbyterianism were Reformed Presbyterians who differed from Seceders by rejecting civil authority and the oath system that it entailed. Clearly, within wider Protestantism the time was at hand for a major revival.

100 *State of Ireland report*, p. 327. **101** Bardon, *A history of Ulster*, p. 249.

While theological and restructuring issues certainly had to be addressed, much emphasis was placed on the conversion of Catholics. Although Methodists had led the way in this area by sending Irish-speaking missionaries to rural Catholic areas, Established Church efforts soon predominated due in no small measure to funding from England. Recognizing the importance of education in conversion attempts, schooling was offered by religious societies such as the London Hibernian Society and the Kildare Street Society. New schoolhouses were erected while thousands of Bibles were printed in Irish and freely distributed. In Ulster, especially, thousands of Catholics did avail of the 'free' education offered by Protestant societies, but how many converted is open to question. Such schools did nonetheless contribute to the ongoing fraternizing of Catholic and Protestant children as evidenced by the 84 Catholics, 20 Church of Ireland Protestants and 5 Presbyterians who attended Knockbaragh Kildare Place school in County Down, for example.[102] The Catholic Church felt compelled to actively respond to the alleged proselytizing campaigns of such societies. The Catholic Church in Ireland, although weak in terms of organization, underwent something of a reformation itself prior to the Famine. Although it is correct to say that the Church's main revival occurred after the Famine with the arrival of Paul Cullen, valuable groundwork had been laid in the 1820s and 30s – much of it as a response to the aggression of the Protestant Second Reformation. Internally the Catholic Church tightened its discipline demanding greater piety from its priests, and embarked on improving church buildings, many of which were basic in the extreme. Priests engaged in well publicized debates with their Protestant counterparts, some of which lasted days on end. Many popular superstitious practices were quashed, the Temperance Society of Father Mathew was hugely successful (at least in terms of the numbers it attracted), while the involvement of priests in O'Connell's campaign for Catholic emancipation is well documented. Many Protestant schools were broken into and ransacked. Windows were smashed in schoolhouses belonging to the Kildare Street Society in Aughaloo and Upper Langfield within a short period of 1838, while the following year the door and windows of the London Hibernian schoolhouse in Termonaguirk were broken and a number of New Testaments in English and Irish were destroyed, along with other books and desks.[103] The by-product of Protestant evangelical zeal was to provoke a feisty response from the Catholic Church and polarize relations between ground-level Catholics and Protestants to a greater degree in comparison to the relatively peaceful existence that had previously existed.

102 Day and McWilliams (eds), *OSM, parishes of County Down I, 1834–6, south Down*, p. 38. **103** NAI: Outrage Reports, Co. Tyrone (1838 and 1839) 89/28, 131/28, 449/28.

STATE SUPPRESSION OF THE ORDER

The fear of a united Catholic campaign hell bent on the destruction of Protestantism in Ireland continued to gather momentum. In the background to such frenzy was the appointment of the seemingly pro-Catholic emancipation Richard Colley Wellesley as lord lieutenant in 1821. Pursuing a policy of conciliation,[104] Wellesley set the tone for apparent Catholic favouritism by immediately dismissing Saurin and replacing him with the liberal William Conygham Plunkett. The visit of George IV to Dublin had seen the new king, recognizing the damaging effects of triumphal celebration, make 'an indirect call for an end to public celebration of Williamite victory'.[105] In July 1822 O'Connell, seizing the moment, requested the ending of the traditional Orange dressing of the statue of King William in Dublin. This was a request to which Wellesley, who had by now recognized the need to curb Orange displays, readily agreed. The orders of Wellesley were furiously resisted by Orangemen who decorated the statue more lavishly than ever thereby ensuring a clash with Catholics that evening. A similar decoration, planned to commemorate the birthday of William, was banned by an irate Wellesley the following November. Despite this, the dressing of the statue proceeded and ended with a clash between Orangemen and the police. The anger of Orangemen manifested itself in December when Wellesley attended, with the cream of Dublin society, a play at the newly opened Theatre Royal. Almost immediately cries of 'no popery' and 'no surrender' rang out from a small section of the audience, while an orange was thrown onto the stage and a bottle at the orchestra. While this was not the most serious incident, it was a serious breach of protocol, and summed up the frustrations of many Orangemen at the administration of Wellesley.[106] It also marked the point of obvious severance between the government and the Order. The relationship that had been established prior to and during the 1798 rebellion had already been on the slide; now it passed the point of repair. Almost immediately the 1823 Unlawful Oaths Act aimed at suppressing secret societies forced the Grand Lodge to abolish the Order's secret oath if the body was to stay within the law. Members were now compelled to take their oath in the presence of a magistrate rather than secretly in their local lodge as previously. Furthermore, under government pressure the duke of York had already been forced to resign as grand master, now many ambivalent Orangemen withdrew from the association. In desperately trying to stay within the law, the Grand Lodge went as far as banning Twelfth of

104 Shunsuke Katsuta, 'Conciliation, anti-Orange politics and the sectarian scare: Dublin politics of the early 1820s', *Dublin Historical Record*, 64:2 (Autumn, 2011), pp 142–59. **105** Hill, 'Loyalty and the monarchy in Ireland', pp 81–102. **106** Chris Morash, 'Boys be wicked', *Irish Review*, 29 (2002), pp 10–21.

July marches in 1824. The Grand Lodge, no doubt hoping to return Orangeism to the moral high ground, dictated to its district masters that:

> it is of great importance that the brethren in your district should act in the most strict conformity with an order which tends so strongly to shew, how much the members of the Orange Association are willing to sacrifice their feelings, or even prejudices, of their fellow subjects, and how desirous they are that no excuse should be left, for ascribing any of the disorders that afflict Ireland, to their conduct of example.[107]

Despite these hopes, such actions were huge blows to the morale of ordinary members. Although lodges were able to survive, Senior argues that confidence was greatly weakened by these seemingly submissive measures.[108] Unfortunately for the Order, government reaction to O'Connell's increasingly strong Catholic Association took the form of banning the Association even though it was non-violent and had made pains to stay within the law. O'Connell in response demanded that the Orange Order should also be banned, a demand which the government readily approved. Despite the many measures taken by the Grand Lodge of Ireland to remain within the law and the presentation of a petition reminding the government of its loyal service in 1798, the Unlawful Societies Act came into effect in March 1825. This Act outlawed the Orange Order exactly thirty years into its existence.

OUTLAWING OF THE ORDER

The ban was reluctantly accepted by the Grand Lodge who issued a circular to its members asking that they 'yield a willing obedience to what is now the law of the land'. This was a request that was difficult for many ordinary members. It was rightly pointed out by Strabane magistrate James Sinclair 'that, it has become rooted in them, so that it would be very hard to eradicate it'.[109] Although some higher Orangemen, such as the Revd Holt Waring of Lurgan, were able to prevent processions from taking place in July, many of the lower classes insisted on parading despite the potential consequences of such law breaking acts. Processions were halted by the military and magistrates in Enniskillen and in Carrickfergus after some negotiation, but in Portadown and Moira the military were unable to deter the Orangemen.[110] Although law and order was maintained in Dublin and Belfast, disobedience was again evident during the marching

107 *State of Ireland report*, p. 353. **108** Senior, *Orangeism in Britain and Ireland*, p. 185. **109** *First report on Orange lodges*, p. 351. **110** *BN*, 15 July 1825.

seasons of 1826 and 1827. The core membership, in general, refused to listen to either their leaders or the threats of the law and continued their summer processions. Commenting on processions that took place in Dungannon during these years, Tyrone landholder Richardson Bell justifiably asked 'how could they assemble themselves together in those large bodies, if they had not lodges [in which] to sit and consult'.[111] While it suited the upper classes such as a defensive Verner to claim that Orange Societies 'ceased to exist upon the passing of the late Act', the Order most certainly did continue despite its government ban albeit as an organization under much lesser upper-class control.[112] Those that remained, such as Fermanagh's Edward Archdall, urged his brethren 'to cultivate the friendship of their Catholic neighbours, to live on terms of amity towards them, for he was sure they all knew to be an Orangeman engendered no feelings of hostility towards any man'.[113] But, for many, this was to prove increasingly difficult in the face of continued Catholic agitation.

THE THREAT OF CATHOLIC EMANCIPATION

The appeal of Archdall was the image of the Order that its upper classes wished to present. But in terms of combating Catholic political mobilization, and the government's ban, such noble rhetoric had the result of largely neutralizing the effectiveness of the Order. O'Connell rather easily sidestepped the ban of his Catholic Association by renaming and re-organizing it thereby allowing him to continue his campaign and raise all-important funds much as before. On the other hand, the Orange Order showed no such initiative and allowed itself to rather fall away as a coherent national organization during this period. The impotence of such a formidable adversary allowed O'Connell to press ahead and upset the Irish electoral system, which had been one of the main obstacles in the way of the emancipation campaign. Although initially reluctant to follow localized initiative, O'Connell eventually backed pro-emancipation candidate Villiers Stuart to run against the landed Beresford interest in the Waterford by-election of 1826. The victorious Stuart, as a Protestant, could sit in Westminster and campaign on behalf of O'Connell, who as a Catholic was ineligible for election. This tactic was replicated in election contests in Armagh and in Monaghan where Henry Westenra took the seat. Moving to the next level of agitation, O'Connell then somewhat hesitantly stood himself for election in Clare in 1828. In again mobilizing the Catholic vote and providing protection

111 *Third report on Orange lodges*, p. 64. **112** *State of Ireland report*, p. 331. **113** *ECEP*, 16 August 1827.

against landlord intimidation, his success was assured as was the success of a number of liberal Protestant candidates who supported emancipation. The ineligibility of the new MP for Clare to take his seat provided a serious problem for the government. The juggernaut of Catholic political mobilization seemed unstoppable at this point. Spontaneous meetings drawing thousands of people occurred, mainly in Munster, and increasingly took on a militant face.[114] Denying the right of O'Connell to sit as an elected representative of the people would surely lead to a situation of major instability or possibly even uprising in Ireland. There seemed little option for the government but to grant Catholic emancipation.

For the Protestants of Ireland, the majority of whom opposed this measure, the demise of the Orange Order had effectively taken away their main agent with which to counter O'Connell and put forward the Protestant viewpoint. While lesser Protestant associations were formed to fill the void left by the Order, they lacked its appeal and were poorly supported overall. The Benevolent Orange Institution created by Revd Sir Harcourt Lees initially excited the *Belfast Newsletter*, which optimistically considered 'the discovery that the fiery spirit of the Association has had a salutary influence on the dormant energies of Protestantism'.[115] This optimism was to prove groundless as the Benevolent Institution and indeed the newly formed Brunswick Clubs did little to encourage lower-class resistance to O'Connell and thus garnered little widespread support from this segment of society. The favoured protest weapons of these groups – political lobbying and petition – held scant appeal for the lower classes who were more *au fait* with physical resistance and the violence that usually resulted. In the words of Senior, these organizations 'did not meet the needs of rural Ulster and achieved very little'.[116] This general inactivity from 1825 until 1828 ensured that even upon the expiry of the Unlawful Societies Act too much ground had been lost and the momentum was firmly with the Catholic party. The non-extension of the Act saw the official revival of the Orange Order. A new Grand Lodge was put in place with fresh laws and regulations being enacted. There were issues of legality to consider that worried some former members. For instance, former grand chaplain, John Graham of Magilligan, was fearful that 'certain individuals are again attempting to draw out the Protestant population into an illegal and dangerous association'.[117] Nevertheless, July 1828 saw a return of large-scale Orange processions throughout Ulster in an almost desperate attempt

114 Gary Owens, '"A moral insurrection": faction fighters, public demonstrations and the O'Connellite campaign, 1828', *Irish Historical Studies*, 30:20 (November, 1997), pp 513–41. **115** *BN*, 1 February 1828. **116** Senior, *Orangeism in Britain and Ireland*, p. 218. **117** NAI: Outrage Reports, Co. Londonderry (1828) 1828/364.

to regain lost ground. Huge turnouts were seen in Lisburn, Dungannon, Rathfriland, Monaghan, Ballybay and Ballymena. The Ballymena correspondent of the *Newsletter* recognized the gravity of the Catholic threat and reported that:

> Protestants, too, though wholly unconnected with the societies, have, on this occasion, without distinction of sect or class, manifested a warmth of feeling, and the growing inclination to make the cause of Orangeism a *common* cause; and this is as it should be, the general aspect of the times, and more particularly the famous humbug exhibited in Clare, has opened their eyes to the necessity of this.[118]

However, the fact that no parades took place again in either Belfast or Dublin rather emphasized that the common Protestant front needed to stall O'Connell was still not present. Indeed, on the eve of the Twelfth, Lees had called on his gentlemen members 'to use their best endeavours, in the various districts, to prevent any infraction of the public peace, by impressing on the Orangemen the necessity of particular caution as to giving offence to the humblest Roman Catholic they might meet in their progress'.[119] In addition to this higher desire to avoid conflict, despite what the *Newsletter* may have thought, many liberal-minded Protestants together with Presbyterians hoping to gain legal equality with their Established Church counterparts actively supported the idea of Catholic emancipation. This naturally further softened the effect of pan-Protestant opposition. The somewhat-belated formation of the Brunswick Clubs in September 1828, while theoretically socially inclusive, again appealed mainly to the upper classes. Although they spread rapidly, the favoured weapon of petition ahead of militant action held little attraction for the Protestant lower classes rendering the movement 'a spectacular failure'.[120] More appealing to the Protestant lower classes, however, was the kind of direct confrontation so opposed by Lees. This occurred at Ballybay, County Monaghan, when thousands of Orangemen assembled, under the direction of the previously mentioned local publican and district master Sam Gray. Their mission was to halt the progress of O'Connell's agent John Lawless and his self-proclaimed 'tour of Ulster', which was designed to drum up untapped Catholic support in the province. Faced by heavily armed Orangemen, Lawless had little option but to heed police advice and end his tour. *This* was the type of action that appealed to the common Orangemen, not political levying carried out in the stuffy halls of Westminster or the mere placing of an 'x' on a petition. As pointed out by Blackstock, 'nationally

118 *BN*, 15 July 1828. **119** *BN*, 8 July 1828. **120** Suzanne T. Kingon, 'Ulster opposition to Catholic emancipation, 1828–29', *Irish Historical Studies*, 34:134 (2004), pp 137–56.

focused politics and local defensive militancy were ultimately incompatible [...] Brunswick faced modern challenges, but many adherents found traditional Orangeism met their concerns better'.[121] But for those Orangemen subscribing to local militancy no opportunity for a repeat action arose. Most likely realizing the effect of antagonizing Orangemen and wary of the effects of violence on British public opinion, O'Connell withdrew his campaign from the Ulster arena and continued his pressure campaign in the relative safety of southern Ireland. As a result of this campaign and the anarchy that was almost sure to follow any rejection of O'Connell's right to sit as an MP, the government in April of 1829 finally granted Catholic emancipation.

ORANGE REACTION

The reaction of most Protestants to what was considered to be a government betrayal was one of fury. For some, this fury manifested itself in violent clashes with Catholics throughout the summer marching season of 1829. Although the duke of Cumberland, as grand master, had hoped for no processions, the Grand Lodge of Ireland did not officially order its members to desist from parading. Large processions took place in Belfast, Comber, Lisburn, Magherafelt, Banbridge, Downpatrick, Monaghan, Ballybay, Coleraine, Tandragee, Armagh, Randalstown, Waringstown and Castledawson, all of which passed off relatively peacefully. However, skirmishes between Orange and Catholic factions occurred in Maghera, Bellaghy, Strabane, Greyabbey, Newry and Clones, while more seriously lives were lost on both sides at Stewartstown, Portglenone and Macken. Indeed, the situation at Macken prompted the *Newsletter* to fear that 'the whole country is in a state of alarm'.[122] This was probably overstating the situation and a semblance of normality returned with little incident of note occurring over the next twelve months. The government nonetheless, fearing a repeat of the violence of 1829, took the step of banning processions the following July. But although the Grand Lodge on this occasion called on members not to march, large parades once more took place. The act of banning processions had little effect as police numbers were simply too few to enforce such rulings, while many magistrates, being members of, or sympathetic to, the Order, took little or no action. Thus, Orange processions continued and indeed accelerated as it soon became obvious that O'Connell was not content to merely settle for Catholic emancipation. In actuality, its granting had changed very little for the vast majority of Irish

121 Blackstock, 'The trajectories of loyalty and loyalism in Ireland, 1783–1849', pp 103–24. **122** *BN*, 21 July 1829.

Catholics other than to demonstrate that collective action on a mass scale *could* achieve results. Buoyed by this, and moving away from the peaceful ethos advocated by O'Connell, many Catholics furiously resisted tithe payments due to the Established Church – a resistance that erupted violently especially in the early stages of the 1830s. This resistance led to the loss of lives at Newtownbarry in County Wexford and at Rathcormack, County Cork, while thirteen members of the police were massacred at Carrickshock, County Kilkenny. Other disaffected Catholics joined the Ribbon Society, which had been reinvigorated during this period and which was again able to provide a serious threat to Protestants and Orangemen at a local level. Cavan's earl of Farnham ominously warned Protestants to:

> avoid being out at night – transact all your business, both of a private and public nature, as much as possible before sun-set. Do not unnecessarily frequent fairs, or other places of public resort, and avoid every needless and improvident expenditure of money, endeavouring to lay by something for the time of need.[123]

Such fear saw a renewal of Protestant upper-class activism, an activism that was not averse to bringing Orangemen on board for protection. Fearing disruption to an upcoming meeting of the Cavan 'Protestant Clergy and the freeholders', the Revd Marcus Beresford recognized 'through the masters of the Orange lodges we could secure a very large attendance of Protestants so early as to occupy every corner of the courthouse before the other party [Catholics] arrived'.[124] This general increased tension caused many moderate Protestants to question their previous positions. A Mr Stubber from Queen's County, 'who had been of liberal principles', bemoaned the change of attitudes prevalent in the Catholic mind that had now been filled with new confidence. He thus explained his 'conversion' to Orange principles:

> If anyone had said to me five years ago 'you will become an Orangeman', I should have looked upon that person as a very false prophet; so opposed was every impression on my mind to such an association; but our opinions change with the times and the position in which we find ourselves placed. I have become an Orangeman, and I will tell you why; before Catholic emancipation, I looked upon the Papists as struggling for what they had a just right to demand; and I was humbugged by the professions of bishops,

123 *BN*, 17 January 1832. **124** National Library of Ireland: The Farnham papers, MS 18,608, Beresford to Farnham.

> priests, and laymen of the party into the belief that they would rest satisfied with equal rights, nor have since seen how one and all have believed those professions, nor have witnessed the conduct or rather misconduct, of the Roman Catholics since the passing of the Relief Bill, nor have come clearly to the knowledge of the ulterior views and objects. It is this knowledge which has led to the increase of Orange Societies, together with the violence and outrage by which they are forwarding their objects [...] it is because I feel the necessity which exists for union among Protestants in defence and property, that I have joined the Orange Society.[125]

For many moderate Protestants who had been sympathetic towards emancipation, the continuing agitation of Catholics went beyond their empathy. It was now considered that these visible physical threats simply had to be met and countered. It seemed that the most obvious way to do this was to form a society or political party to make the Protestant case on the national stage.

THE PROTESTANT CONSERVATIVE SOCIETY

At a political level, the next target for O'Connell was a repeal of the Union and a return of a Dublin parliament. This would now, of course, be dominated by Catholics – an almost doomsday-like scenario for Protestants. As part of an overall greater programme of reform, the government seemed intent on eroding the Protestant position of supremacy in Ireland. This would possibly go a long way to providing a remedy to the perceived wrongs that Catholics highlighted. Against this backdrop of continued Catholic agitation, and with a continued influx of more liberal-minded Protestants, a new political society emerged in November 1831 that 'constituted the first practical response to the new politics [of reform]'.[126] Headed by MP and Donegal Orange leader, the Revd Charles Boyton, the Protestant Conservative Society (PCS) was quickly patronized by landed proprietors such as the earl of Enniskillen and Sir Arthur Brooke, both high Orangemen. The Society rapidly attracted rural gentlemen and their patronage. This patronage was vital as the involvement of the lower orders was considered key in the defence of Protestantism in Ireland.[127] Set up as an association to best serve the interests of Protestants, there was a close connection between this new society and the Orange Order. Boyton proudly proclaimed that 'everything connected with this Society, the character and names of the members

125 *First report on Orange lodges*, pp 198–9. **126** K.T. Hoppen, *Elections, politics, and society in Ireland, 1832–1885* (Oxford, 1984), p. 280. **127** Ibid.

who compose it, the object it proposes, the plan of its operations, harmonize expressly with the avowed objects of the Orange Association'.[128] While it could be argued that Brunswick Clubs had possibly been too docile in their attempts to oppose government concessions, from its onset the PCS was much more active. While O'Connell had to an extent organized mass mobilization of the Catholic lower classes in 1828, he and his Catholic Association had shied away from officially sanctioning the large-scale meetings of Catholics that followed his election victory. Conversely, no such ambivalence emerged from within the PCS, which immediately began the organization of a series of countrywide meetings to demonstrate its discontent, and its numerical strength, to the government. Throughout January and February 1832, a number of these were held throughout the country which attracted tens of thousands of Protestants of all classes. One of the biggest of these was held in Enniskillen, an examination of which demonstrates the coming together of the Protestant classes in popular protest.

This meeting was no simple protest meeting hastily convened by the lower classes. On the contrary, it was well organized by the upper classes who ensured that the lower classes were first mobilized but more importantly kept in an orderly manner. In the same vein as O'Connell's reasoning, there could be no signs of violence present at any of the PCS meetings if a moral high ground was to be maintained. Such a gathering of the lower classes could be potentially explosive. Referring to the Catholic meetings of 1828, Owens asserts, 'what made these spectacles particularly remarkable however, was that their participants were mainly drawn from the very lowest ranks of rural society and represented groups which had been hitherto excluded from the political process'.[129] The same conclusion can be drawn from the meetings of the PCS. While O'Connell would later use priests as controlling agents at his mass repeal meetings of 1843, on the other side of the spectrum, the PCS used landlords and their agents to maintain discipline and control. This was made much easier because of common class membership of the Orange Order.

This control allowed for a well-organized and choreographed meeting to take place. A significant venue in popular Protestant memory, the town itself was brightly decorated with flags flying from most buildings. Four parties of Orangemen, each comprised of several lodges, were led into the town in military parade 'by the leading noblemen and gentlemen of their respective neighbourhoods'.[130] At the head of these processions, which entered the town from different directions, were notable Orange leaders such as Brooke, Lord Viscount Cole, the marquis of Ely and his son Lord Loftus, and Mr William

128 *DEP*, 22 March 1832. **129** Owens, 'A moral insurrection: Faction fighters, public demonstrations and the O'Connellite campaign, 1828', pp 513–41. **130** *DEP*, 28 January 1832.

D'Arcy of Necarne Castle. It was reported 'there were many others who had to come greater distances [...] headed by most respectable gentlemen'.[131] It is obvious that considerable planning had taken place in organizing the logistics of such a grand entrance. With long distances to travel for some tenantry, transport and food would have to have been provided by their landlords. In the case of contentious election contests, landlords were known to provide food and alcohol to their mobilized tenantry.[132] There is no reason to think otherwise of this assemblage. This is an example of the successful working of the two-way relationship between landlord and tenant, a relationship that required the landed class to provide an incentive to its tenantry and co-religionists if loyalty was to be assured. This loyalty was indeed forthcoming as the Orangemen 'with flags floating in the air, and marching to the music of various respectable bands' soon swelled the crowd to an estimated 50,000. Owens rightfully asserts that estimates of crowds during this period need to be scaled down but even so, it is evident that a substantial crowd was present.[133] By twelve noon, 'the scene was truly imposing, the colours of the various lodges were now seen flying from the windows of the several houses at which the parties rendezvoused', and such was the crowd that the meeting had to be moved from the courthouse to the outdoor fair green where a hustings was hurriedly constructed.[134] With the meeting commencing at one o'clock, the several speakers made clear the necessity for unity among Protestants, and their determination to fight government reform. It was made explicitly clear that the Orange Order was to provide the means to halt Catholic progress, which was being seemingly accommodated by the government. William D'Arcy viewed 'the Orangemen of Ireland as the best and trust [*sic*] supporters of the Protestant interests in this country; and we call upon them to afford that protection which they have hitherto done'.[135] Edward Archdall quoted from Cromwell and advised his fellow Orangemen to 'put your trust in the Lord, and keep your powder dry', while Lord Loftus asserted that it was 'to the Orangemen and Protestants of Ireland we look for assistance and support'.[136] Such calls abounded during the course of the meeting and were greeted eagerly by the large crowd, although it is quite likely that very few of them actually heard the sentiments of the speakers. As the high sheriff concluded the meeting by calling for 'three cheers for the Protestants of Ireland', 'the various lodges assembled at their places of rendezvous, and formed themselves into four great district parties, in which order they marched out of town playing "Protestant Boys" and "The Boyne Water". On their departure they were headed by the Noblemen and

131 Ibid. **132** Hoppen, *Elections, politics, and society in Ireland, 1832–1885*, pp 399–400. **133** Gary Owens, 'Nationalism without words: symbolism and ritual behaviour in the repeal "monster meetings" of 1843–5' in J.S. Donnelly, Jr and Kerby A. Miller (eds), *Irish popular culture, 1650–1850* (Dublin, 1999), pp 242–69. **134** *DEP*, 28 January 1832. **135** *BN*, 31 January 1832. **136** Ibid.

Gentlemen in like manner as before described on their entrances'.[137] In terms of mobilizing the Protestant lower classes, the meeting was a great success, comparable to the meetings of O'Connell. The difference was that the PCS had the backing of a largely militant organization that was well armed and prepared to use violence to stem government reform. It remained to be seen whether this massive force would be used by the PCS.

SUCCESS OR FAILURE?

Following the upsurge in Protestant mobilization, the PCS continued its close connection with the Orange Order. Nobles such as the earl of Roden and the marquis of Ely quickly joined the Order, and the links between the organizations continued to strengthen. The PCS defended Orangemen facing prosecution by employing lawyer W.R. Ward to fight their cases.[138] Funding was facilitated by the collection of a 'Protestant rent', which was generously supported by the likes of Enniskillen and Roden, who both donated £100 in July 1832.[139] The collection of this 'Protestant rent' yielded an average £570 per week in 1832 and meeting proceedings were widely reported in the press in order to maximize the cause.[140] A petition was sent to Westminster with Derry MP Robert Bateson, asking for a removal of the government ban on processions that had been enacted for the summer marching season. Although the petition was unsuccessful, the work of the PCS was greatly appreciated by the Orange lodges, many of whom echoed the sentiments of Waterford lodge, no. 924, which resolved, 'that we conceive it our bounden duty to co-operate with that excellent society in forwarding and establishing, by every possible means, its interests and proceedings'.[141] Part of this co-operation involved lodges collecting subscriptions, which were gladly accepted by the PCS.[142] Roden noted, 'it is a matter of great satisfaction to this society to find that it has been so well supported by the Orangemen of Ireland'.[143]

Despite this close alliance, the PCS was doomed to failure. The mass meetings had certainly mobilized the Protestant community and likely gave many a political awareness they may not have had previously, but their actions gained little support within government circles. Rather than bow to Protestant pressure, the government instead enacted several reforms throughout 1832 and 1833 considered sympathetic to Catholics. Changes in the electoral system broke open previously closed boroughs, a new system of education threatened to implement

137 *DEP*, 28 January 1832. **138** *DEP*, 26 July 1832. **139** Ibid. **140** J.H. Whyte, 'Daniel O'Connell and the Repeal Party', *Irish Historical Studies*, 11:44 (September, 1959), pp 297–316. **141** *DEP*, 30 August 1832. **142** *DEP*, 25 October 1832. **143** *DEP*, 3 January 1833.

non-denominational schooling, the magistracy was drastically culled, the yeomanry disbanded, the central constabulary continually expanded, while the Irish Church Temporalities Act savagely attacked the protected position of the Established Church. With the passing of so many acts of reform, it could be argued that the PCS failed in its objectives. Following the passing of the Church Temporalities Act, *The Warder* probably correctly summarized that the PCS had been set up too late and that 'it had failed of the great object which it sought to effect'.[144] PCS activity continued at an official level irregularly but the great mobilizations of early 1832 were not repeated; in fact, the PCS had suspended its activities by October 1833. Large-scale coming together of Orangemen continued throughout the marching seasons of 1833 and 1834 but very much as a specifically Orange entity rather than as PCS-organized events.

But what the PCS did contribute to was 'rapid adjustment and organizational drive' while helping cement the links between Orangeism and Toryism as part of a pan-Protestant front.[145] Hoppen explains that Toryism became much more than a political movement alone, it in fact 'became an explicit propellant of action' during the 1830s and 40s.[146] The lower classes were actively courted and brought on board, especially in regard to elections. Voter registration drives were fine-tuned by the likes of Belfast's John Bates whose underhand valuations of property ensured Tory electoral dominance in the city. Even greater efforts were made in the south where registration election societies were set up in many areas, greatly supplemented by English funding.[147] But perhaps the most telling contribution of the lower-class Protestants was their presence at election contests. Although few of their number had a vote, the intimidation factor provided by these Orangemen in support of Tory candidates was a feature of election contests throughout this period. It is difficult to measure the extent to which Orangemen were politicized but with such a litany of issues to protest, it must be considered that attitudes were greatly sharpened in the post-emancipation period.

PROTESTANT EMIGRATION AND COLONIES

Overall, a bleak picture was being drawn for Protestants in Ireland throughout the 1830s, many of whom were choosing emigration as the safest option. It was estimated that between 1829 and 1832, 94,000 Protestants had left Ulster alone.[148] The *Newsletter* lamented that Protestant emigration 'has caused us no ordinary regret, especially when we recollect the tenacity with which R. Catholics

144 *The Warder*, 11 September 1833. **145** Hoppen, *Elections, politics, and society in Ireland, 1832–1885*, pp 278–80. **146** Ibid. **147** Ibid., p. 300. **148** 'Protestant emigration', *The Dublin University Magazine*; *The Belfast Newsletter*, Tuesday, 14 May 1833; CMSIED 200296.

cling to their natal soil, and the possibility that in the progress of time, unless Protestants materially change their migratory habits, even Protestant Ulster will cease to deserve the name'.[149] It was also feared that the middle classes made up the bulk of these emigrants thereby leaving the ill-disciplined and illiterate extreme lower classes as the standard bearers of Protestantism. Government official R.M. Muggeridge recalled how:

> in a conversation with one of the Government emigration agents, at a principal northern port, I learned that the total emigration which had taken place from that port in the five years 1834–8, amounted to 14,233 persons, every one of whom had paid their own expenses, and whom were represented by him as 'a great loss to Ireland'. They were also I found, with very trifling exceptions, all Protestants, and many of them small capitalists, and as he expressed it, 'exactly the sort of persons it was most desirable to keep at home'.[150]

Muggeridge went on to warn that they should not 'loose [*sic*] sight of the possibility of the places of good men being supplied by other less useful members of society'.[151] In a bid to counter such a drain Protestant colonies had already been established in Donegal, Armagh and Cavan, and were considered a viable option in halting emigration of disenchanted Protestants. This was, in the words of Derry Protestant landlord H.B. Beresford, 'of all things the worst to be dreaded'.[152] One of the key players in this project was Marcus Beresford, who in expressing his sorrow that so many Protestants were emigrating in 1826, had wished 'there was an enactment to stop them'. He was, however, 'quite sure that the union there has lately been cemented between all classes will be a great means of preventing them'.[153] Prominent Orangemen, the earls of Enniskillen and Farnham, Donegal MP Edmond Samuel Hayes, as well as William Blacker threw their weight behind this colony scheme. This scheme also sought to reinforce the second coming of Protestantism that had being sweeping Ulster since the 1820s. It must also be pointed out that some landlords used religious zeal to bring their tenants back to a state of compliance. Evangelicalism suited many of the upper classes who actively funded its growth and used it to suit their own ends. According to Myrtle Hill, 'for those who had much to lose from the political and religious challenges of their generation, the Biblical promise of eventual victory

149 'Emigration to America', *The Belfast Newsletter*, Friday, 6 April 1832; CMSIED 980444. **150** *Hand-loom weavers report*, p. 772. **151** Ibid. **152** PRONI, Barre Beresford, Cheltenham to Sir George Hill, D642/221; CMSIED 800423. Irene Whelan, *The Bible war in Ireland: the 'Second Reformation' and the polarization of Protestant–Catholic relations, 1800–1840* (Dublin, 2005), p. 237. **153** National Library of Ireland, Farnham papers, MS Beresford to Farnham, 18,608.

was particularly appealing; and in Ulster both the earl of Roden and the duke of Manchester [Mandeville] kept a wary eye on the Book of Revelation and the "Sign of the Times"'.[154] Living on the estate of Mandeville in north Armagh certainly had its advantages. Samuel Lewis' *Topographical dictionary of Ireland* reported that:

> a very extensive and important charitable establishment has been founded on the moral agency system by Lord and Lady Mandeville, upon the estate of Tanderagee, the benefits of which are open to the whole of their numerous tenantry, in the improvement of whose moral, intellectual, and social condition, it has, though comparatively in its infancy, already produced the most beneficial effects. The establishment includes a loan fund, a clothing fund, three dispensaries, an orphan asylum, a circulating library, and 25 public schools, to each of which is attached a lending library. The loan and clothing funds are conducted by the moral agent resident at the castle; the dispensaries are in the towns of Tanderagee, Portadown, and Tullahappy, and are open one day in every week, under the care of a physician, who devotes the whole of his time in dispensing medicines and in visiting the poor tenants at their own dwellings.[155]

There was also an:

> orphan asylum, at Tanderagee, [which] is open to the female orphans of the Protestant tenantry, who are boarded, clothed, and educated for service in respectable families. The schools, for which spacious and handsome buildings, with houses for the master and mistress, have been erected, are scattered over the whole estate; those in this parish are at Tanderagee, Corvernagh, Cargans, and Ballymore, in which are about 260 children and 100 infants. There are also schools at Portadown and Mullantine, in the parish of Drumcree, and also in the parishes of Seagoe, Kilmore, and Killevy; to each is attached a Sunday school, and the aggregate number of children in all the schools exceeds 2000. An annual festival takes place at the castle, where all the children assemble and are hospitably entertained by Lord and Lady Mandeville; on the last occasion, more than 2000 children attended.[156]

Such an apparent well-ordered estate surely was financially costly but the loyalty of tenants was assured for Mandeville. As pointed out by Miller, evangelicalism was used by some landlords to purge radicalism and secularism from lower-class

154 Myrtle Hill, *The times of the end; millenarian beliefs in Ulster* (Belfast, 2001), p. 34. **155** Lewis, *Topographical dictionary of Ireland*, pp 593–4. **156** Ibid.

Protestants, while also uniting them against Catholic political demands.[157] In 1831, for example, 10,000 Orangemen marched around the castle of Mandeville, who was the Armagh Orange grand master, in Tandragee 'to pay compliment'. This was followed by a similar gathering of 8,000 the following year.[158] In 1833, an effigy of the despised liberal magistrate William Hancock was burned at the castle gate of Mandeville, while his tenants were also instrumental in the wrecking of Annahagh village following the Armagh election victory of Colonel Verner in 1835. Hempton and Hill contend that 'the personalizing of estate management and the obvious temporal advantages to be gained by conforming to the landlord's expectations, forged a bond between landlord and Protestant tenant'.[159] This would appear to have been the case on the Mandeville estate. By providing for the needs of his tenants, Mandeville ensured their loyalty, a loyalty which could be mobilized to intimidate and provide physical force against Catholics and liberal incursion when considered necessary.

The Protestant Colonisation Society, formed in 1829, was initially strongly tied to the Order and hoped to improve conditions by establishing co-operatives that would enable self-sufficiency of Protestant tenants. The Grand Lodge encouraged support and hoped that each member would donate 6*s.*, which would raise £60,000 and enable 1,000 Protestant families to move to productive land.[160] By introducing new farming methods, hard work and discipline, the likes of Farnham and Enniskillen, key members of this organization, hoped to better the condition of their tenants.[161] This lead was followed throughout the country especially in Connacht where the archbishop of Tuam played a prominent role. The colonies also doubled as missionary centres that sought to reinforce the Protestant religion; this ensured much cohesion with the religious aspect of the Order, which itself placed great emphasis on prayer and the Bible. The instruction provided by the ever-increasing number of clergy that had joined the Order offered an additional spiritual level of comfort for its members. Although ultimately both Protestant colonization and the hoped-for conversion of Catholics was largely unsuccessful, these campaigns did offer better living conditions, spiritual comfort and hope for some Protestants.

But, in general, colonization campaigns were recognized to be of little use by most Orangemen, the very idea being in fact a cause for concern on occasion. Indeed, a letter promoting colonization from the infamous veteran of 1798, J.C. Beresford, had not been well received by the Grand Lodge. It sternly noted that 'it appears to us so completely inconsistent with the essential principles of the

157 Miller, *Emigrants and exiles*, p. 87. **158** *Second report on Orange lodges*, p. 16. **159** David Hempton and Myrtle Hill, *Evangelical Protestantism in Ulster society* (London, 1992), p. 65. **160** *L Sen*, 30 September 1829. **161** Whelan, *The Bible war in Ireland*, p. 252.

Orange Institution, that we cannot by any means consider a gentleman, entertaining such sentiments, a fit and proper member of the Grand Orange Lodge'.[162] Beresford, unlike his well-regarded father, was considered 'cruel, mean-spirited and arrogant [...] his hatred of Catholics bordered on the pathological'.[163] While popery and the teachings of Catholicism were disliked by many Protestants, absolute hatred of Catholics was not prevalent nor was it part of official Orange doctrine. The 'errors' of Catholics were blamed on general ignorance and their lack of enlightenment rather than blatant sectarianism. This was a stance many upper Orangemen were keen to publicly forward hence the condemnation of Beresford. It must be recognized that such evangelicals as Beresford did not by any means make up a majority within the combined Protestant religion. There was, as highlighted by Hempton and Hill, 'mutual antipathy between "sound, pious and rational Christians", and the whole body of evangelical "enthusiasts"'.[164] Evangelical preachers were often not 'qualified' to interpret scripture and were frowned upon by Church authorities for operating outside of their sanction and for being the instigators of sectarian violence. Thus, for the Order, many of whose members were still orthodox Protestant at this point, such sentiment as expressed by Beresford was unhelpful and contrary to their Christian beliefs.

On the other hand, it is difficult to know how popular Beresford's sentiments actually were. Granted, the Order officially condemned his blatant sectarianism but the Order was under increasing scrutiny from the government at this time. It had little option but to condemn the sectarian utterances of extreme members such as Beresford. Wright considers that the condemnation of Beresford was part of the Order's grand condemnation of colonization and its policy of removing Catholic tenants for Protestants.[165] Without any clear evidence, it is difficult to say to what extent Beresford's views were popular. It is also difficult to say whether the Order was merely covering itself from the inevitable political attack that would follow, or if it was genuine in its sentiments. Either way, such public bickering did little to enhance the reputation of the Protestant Colonization Society.

In addition to this issue, the necessary funds were not forthcoming. Even 6*s.* was beyond the reach of the lower classes, while landlords of the less extreme nature seemed to take little interest. Addressing the PCS in 1834, the Revd J.B. McCrea 'deplored the decay of that excellent institution, the Protestant Colonization Society, which had originated with the patriotic Orangemen, but

162 *First report on Orange lodges*, p. 225. **163** Kevin Haddick-Flynn, *Orangeism, the making of a tradition* (Dublin, 1999), p. 186. **164** Hempton and Hill, *Evangelical Protestantism in Ulster society*, p. 66. **165** Frank Wright, *Two lands on one soil* (Dublin, 1996), p. 95.

was now almost destitute from the supineness [*sic*] of the landed proprietors'.[166] For a variety of reasons, Protestant colonies were not the success hoped for and had rather petered out by the end of the decade.

RENEWED PROTESTANT MOBILIZATION

Yet amid the uncertainty, new hope was rather unexpectedly offered to the discontented Protestants of Ireland. The king, William IV, thoroughly unhappy with the general reform of the Whig government, dismissed its entire ministry, as was his prerogative, in December 1834. The Protestant Conservative Society was re-ignited and began another campaign of Protestant mobilization. Mass Protestant meetings followed around Ulster in late 1834 and early 1835 in towns such as Hillsborough, Dungannon and Enniskillen, attracting tens of thousands of Protestants eager to display their support of the king's actions. Other Protestant associations such as the Protestant Association and the National Club worked in tandem with the PCS and the Orange Order as 'complimentary extra-parliamentary pressure groups of the post Reform Bill period'.[167] This assistance, and the resulting return of Peel as prime minister, was gratefully received by the Orangemen of Ireland. In an address of gratitude to the king, Trinity College Orange lodge happily declared that its 'confidence [...] has been re-assured by the prompt confirmation of these sentiments, given by Your Majesty's dismissal of a Ministry, from whose line of policy we had every reason to be in the highest state of alarm for the existence of those Protestant institutions and privileges which form the basis of this free and enlightened Empire'.[168] Queen's County's Stradbally Orange lodge reiterated its:

> Fixed determination 'to assist, if necessary, with our blood in upholding those prerogatives which the British Constitution has conferred upon the Sovereign' and thanked His Majesty for having dismissed 'the ministers who were inimical to our Protestant Institutions, and who had allied themselves with the open and avowed enemies of our Religion, and for having placed in their stead Ministers whom we alone can depend on'.[169]

The king was, of course, the ultimate figurehead to Orangemen whose loyalty was pledged to the Crown and not the government of the country. Had not

166 *L Sen*, 15 November 1834. **167** Gilbert Cahill, 'Some nineteenth-century roots of the Ulster problem, 1829–48', *Irish University Review*, 1 (1970–1), pp 215–37. **168** *Orange lodges. Copies of addresses to the king from Orange lodges in Ireland; with the answers returned thereto*, HC 1835 (30), xlv.453, p. 1. **169** *Orange Societies. Addresses from the Brotherhood Club, and Orange Stradbally lodge; with the answers*

George III vetoed prime minister Pitt's pledge to grant Catholic emancipation in 1801 thus ensuring a protection of Protestant interests?

Yet the sense of relief and the hope of a reassertion of royal authority that resulted from the king's actions was to be short lived. The new Tory government of Peel was in the hopeless position of being in a minority in the House of Commons and quite simply could not last. The inevitable election contests were marred by sectarian conflict as some ultra Protestant candidates utilized Orangemen to ensure their political success by use of intimidation and violence. The anti-Catholic rhetoric of speeches by men such as the Presbyterian minister Henry Cooke, who had captivated the Hillsborough assemblage, simply added to Protestant disaffection. Such rhetoric succeeded in strengthening the desire of many Protestants to fight government changes and O'Connell. Cooke's oratory at Hillsborough was remarkable especially given that it called for a unity between Presbyterians and Church of Irelanders who were far from natural allies. Once again, evangelical zeal mixed itself with politics. The elections returned the Whigs to power under the leadership of Lord Melbourne but it was a power now dependent on its majority on the Irish MPs under O'Connell's control. Indeed, the position of O'Connell was further strengthened by the signing of the Litchfield House compact. This agreement created a united political front against the Tories and ensured further reform in Ireland. This compact, somewhat forced upon the Whigs given their precarious grasp on power, put O'Connell in an extremely strong position as it made the prime minister 'a prisoner of O'Connell's Irish "tail" – the famous "tail" that wagged the dog'.[170] Under the terms of the compact, the issue of repeal was dropped by O'Connell in return for the continuation of Whig reform. But for most Protestants it must have seemed that O'Connell's ultimate goal would eventually occur if the present situation was allowed to continue.

With a backdrop of such uncertainty and fear, processions did continue despite increasing police interference and took on even more importance as a show of strength to both the government and Catholics. New members flocked to the Order, so much so that by 1835 it had surpassed the numerical strength it had enjoyed prior to the government ban of 1825. It could now claim a membership of over 200,000, which although numerically heaviest in Ulster could draw on considerable support outside of its northern bastion. As part of the Protestant united front, 'southern' meetings had already taken place in Dublin, Sligo, Cork and Wicklow. Now, driven on by prominent members of the elites such as Robert Hedges Eyre, the recently enrolled earl of Bandon, Lord Longford,

thereto, HC 1835 (84), xlv.449, p. 3. **170** Cahill, 'Some nineteenth-century roots of the Ulster problem, 1829–48', pp 215–37.

the marquis of Thomond, Sligo MP E.J. Cooper, Viscount Powerscourt and Randall Plunkett, many Protestants in southern Ireland felt that the Order was at this stage their only defence mechanism. As reiterated by d'Alton, 'in short, it [the Order] was to act as an internal support for a section of the Irish people who felt that, for many reasons, they needed that support'.[171] Although Bandon was the deputy lieutenant of Cork, he made no secret of his discontent at the government. This discontent was heightened following Lord Mulgrave's refusal to sanction the election of Mr Robert Deane as lord mayor of Cork in 1835 because of his 'notorious Orangeism'. This was considered a move 'calculated to publicize the Whigs' stand against Orangeism in institutional positions of state'. An enraged earl attended a November dinner of 700 Orangemen in the city.[172] Here he summed up the feelings of many of his brethren in his criticism of the government. He summarized that the reforms of the government:

> If not happily intercepted by the awakened loyalty of the Protestants of the United Kingdom, would appear to overwhelm the Altar and the Throne in one common ruin – to erect Popery in their stead – to separate the sister countries, and to re-enact, perhaps, the horrors of 1641, amid the orgies of a besotted laity, an intolerant priesthood, and the fraudulent practices of a self-convicted and mendicant Agitator.[173]

Already, some 5,000 people had attended a Protestant meeting in Bandon as part of a series of the Protestant meetings organized throughout the country designed to mobilize support and demonstrate opposition to the government. Driven by such feeling and by the 'sudden acceptance of the Order as socially respectable' by the upper classes, the county of Cork was now home to 21 lodges under the stewardship of Eyre of Macroom Castle. Although the Poor Law Commission bemoaned that Bandon was 'peaceable except when disturbed by the Orange processions, which may be reckoned upon to a certainty once a year', Somers Payne, a Cork gentleman, was:

> Fully persuaded of the happy and beneficial results attendant on the extension of the society [...] as it is justly viewed as a bond of union loudly called for by the unfortunate existing state of society, and considered, under Providence, one chief safeguard and protection; indeed without such a connecting link, I feel assured that the number of Protestant emigrants would have greatly increased, as in the adverse days of oppression, it is

171 Ian d'Alton, *Protestant society and politics in Cork, 1812–1844* (Cork, 1980), p. 210. **172** d'Alton, *Protestant society and politics in Cork*, p. 208. **173** *The Spectator*, 21 November 1835.

> almost incredible to think how a poor Protestant is cheered and comforted by the conviction that he has at least some kind of friends to look to for advice and support.[174]

This lead was followed in the south-east which had seen Wicklow and Wexford, with almost 40 lodges between them, take over from Carlow as the strongpoint of Orangeism in south Leinster. Deputy grand treasurer H.R. Baker explained that previous to 1832 there was but one lodge in the county of Wexford, now however:

> The questions about the non-payment of tithe and the repeal of the union were very much discussed in that county, and the outrages were very numerous, so much so that I heard it from gentlemen of great consideration in the county that it was quite dangerous for a Protestant, even in the daytime, to ride along or travel the roads unarmed; they then formed Orange lodges, and now, I understand, they consider that they can go about the county by day or night, from the mere moral effect of knowing that there is a body of men ready to support the police with perfect safety.[175]

Further north, a sufficient force of Orangemen from Westmeath and Kildare was able to join with their Meath and Cavan brethren to seriously disrupt the Meath election contest in January 1835.[176] Lodge numbers in Dublin had dropped possibly because the upper classes had disassociated themselves in the previous years but a strong working-class element remained active spurred on by the firebrand evangelical Revd Tresham Gregg. Connaught saw Leitrim, with 29 lodges, head numbers while Longford and Queen's County, with 8 lodges each, ensured that the Order in the midlands maintained a solid existence. The town of Mountmellick had regularly been the scene of Orange parades during the 1820s and had been the setting for frequent party clashes as Orangemen zealously defended their right to place a flag on the mountain. The town had also seen relations deteriorate as Catholics had boycotted Protestant businesses during the campaign for Catholic emancipation. Although 'exclusive dealing' was not officially endorsed by the Catholic Association, some higher members were supportive.[177] This policy also was affected in areas of north and mid-Leinster,

174 *First report on Orange lodges*, p. 200. *Poor Law Commission*, p. 172. **175** *First report on Orange lodges*, p. 198. **176** *Third report on Orange lodges*, p. 30. **177** J.H. Hill, 'Carrying the war into the walks of commerce: exclusive dealing and the southern Protestant middle class during the Catholic emancipation campaign' in F. Lane (ed.), *Politics, society, and the middle class in modern Ireland* (Hampshire, 2010), pp 65–88.

and had the effect of heightening sectarian tensions. Such tensions had polarized many Protestants in Mountmellick, so much so that the town was described as 'the very hot-bed of southern Orangeism'.[178] Baker was now able to claim that 'there is hardly a gentleman of property or station in the county who is not a member'.[179] These figures were of course dwarfed by Ulster numbers – Tyrone just short of 200 lodges, Antrim and Armagh exceeding 200 each – but they did demonstrate a countrywide organization. The Orange Order was now well placed, sufficiently powerful and popular enough to provide a serious obstacle to the campaigns of O'Connell and the concessions to Catholics of the Whig government.

* * *

The Orange Order, while travelling somewhat of a bumpy road, had risen to enjoy vast numerical support in its forty years of existence. Unsurprisingly, the vast majority of its members were drawn from the lower classes but possibly unforeseen was the involvement of the upper classes in such a movement of the masses. The benefits to rank-and-file Orangemen of such involvement of these better classes was offset to a certain degree by the loss of government sanction and acceptance. The Order was hereafter faced with threat not just from Catholic quarters but also from the very government of the king – a king to whom they professed loyalty. The twin threat of government suppression and further Catholic encroachment would be faced and vigorously fought by Orangemen in an ever-shifting social, political and economic arena.

178 *KI*, 14 July 1827. **179** *First report on Orange lodges*, p. 198.

CHAPTER TWO

Dissolution and reformation

If 1835 can be considered the zenith of Orange popularity in Ireland, then it is safe to say that its nadir was reached within a surprisingly short period. The ever-contracting tether of reluctant government acceptance would finally snap and throw the Order into chaos and confusion as it was pushed into a period of official non-existence. However, a number of factors either emerged or actually remained in place to ensure that the need for such an association remained vitally important for large numbers of Protestants in Ireland. These factors, together with the fact that the fraternalism offered by such an association was simply too central especially in lower-class Protestant society to disappear, meant that this was an organization destined to re-emerge in the not-too-distant future. The conditions that resulted in the reformation of the Orange Order, and the obstacle-laden path that led to its official nationwide revival, will form the crux of this chapter.

DISBANDMENT

The importance of the Order in everyday Protestant life, and as a bulwark against further giving way to Catholics, faced a monumental threat with the dissolution of the association in the face of a government enquiry into the body in 1835. Many within the Whig government of Lord Melbourne, such as Scottish radical Joseph Hume, despised the Orange Order and all that it stood for and called for an official government inquiry into it. This call was echoed by Daniel O'Connell, eager to see such a powerful opponent banned. He was, of course, backed by his supporter MPs upon whom the government was becoming increasingly dependent to maintain its House of Commons majority. To most Orangemen this inquiry was yet another step in keeping with what they believed to be the unjustified yet continued government attack on the Protestants of Ireland. The commission appointed to carry out the inquiry was heavily loaded against the Order and found accordingly against the Orangemen in its report. This report simply confirmed what most people already knew: that Orangemen were prominent in the legal and civil services of the country and that they played a pivotal role in the state apparatus. Also highlighted was the extent of the organization and its popularity within the Protestant community, again not too damning common knowledge. More damagingly however, the report confirmed the extent to which Orange lodges existed within the army – a possible, if unlikely, threat to national security. Oath-bound societies were banned within the military services and although this was a measure aimed at Catholic Ribbon secret societies, it also by default included the Orange Order. Given that the grand master of the Orange Order, the duke of Cumberland (brother of the king), was a field marshall in the army, this revelation caused considerable embarrassment to the royal family. This embarrassment was further heightened by the actions of one Captain Fairman who had approached influential Orangemen in mainland Britain with vague plans to oust the rightful heir to the Throne, Princess Victoria, and replace her with Cumberland. While these approaches by Fairman were generally dismissed by most Orangemen as the wild fantasies they were, the very fact that they took place at all was pounced upon by opponents of the Order including many of those within the government. That Fairman refused to produce his personal diaries to the government fuelled suspicion and left the government with little option but to plan the outlawing of the Orange Order.

Before this could happen, the Grand Lodge of Ireland took matters into its own hands. The prospect of being banned would be one of humiliation and many of its upper-class members hoped to avoid this scenario. Thus, the Grand Lodge of Ireland voted on whether to remain in existence or to wind itself up before the government could act. The result of the vote, which took place in February 1836, was by no means unanimous. Seventy-nine of the delegates voted in favour of dissolution, fifty-nine voted that the Order remain in existence. Many influential Orangemen, including the by-now MP for County Armagh Colonel William Verner who had vigorously defended the Order in the House of Commons, were unhappy at the prospect of dissolution. Nevertheless, the majority had their way and issued a 'manifesto' to its membership justifying its decision. The Grand Lodge conveyed confidence that this was merely a temporary decision; point vii of the 'manifesto' expressed confidence:

> that the moral effects of Orangeism will not pass away with its organization – that Orangemen will still remain united in reality, although not in name, and that if danger should become imminent there will be no difficulty in reorganizing our system – an assurance which seems justified by the former revival of the Institution after an interruption of three years.[1]

1 Richard Niven, *Orangeism as it was and is* (Belfast, 1899), p. 85.

The previous ban enacted in 1825 had been short term with the Order emerging stronger from it than it ever had been. There was no reason to suspect any difference on this occasion. With an avenue for revival left open, the Grand Lodge of Ireland ordered the wind-up of the Orange Order in February 1836 after forty-one years in existence.

REACTION

This decision, despite the assurances of the Grand Lodge 'manifesto', was greeted with some indifference by most of the lower-class membership. While the upper-class membership had met and debated the crisis facing the Order, the rank and file had not been consulted in any way. There was not, of course, anything unusual in this given the rigidity of the social norms of the day that denied the lower classes a voice in most aspects of life. However, implementing the disbandment of the Order was well-nigh impossible. The embarrassment of the upper classes was not shared by this core membership of the Order who did not, of course, frequent the social scenes of London and Dublin. For the upper classes it was convenient, in order to deflect criticism, to assert that the Order no longer existed. Claiming in 1840 that there were now no Orange societies in Ireland, king's council and Conservative MP for Coleraine Edward Litton described how:

> As soon as his late Majesty, William 4th, had expressed an opinion unfavourable to the existence of that society, all the noblemen and gentlemen who had been the leaders of that loyal body – for so he might term it, although he never had been an Orangeman, nor ever would belong to any secret political association in his life – assembled, and though by law they might have continued their meetings, abandoned the privilege, in deference to the wishes of the Crown.[2]

This assertion may have had some substance as far as the noblemen and gentlemen were concerned but it rang hollow for those outside this class sphere. For the upper classes, the void left by the demise of the Order was replaced by membership of Conservative Societies and continuing participation in politics. The Irish Metropolitan Conservative Society, closely linked with Trinity College, was founded in 1836 to replace the PCS with Charles Boyton again taking control. Although the IMCS was less extreme than the PCS it was considered by some, such as Dublin MP and late Orangeman George Alexander Hamilton, as

2 *Hansard, HC Deb, 29 January 1840, vol. 51, cc 737–835.*

something of a replacement organization for the Orange Order. Although this was publicly denied by Orangeman Randall Plunkett MP of Dunsany Castle, and by the *Dublin University Magazine*, the links between both groups could not be ignored.[3] But whether the IMCS was a cover for the Orange Order or not, it was of little use to lower-class rank-and-file Orangemen, whose social status excluded them from such an organization.

At ground level, away from the glare and the politics of high society, the prospect of life without the Order was not one that many ordinary Orangemen were prepared to accept. The common thought emerged that the lodges did not *need* a central body or indeed the upper classes to function. After all, what right did less than 200 delegates have to decide the future of a body that contained a reported 200,000 members? Thus, the majority of lodges remained in operation on an independent basis following dissolution and continued as normal, albeit without many of the upper classes and without an efficient central body of control. The Grand Lodge of Armagh, with Colonel William Blacker at its head, had taken on the functions of the Grand Lodge of Ireland in June in order to 'preserve the Orange system from annihilation'.[4] Although its impact was limited, the summer of 1836 saw parades continue as usual although on a smaller scale and bereft of much upper-class leadership and sanction. No processions were reported in the popular media during the summer of 1837 as the death of the king, William IV, and the subsequent accession to the throne of Victoria, took journalistic precedence but Under Secretary Drummond did acknowledge that in County Antrim for instance 'there were so many found guilty [of walking in illegal processions] that there was some difficulty in finding room for them in the gaol'.[5] Pointing to the fact that a new lodge had been established at Ballyhenry, outside Belfast, the *Northern Whig* lamented 'that the Orange system is, at this moment, in active operation, nobody in Ireland doubts'.[6] This assertion was confirmed by Antrim barrister Francis Workman-MacNaghten who had hoped that 'the moon of Orangeism had waned into her last quarter' but was forced to conclude 'but now she has filled her horns again'.[7] Backing this up was the Grand Lodge of Armagh's call for a nationwide revival since, 'that as now the experiment of the dissolution of our Institution has been fully tho' fruitlessly tried, we deem the present a fitting opportunity to call upon our Brethren throughout the country to re-organize the [Grand] Lodge of Ireland'.[8] By the actions of these Orangemen in the immediate post-dissolution period it became patently obvious that this society would not be allowed to die.

3 *Dublin University Magazine*, 9, January–June (Dublin, 1837), pp 6–12. 4 Grand Orange Lodge of Ireland, Edward Rogers, *Memorials of Orangeism*, vol. ii. 5 *State of Ireland in respect to crime*, p. 988. 6 *NW*, 28 October 1837. 7 Francis Workman-MacNaghten, 'Some observations on the present state of Ireland' (London, 1837). 8 Rogers, *Memorials of Orangeism*, ii.

EARLY SEEDS OF REVIVAL

The call from Armagh was heeded in November of that year by those among the upper classes who had continued in their Orange capacity. At a meeting in Tim's Rooms, Grafton Street, Dublin, a new Grand Lodge of Ireland was established with County Down's Lord Roden voted as its grand master. A large landholder in counties Down and Louth, Roden was the very type of high-profile figure needed by a new Grand Lodge seeking to re-establish itself. Although he had only joined the Order in 1831, his evangelical fanatism and ultra-Tory standpoint ensured that he remained loyal to the Order through its period of 'dissolution'.[9] As a former MP for Louth (1810–20), he had voted against successive Catholic relief measures in parliament. The granting of Catholic emancipation had pushed Roden to call on Protestants of Ireland to unite despite class or denomination.[10] Instrumental in organizing the Protestant mass meetings of 1834 and 35, 'his large stature and booming voice generally made an impression'.[11] The pressing question was whether Roden could use these ideal attributes to return Orangeism to its previous position.

The committee that drew up a manifesto for this new Grand Lodge of Ireland was adamant that a defensive association was essential for Protestants and 'that the only effectual means of doing so is the restoration of the Orange Institution'.[12] This was perfectly legal, of course, as the Order had not been outlawed by the government although the Party Processions Act banning assemblies did remain in place. The *Dublin Evening Mail* advised caution however and called for a 'pause [...] and time for deliberation on a step so momentous'.[13] This hesitancy, based on a desire not to provide ammunition to opponents, was shared by many among the educated classes. As a result, the new Grand Lodge of Ireland, bereft of many central figures, meandered rather than sped onwards. Nonetheless, and despite the advice of the *DEM*, at a meeting in December of 1838 the Grand Lodge stated its intention to fully revive the Order. Some of those upper classes interested in revival, such as Verner, considered that they had dissolved the Order on the premise that the 'government would put down all other political societies in Ireland' including those of O'Connell as well as Ribbon societies. This had not happened and as far as Verner was concerned the government 'had been guilty of a breach of faith towards himself and other leading members of the Orange Association'. Lord Lieutenant Morpeth, Verner declared, 'had deceived the Orangemen whom he had induced to relinquish their societies upon false pretences'.[14] Despite such feelings of betrayal, once again

9 Bridget Hourican, 'Robert Jocelyn', *Dictionary of Irish biography*, online edition, accessed 5 September 2019. **10** Ibid. **11** Ibid. **12** *ECEP*, 23 November 1837. **13** *ECEP*, 23 November 1837. **14** *Hansard, HC*

caution was advised, this time by the *Standard*, which urged no return to the secrecy and mystery of Orangeism that had provided such tinder for the attacks of opponents. The paper feared that a revival of Orangeism would sweep away the newly invigorated Conservative Societies as they would 'be found incompatible', and implored 'our Irish brethren to think deeply before they revive the Orange Institution'.[15] While the upper classes took heed of such advice and continued to hesitate, the lower classes showed little such indecision. Joining such 'new' societies was impossible because of financial cost and class barriers – limitations not present in the Orange Order. The attraction of the Order was highlighted in the Grand Lodge report of the previous year which underlined that:

> in the Orange Institution, each brother felt support from those beneath him, protection and encouragement from those above; the interests of all were so truly identified, so happily amalgamated, that the unequal distribution of wealth and power, so far from causing envy and distrust, was not speculatively known, but practically felt to be the necessary arrangement of the parts that gave uniformity, strength and harmony to the whole.[16]

Such ties were impossible to procure in replacement societies, which in reality only targeted and catered for the wealthy. Thus, a report on the state of the Order around the country provided by the new Grand Lodge could highlight continued growth. Some counties such as Sligo and Leitrim had fallen into disorganization, others including Kildare and King's County had not posted their returns, but lodges had most assuredly continued in most counties. It was a given that the Order would continue in Ulster because of its high Protestant population – Antrim and Armagh for example were reported to have 213 and 212 lodges respectively in 'active operation', while 200 lodges continued to function in Down and 109 in Derry. These figures are hardly surprising; what is more striking however was the continuing activity of Orange lodges in the south of the country. It was reported that Limerick had 'distinguished itself by an open and manly upholding of the principles of Orangeism', Wexford had seen the continuation of 'true Orange spirit', while Queen's County 'continues to be distinguished for its zeal and activity'.[17] In Longford, the admittedly partisan priest Father Edward McGavern insisted that 'all of the lower order of [Protestant] people in Longford are Orangemen' and that 'all the Protestant gentry are Orangemen'. McGavern had no doubt that lodges continued to meet openly pointing to:

debate, 11 March 1839, vol. 46, cc 308–21. **15** *ECEP*, 22 November 1838. **16** *ECEP*, 23 November 1837. **17** *BN*, 4 December 1838.

> the last 12th of July [when] they attended a meeting in my parish, and had colours, and the police came to take them down, and they took them down by force; after the police went away they put them up again; and I understand they have dinners now; they do not call them Orange meetings, but they go under another name [...] I do not know exactly what name; they generally wish to conceal it.[18]

In such counties of Catholic domination, Orangeism was tenuously clung to as a defence mechanism against Ribbon attack; a withdrawal from the protection afforded by local organization could leave Protestants open and exposed to such assaults. In lamenting the decline of the Order in Leitrim, the Grand Lodge had 'little hesitation in enumerating the occurrence of four murders of Protestants within the present month, as among the results of this departure from the pale of the Orange Institution'.[19] Paradoxically, the Ribbon Society, which was sworn to oppose Orangeism, was helping to consolidate and even rebuild the Order. Commenting on Mayo, it was stated that 'the necessities of the times are forcing the institution even into this popish county'. Further encouraging news was received from Cork, which retained over 20 active lodges, as 'amongst the gratifying results of the spread of the institution in this county is the establishment of an Orange Orphan Society, which has rescued from destitution, and perhaps lapse into popery, the children of many excellent brethren'.[20] The fear of 'losing' children to Catholicism was one of the biggest fears of those involved in the Second Reformation; once again the Order was playing its part in countering the Catholic threat. At the half yearly meeting held on 22 May 1839, the Grand Lodge announced that 'it is their pleasing duty to announce that the Orange Institution, has, during the last six months, extended beyond their most sanguine anticipations'.[21] The figures provided by both reports must, of course, be viewed in the context of a Grand Lodge painting a brave face on the state of Orangeism in the country especially as its enemies continued to strengthen. This Grand Lodge of Ireland never returned the Order to its former glory or popularity during this period and in reality, served as a mere rump Grand Lodge with little or no control over its core membership. While parades did continue, it was considered in many upper circles that 'the creatures who compose those processions are the very basest of society'.[22] Aside from parading, these 'base' members of society continued to use the Orange cloak to fulfil their shared needs. The trial of Belfast publican Robert McMillan revealed a level of activity far removed from leadership approval. When police raided the Orange decorated

18 *State of Ireland in respect to crime*, p. 246. **19** *BN*, 4 December 1838. **20** *BN*, 4 December 1838. **21** *ECEP*, 6 June 1839. **22** *LJ*, 17 July 1838.

public house of McMillan, they found a group of 40–50 people, including several women, present. Witness George Sibbins testified that, 'the persons were admitted by tickets [...] they were printed and had a seal on them, representing a man on horseback. I think it is generally known as the picture of King William on horseback. The words "private ball" were at the bottom [...] I think the tickets cost 2*s.* 6*d.* or 3*s.* each. They would admit a young man and a young woman'.[23] Fellow witness Jacob Ferguson had no qualms in declaring that 'we had no object, in meeting in McMillen's that night, except pleasure'. The funds raised (around 50*s.*) were not donated to the Order but kept between the group and provided 'for a comfortable little party, and that was all we wanted'.[24] Ferguson also claimed that one of the women (Ellen McManus) was a Catholic, which would hint that cross religious socializing could also occur in the urban context. Such events organized by the lower classes ensured that the Order did not die during this period and 'maintained a lively underground existence'.[25] Organization most certainly did continue at a local level and activities did endure despite the general inadequacy of the new Grand Lodge of Ireland. Throughout the Order's short history, Orangemen had demonstrated an independence of mind, and central instruction was frequently disobeyed. This was demonstrated by the amount of processions held against the will of the Grand Lodge during periods of previous crisis and government restriction. Whether or not a central body was in place seemed to be of little relevance to many rural lower-class members. Indeed, Mattison makes the point that dissolution had actually been beneficial for the 'rogue' degrees that had so bothered the Grand Lodge.[26] Without a central authority to supress them, these degrees gained in popularity especially in rural areas. It could be argued that Protestant disobedience of authority, even clerical authority, is inscribed in its history and Orangemen were no exception to this thinking of an independent, some might say cantankerous, nature. This tied in with the 'contract' regarding deference. If upper-class sanction was not forthcoming, figures of local authority *could* legitimately be disobeyed if a sufficiently contentious problem arose. Cootehill Orangemen best exemplified Orange intransigence as they, contrary to the orders of one Revd Douglas, had placed an Orange flag on the church steeple after forcing entry. At the following service, the entire congregation rose and walked out of Douglas's sermon in protest at his stance. The flag remained for several days on the steeple as 'the police dared not interfere, because it was known that 180 men were resolved to keep up the flag'.[27] This determination and ability to act independently

23 *NW*, 29 August 1840. **24** Ibid. **25** K.T. Hoppen, *Ireland since 1800* (Harlow, 1989), p. 82. **26** Mattison, '"From Dolly's Brae to Westminster", the loyal Orange Institution in Ireland, *c.*1849–1886', pp 35–6. **27** *Hansard, HC debate, 9 August 1843, vol. 71, cc 426–70.*

personified many Orange lodges at local level and ensured their ability to continue alone. Expenses incurred by the Glenawly lodge in Fermanagh during July of 1838 indicate that outside help was not greatly needed in any case. For their Twelfth celebrations £5 5*s.* 5*d.* was spent on an array of items including 4 gallons of spirits, a quarter barrel of ale, 21 lbs of bacon, 72 lbs of beef, 20 loaves of bread, along with sugar, mustard and pepper, and the allocation of 3*s.* to a woman for cooking and cleaning the room, hardly the outlay or organization of a lodge in disarray. Meetings of the lodge were held on a monthly basis throughout 1838 and 1839 and despite such expenditure, a regular float of around 15*s.* was maintained by the treasurer.[28] Indeed, according to the *Londonderry Journal* a general revitalization was underway as it reported that 'we find that the revival of these lodges, in various parts of this district, is ostentatiously announced by their accustomed organs. They were never dead, nor so much as asleep, we were very well aware, and the announcement to which we allude, only lets us know that they are about to resume all their former activity'.[29] Blackstock asserts that 'some lodges just secreted their papers awaiting revival, their office-bearers remained, not as elected officials, but as an interim permanent staff to muster the members "in any case of emergency".'[30] Lord Lieutenant Morpeth, citing a planned attack on a chapel in Loughgall, considered that Orange lodges in the area had never ceased to exist and were in fact even 'more numerously attended' than previously.[31] The re-organization of the Ballintra district in County Donegal gave credence to such assertions. At a meeting in January 1839 it was claimed that:

> at no former period was the meeting so numerously attended, representatives being present from all the lodges in the district; there were several applications for new warrants, and others which were for some time past dormant, have been revived. All the masters of the lodges reported an increase of their numbers since the revival of the Orange Institution.[32]

Literacy and the printing press also played its part in keeping Orangeism alive. 500 copies of the following notice were distributed throughout Killyman in east Tyrone and left no doubt in the minds of its intended readers that they were needed now as much as ever.[33]

Located in the heart of mid-Ulster, the contested and over-populated area of

28 PRONI, Account book of Glenawly Orange Lodge, Co. Fermanagh, D1433/1. **29** *LJ*, 13 March 1839. **30** Alan Blackstock, 'The trajectories of loyalty and loyalism in Ireland', pp 103–24. **31** *Hansard, HC debate, 1 May 1838, vol. 42, cc 755–95.* **32** *NS*, 2 February 1839. **33** NAI: Outrage Reports, Co. Tyrone (1839) 3847/28.

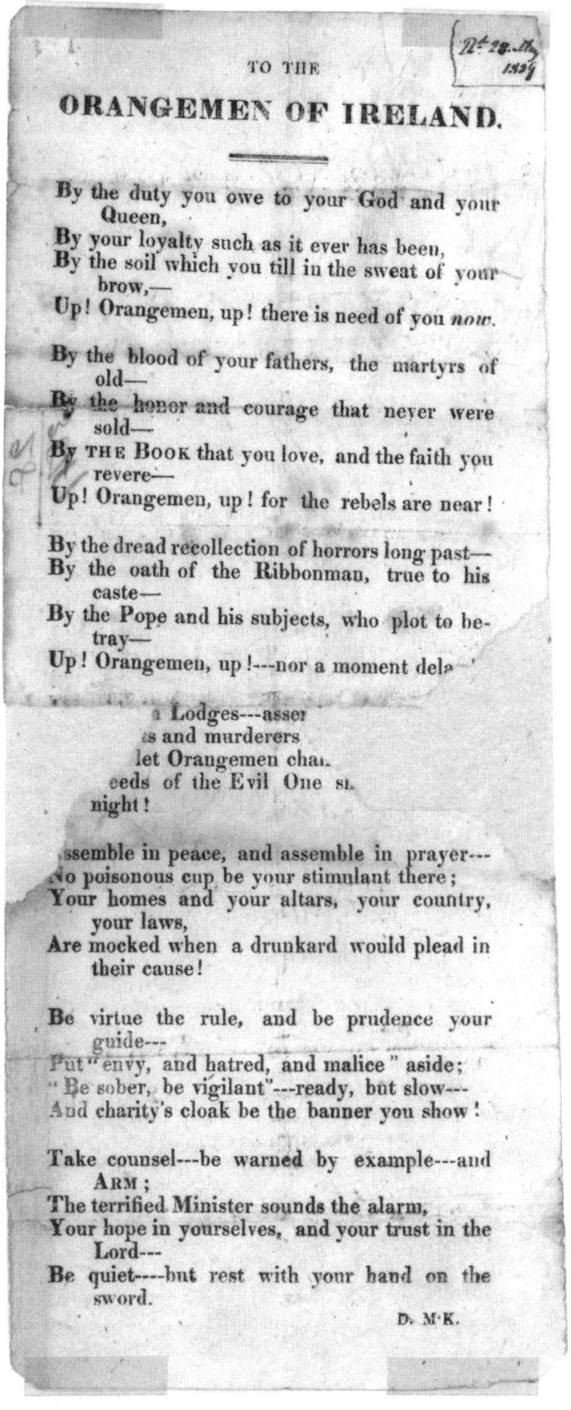

TO THE

ORANGEMEN OF IRELAND.

By the duty you owe to your God and your
Queen,
By your loyalty such as it ever has been,
By the soil which you till in the sweat of your
brow,—
Up! Orangemen, up! there is need of you *now*.

By the blood of your fathers, the martyrs of
old—
By the honor and courage that never were
sold—
By THE BOOK that you love, and the faith you
revere—
Up! Orangemen, up! for the rebels are near!

By the dread recollection of horrors long past—
By the oath of the Ribbonman, true to his
caste—
By the Pope and his subjects, who plot to be-
tray—
Up! Orangemen, up!---nor a moment dela

a Lodges---asser
s and murderers
let Orangemen cha
eeds of the Evil One s
night!

ssemble in peace, and assemble in prayer---
No poisonous cup be your stimulant there;
Your homes and your altars, your country,
your laws,
Are mocked when a drunkard would plead in
their cause!

Be virtue the rule, and be prudence your
guide---
Put "envy, and hatred, and malice" aside;
"Be sober, be vigilant"---ready, but slow---
And charity's cloak be the banner you show!

Take counsel---be warned by example---and
ARM;
The terrified Minister sounds the alarm,
Your hope in yourselves, and your trust in the
Lord---
Be quiet----but rest with your hand on the
sword.

D. M'K.

2 Orange pamphlet distributed in Killyman, Co. Tyrone, NAI: Outrage Reports, Co. Tyrone (1839), 3847/28.

Killyman was home to the notorious 'Killyman wreckers', the Orange faction that had destroyed the village of Maghery in 1830.[34] While it is unlikely that revitalization was necessary in this particular vicinity, revival did continue throughout the country. Although the government could rightly claim that the number of processions had greatly decreased, it was clear that the Orangemen of Ireland had no intention of turning their backs on their principles, a fact pointed out by one Mr Nash at a Dublin meeting of the Irish Metropolitan Conservative Society. Nash reminded members that although 'the society is dissolved, the principle, the fidelity of Orangeism will exist as long as Protestantism endures'.[35] The fact that Protestantism and the lives and livelihoods of its adherents did appear to be under attack from several quarters ensured that Orangeism was far from a finished entity.

URBAN SECTARIAN CLASHES

Meanwhile, as the economic situation worsened, the influx of country workers of both religious persuasions into Belfast contributed to the continuation of the Order and its growth in the town. Lamenting the demise of the linen industry, Sir Robert Bateson claimed between six and ten thousand people were out of work in the city and pointed out that:

> the people who followed the unfortunate trade in question were in the state of greatest distress, and many were actually starving. In Belfast, with which place he was most intimately acquainted, many thousands of persons who had been remarkable for their industry, sobriety, and orderly demeanour, were now reduced to want and wretchedness.[36]

Increasing Catholic incursion into this hitherto Protestant-dominated urban arena brought about stubborn resistance from its Protestant working-class residents who had no desire to surrender precious jobs, or indeed territory, to these rural Catholics. A sharpened sectarianism not necessarily present in rural areas became more evident in the city. Sectarian riots in Belfast could be traced back to the early years of the century as workers brought their rural habits and traditions to a city setting. Riots occurred throughout the 1830s and 40s, most notably in a two-week affray in 1843. Although not primarily instigated by Orangeism (economic matters also played a key part as did Protestant fear of repeal), tensions were greatly added to by the visible presence of Orangemen

34 See page 39. **35** *NG*, 20 November 1839. **36** *Hansard, HC debate, 4 July 1837, vol. 38, cc 1790–7.*

during the summer marching seasons. No worthwhile central body was in place to advise on the folly of sectarian clashes although, given the past record of selective obedience, it is doubtful whether such instruction would have made a difference.

THE REPEAL ASSOCIATION

Thus, the core membership continued to act independently and certainly made its presence felt in response to the re-invigoration of the Repeal Association in 1840. O'Connell, who had lost his already waning influence within government circles following the Tory return to power, now turned his attention back to repealing the Union with Britain and re-establishing a parliament in Dublin. The general election of 1841 saw violent clashes between Orangemen and Repealers as O'Connell sought to make inroads into Protestant Ulster. One of the most notorious occurred in Dungannon during the contest between the Tory Lord Northland and the repeal sympathizer John Falls. Following threats on his life and widescale rioting, Falls was forced to withdraw from the contest. Attempts by O'Connell to muster support earlier in the year culminated in an ill-fated visit to Belfast. This much-disrupted trip served to merely highlight the extent of his lack of support in Ulster and further galvanize opposition. Forced to flee from a hostile Belfast in disguise, Ulster was quite frankly an arena in which O'Connell could make little headway. In contrast to the monster meetings that attracted tens of thousands in support of the repeal issue held throughout 'southern' Ireland, other than a meeting held in Clones, County Monaghan, few of a large scale were held in Ulster. Conversely, and again borrowing from the tactics of their nemeses, counter anti-repeal meetings were organized to demonstrate the depth of opposition towards O'Connell. In June 1843, a reported crowd of 6,000 including a large contingent of Orangemen attended one such meeting in Dungannon. As news reached the town that a small Orange party had been attacked at Carland village on route to the meeting, a section of these Orangemen broke away from the assembly and sped to the scene to assist their comrades. Much of the village was destroyed by the frenzied Orangemen, a number of whom were later jailed. O'Connell, embarrassed and angry at the damage caused to his campaign by the incident that had been sparked by Catholic quarry labourers, offered to replace an Orange drum that they had badly damaged. The Repeal Association sent a replacement drum, which was rejected out of hand by the Pomeroy district who returned it by coach and bluntly resolved:

> That the drum presented for our acceptance has no value in our estimation […] we will enter into no relation with Repealers, in their capacity as Repealers […] we will never be misled by their invidious overtures! – and that, in proof of this determination, we reject this drum, which the Repeal Association have been so weak as to suppose that men, such as we are would have accepted.[37]

This uncompromising refusal was indicative of the attitudes of the Order to the continual stream of Repeal Association advances. In any event, O'Connell's repeal campaign rather petered out following the decision made by the government to ban a planned monster meeting at Clontarf in 1843. The limitations of O'Connell's insistence of non-violence were dramatically exposed and left the Repeal Association with an extremely narrow path upon which to continue its agitation. For the majority of the Protestants of Ireland the threat of repeal would linger in the background. But it was to a much less threatening extent than previously as it was apparent that the government was, on this issue, not prepared to yield to mass Catholic pressure.

THE GRAND LODGE OF ULSTER

Much more worrying and physically threatening to Protestants, especially in the northern half of the country, were the continuing activities of the Catholic Ribbon secret society. Therefore, despite the passing of the main threat posed by O'Connell, significant apprehension still existed within the Protestant community. This apprehension prompted a decision to reform the Grand Lodge of Ulster in February of 1844 in order 'to give mutual support and defence in these perilous times'.[38] At its first half yearly meeting, held in Coleraine on 24 June, 'the principal business which occupied the attention of the lodge was the receiving of returns from the district masters, and also deputations from those counties who wished to enrol themselves under the loyal banner, viz., Fermanagh, Antrim, Derry, etc.'[39] This would indicate a strong interest in an overall revival of the Order, which it was hoped would exist on a more solid foundation than the existing ineffective Grand Lodge of Ireland. The revival of the Grand Lodge in 1837 had achieved little. Core membership paid scant heed, while the better classes retained a distance. Thus, the existing Grand Lodge of Ireland was a rather impotent body. A new strong and well-organized Grand Lodge of Ulster was

37 *BN*, 8 August 1843. **38** M.W. Dewar, M. Brown and S.E. Long, *Orangeism, a new historical appreciation* (Belfast, 1967), p. 133. **39** *NG*, 3 July 1844.

clearly the force needed to revive the Orange Order. Hence, little protest to re-organization was forthcoming from Dublin headquarters. The Grand Lodge of Ulster soon faced a familiar problem, however. The issue of respectability, which had been a problem for the Order since the beginning of the century, raised its head as the summer marching season loomed. The Party Processions Act still remained in place and the new Grand Lodge of Ulster had no desire for its membership to antagonize the government. With this in mind, the Grand Lodge drew up a circular for all members to refrain from demonstrations on 1 and 12 July, 'thereby showing that they are not only determined to obey the law, but also to guard themselves from the imputations of those who would glory in their discomfiture'.[40] This call was echoed by Colonel Verner who demanded that, 'you will respect the laws – you will respect yourselves – and while you return thanks to Him who preserved you through the dangers that are past, you will preserve in the strength He gives, in an obedience which has been so signally rewarded'.[41] Cavan's highly influential earl of Farnham, who had in 1836 seconded the resolution to dissolve the Order, reminded members 'you are bound to obey it [the Party Processions Act]; and that if you do not obey it, you cease to be true to your loyal principles', while Henry G. Johnston, the Monaghan grand master, issued a similar address and proclaimed that 'there will not be in Monaghan a procession, from the first to the twelfth July, both days included'.[42] The wishes of these senior figures were generally adhered to by the membership, and no parades took place on the Twelfth of July. The *Coleraine Chronicle* was happy to announce that 'in abstaining from processions and in avoiding the display of party emblems, the Orangemen have raised themselves in the estimation of every right thinking man in the community'.[43] This, of course, was the main aim of not parading – the desire to regain respect and standing. Despite this good conduct, a bill was soon brought before parliament to extend the Party Processions Act for another five years. Although this proposal was not proceeded with, it brought an angry response from many Orangemen who considered that their good behaviour warranted a response of good faith from the government. Rathfriland Orangemen complained 'that we most seriously lament the apathy shown by members belonging to the late Orange Institution, at the time of Sir James Graham's [Home Secretary] motion to have the anti-procession act renewed – when not a single member had the manhood to step forward and oppose and shew [*sic*] the injustice of such a measure'.[44] The tone of this grievance would indicate that at a political level, few pre-1836 Orange members had re-joined at

40 Ibid. **41** *NG*, 2 July 1844. **42** *BN*, 28 June 1844. *NG*, 3 July 1844. **43** *DEM*, 15 July 1844. **44** *BN*, 19 July 1844.

this stage despite the foundation of the new Grand Lodge of Ulster. During the period of dissolution, 'the maintenance of a sense of cohesion was largely due to the determination of the lower orders, the bourgeoise, and a number of key gentry figures, such as the Verners and the Blackers, who provided a "dynastic" link with the origins of the Institution'.[45] The elites who had backed away in 1836 showed reluctance to re-join the Order as yet and reconnect with those who had kept Orangeism alive. For now, they maintained a careful distance from the Grand Lodge of Ulster.

A PROTESTANT COALITION

The return of the Tory government to power in 1841 ought to have been a relief to Protestants in Ireland. This return spelled the end of O'Connell's influence in government, the Liberator being no friend of the Tories. The Whig government had held power for almost all of the 1830s and did enjoy support from liberal-minded Protestants. However, the majority of Irish Protestants had aligned themselves with the opposition parliamentary party and indeed with the 'Protestant Association'. This was a coalition group representing different strands of extreme Protestant opinion, which had been re-activated in 1835 to celebrate the Protestant jubilee by ultra-Protestant Tory supporters as a protest weapon against the liberal Melbourne administration. The Revd Marcus Beresford described Protestant feeling in England during a tour he undertook in Staffordshire on behalf of one of these coalition groups, the Protestant Reformation Society. He enthused that:

> we were well received especially by the Clergy who opened their pulpits to us and came in numbers to our meetings. No religious society ever attracted such crowds in that county [...] From what I saw I am convinced there is a splendid and unfathomed mine of good Protestant feeling in England which only requires to be well worked. When I spoke of the persecution suffered by Protestant clergy and people I excited a feeling that must be seen to be understood![46]

Such evangelical hysteria propelled much anti-Catholic feeling on the mainland. This hysteria was added to by the continuing influx of unwelcome Irish Catholic workers, the ongoing tithe war, and government investigation into Church

45 Mattison, '"From Dolly's Brae to Westminster"', p. 8. **46** National Library of Ireland, Farnham papers, MS 18,608, Beresford to Farnham. Hempton and Hill, *Evangelical Protestantism in Ulster society, 1740–1890*, p. 91.

reform. Ireland seemed to have become the 'new' Catholic enemy that Spain, France, and the Jesuits had formerly been.[47] Opposition groups frequently played the 'no-popery' card in matters of Irish relevance debated within parliament, and had, to a certain extent, come to treat 'the Irish question as a popery issue'.[48] The year 1835 had also seen the emergence of Protestant Operative Associations, with prominent clergy involvement, around the United Kingdom especially in urban centres of Irish Catholic immigration. Following this lead, a Cork city branch of the POA had been formed in 1837 to counter the liberalism of the chief employer in the city, F.B. Beamish, while the Dublin branch of the POA, formed in 1841, was led by the hot-headed Reverend Tresham Gregg. The connection between the Orange Order and the DPOA was cemented by Gregg's involvement in both groups. A powerful orator, Gregg was able to harness the grievances of Dublin working-class Protestants, particularly in the Liberties area of the city, who had been drastically affected by the severe economic depression in the early 1840s. The position of these workers was in steady decline especially with the collapse of the silk industry and with the increasing concessions being granted to Catholics. Whig reform had allowed for a wider Catholic vote in the city resulting in a virtual Catholic takeover of Dublin Corporation. Such Catholic dominance had resulted in O'Connell becoming the first Catholic lord mayor of Dublin since 1689, sure evidence in the minds of city Protestants of government favour towards Catholics. Crowded together with these Catholics in inner city Dublin, many working-class Protestants, largely ignored and feeling abandoned by the upper classes, embraced Gregg's apocalyptic beliefs and his hatred of popery.[49] As many as 3,000 of these working-class Protestants joined the DPOA making it a considerable force in the city. It is reckoned that most of the members were also Orangemen.[50] Other Operative Associations were formed in Belfast, Bandon and Youghal. Cork numbers are difficult to ascertain; the *Cork Examiner* was certainly sceptical of the praise bestowed on the Cork Associations by Gregg sneering that, 'except in the columns of the [ultra Protestant] *Constitution*, it would be difficult to find the *locus in quo* where those reside who have attracted the admiring regards of Parson Gregg!'[51] Hoppen, however, points out that the Youghal POA 'attracted support, not only from the artisans at a penny a fortnight, but also from wealthier men at higher subscriptions'.[52] Certainly, the formation of three such associations in the county highlights a considerable

47 Desmond Bowen, *The Protestant crusade in Ireland, 1800–1870* (Dublin, 1978), p. 197. **48** Gilbert Cahill, 'The Protestant Association and the anti-Maynooth agitation of 1845', *The Catholic Historical Review*, 43:3 (October, 1957), pp 273–308. **49** J.H. Hill, 'The Protestant response to repeal: the case of the Dublin working class' in F.S.L. Lyons and R.A.J. Hawkins (eds), *Ireland under the Union, essays in honour of T.W. Moody* (Oxford, 1980), pp 35–68. **50** Ibid. **51** *CE*, 15 May 1843. **52** Hoppen, *Elections, politics and society in Ireland, 1832–1885*, p. 311.

Protestant support base (2,000 members attended a meeting in September 1841) and an Orange Order crossover did exist in Cork. The POA was prominent within this wider Protestant coalition, as was clerical membership. Similar to its involvement in the Orange Order, it was heightened by Whig measures reducing the power of the Established Church and also because of the wave of evangelical fervour and anti-Catholicism that swept mainland Britain throughout the 1820s and 30s.

THE MAYNOOTH CONTROVERSY

The full force of this opposition was soon to be felt by the new prime minister, Sir Robert Peel. Peel, who had been chief secretary when Catholic emancipation had been passed, had never been fully forgiven by the Protestants who had opposed it despite his later issuing of the Tamworth Manifesto, which advocated modernized Toryism. This mistrust was again unleashed in 1845 over Peel's controversial Maynooth bill. This bill, introduced to parliament on 28 March, proposed to increase the government grant to the Catholic priest training college in Maynooth from £8,000 to £26,000 per annum. It also offered the seminary £30,000 for essential repairs. This action 'stemmed from Peel's general policy of conciliation as a way of dealing with the explosive Irish situation in the early 1840s'.[53] Despite O'Connell's withdrawal at Clontarf, the repeal movement was still considered a dangerous threat to the stability of the empire.[54] Peel's answer to this was to separate the Catholic clergy and the middle classes from the movement. The Maynooth grant, he hoped, would achieve this by first conciliating the clerical hierarchy, and second, by providing proper education to priests. At this stage, despite some tightening of regulations, many ground-level priests were still not properly educated or trained. Peel hoped that education and a subsequent wider view on life would see the clergy drift away from nationalist politics. Most likely, clerical absence would then eventually destroy the repeal movement. Peel also sought to woo moderate Catholics by offering higher education in his new interdenominational Queen's Colleges. In order to continue his conciliatory policy of placing Catholics into positions within the state apparatus, a new educated Catholic youth was needed. Once again, Peel hoped that education was the key 'to conciliate moderate Catholic opinion and syphon off some quantity of O'Connell's abundant support'.[55]

53 Neil J. Smelser, *Social paralysis and social change: British working-class education in the nineteenth century* (Oxford, 1991), p. 100. **54** Donal Kerr, 'Peel and the political involvement of the priests', *Archivium Hibernicum*, 36 (1981), pp 16–25. **55** E.R. Norman, 'The Maynooth question of 1845', *Irish Historical Studies*, 15:60 (September, 1967), pp 407–37.

A conciliatory policy was not what an outraged Protestant populace demanded. A feeling of betrayal raged among the many denominations of Protestantism within the United Kingdom. The proposed increase of financial aid to the Catholic Church was almost treasonous in the eyes of some who still regarded Catholics as disloyal second-class citizens ready to rebel at any given moment. Others considered the proposal in the light of the repressive measures introduced against the Established Church over the previous decade, and saw it to be further evidence of government favouritism. Dissenters campaigning to stop state aid to all religious bodies joined in the protest, advocating that these should all survive on voluntary donations. Many within Peel's own party were opposed to the bill, which had the effect of practically splitting the government in two. Almost immediately a central anti-Maynooth committee was formed under the guidance of the Protestant Association. From its base at Exeter Hall in London, the Protestant Association launched a campaign of meetings, propaganda, literature and petition against the proposed measure. An anti-Maynooth meeting held in Dublin's Rotunda was attended by 2,000 people, most of whom signed a petition that was presented to the government. The following month a 'great anti-Maynooth' demonstration was held in Lisburn, County Antrim. At this meeting Thomas Johnston Smyth, JP, summed up the general Protestant fear by considering that the 'grant is only an instalment of a still greater concession. Looking at it in this point of view, I am led to ask "where will it stop?" It is, I think, only the beginning of the end'.[56] Orangemen from surrounding areas had contributed to the meeting by marching around the Market House playing party tunes. A fearful Home Secretary, Sir James Graham, had already privately considered re-mobilizing the yeomanry to deal with the repeal threat.[57] This force would have naturally once again been heavily laden with Orangemen and could have seen a repeat of the barbarity of 1796–8. Once again, an attempt to improve the condition of Ireland for the Catholic community had been turned into a religious crusade. In the words of Cahill, Peel 'stirred a hornet's nest' with his bill and succeeded in galvanizing a new pan-Protestant front that had lain somewhat dormant since the great meetings of 1834 and 1835.[58] With the help of Whig members of parliament, Peel succeeded in having the bill passed in May but the damage he had caused within his own party severely damaged his own leadership. This damage would effectively lead to the fall of his government the following year over the proposed introduction of a coercion act that followed the weakening effects of the controversial repeal of the Corn Laws. The fact that this Maynooth controversy was overseen by the Tory

56 *BN*, 20 May 1845. **57** Kerr, 'Peel and the political involvement of the priests', pp 16–25. **58** Cahill, 'The Protestant Association and the anti-Maynooth agitation of 1845', pp 273–308.

government surely added to the feeling that Protestants in Ireland stood alone, abandoned by their natural political allies. Government actions, both Whig and Tory, contributed to an increasing perception that Orangeism was the only defence against the ultimate destruction of Protestantism.

RETURN TO LEGALITY

Having, for the time being, survived the Protestant backlash, Peel probably wisely chose to let the Party Processions Act lapse the following month. In general, Orangemen had been well behaved since 1836 and the earl of Wicklow (William Howard, lord lieutenant of the county) 'was perfectly convinced that there was not the slightest danger to be apprehended, if this Act were not renewed'.[59] Home Secretary Sir James Graham, 'had reason to hope that the Protestants of the north would, on the approaching anniversaries, abstain from processions as they had so wisely done for several years past'.[60] It was felt in government circles that if influential Orangemen played their part and advised their brethren then the expiry of the act would see no return to the violence and conflict that had marred parades and processions in the past. This support and advice was forthcoming from the likes of Verner, Farnham and Roden. In the lead up to the summer marching season of 1845, Roden professed that, 'I should rather that you quietly met, in your respective neighbourhoods, determined to maintain true Protestant principles among yourselves and your children, rejecting alike the insidious snares of a false Protestantism within the Church, and the errors of Romanism, from which we have happily been delivered'.[61] Verner declared that:

> In this altered state of things, I confess myself unwilling to offer any advice which might seem in the remotest degree to resemble dictation. I would, in truth, rather consult the wishes of my friends than set myself against them. I would venture only to say this – public processions have, upon the part of Protestants been discontinued for some years – a different mode of celebrating the triumph of civil and religious liberty has been adopted. May it not be wise to persevere in a line of conduct which has proved so highly credible – by which adversaries have been conciliated, and friends more strongly attached; and which, if it not be voluntarily continued, will show that a spirit of forbearance, which would give wanton offence to no man, is united in the hearts of our friends with the truest loyalty and the most ardent attachment to Protestant principle.[62]

59 *Hansard, HL debate, 16 July 1844, vol. 76, cc 876–8.* **60** *Hansard, HC debate, 1 July 1844, vol. 76, cc 136–7.* **61** *BN*, 1 July 1845. **62** *BN*, 8 July 1845.

This attitude of these influential upper-class figures was indicative of the general mood of the better classes that had frequented the Order prior to its winding up. While the way was now clear to re-join the Order, many felt reluctant to do so at this initial stage. After all, the Order had not yet officially reformed and the Grand Lodge of Ireland, which in any case was now overshadowed by the Grand Lodge of Ulster, had not proven itself worthy of taking on the mantle of its predecessor. This hesitancy was condemned by Gregg who had organized a *soirée* in the Rotunda Gardens on 1 July. Although the meeting was well attended by clergymen including Robert Hedges Eyre Maunsell from County Cork (grand-nephew of 'southern' Ireland's leading Orangeman Robert Hedges Eyre),[63] the Irish gentry were notable by their absence. This prompted Gregg to ask his audience 'where were the Irish members (of parliament)? – (groans). He would say that it was the business of the Irish gentry to attend on the occasion of this great demonstration of the Protestants of Ireland [...] Why were not the city members present? Where were the county members? Where was the nobility? If all were there who should attend, there would be no space for the vast assemblage'.[64] Nevertheless, despite such harangues, for many of these upper-classes a wait and see policy suited them at this stage.

Meanwhile, the Ulster Grand Lodge meeting in Coleraine also called on members not to parade on 12 July but instead to fight Ribbonism and popery.[65] Similar calls to refrain were made by prominent members, the marquis of Ely, Revd Holt Waring and magistrate Robert M. Dolling of Magheralin.[66] However, this was not an avenue that all Orangemen were willing to take. Despite advice to the contrary, a meeting attended by 300 lodge masters under the auspices of James Watson was held in Lisburn 'to adopt measures for the celebration of an event so dear to their recollection, and so closely connected with their fondest sympathies'. The extremist *Belfast Protestant Journal* reported that:

> There was a unanimous feeling in favour of processions [...] arrangements were made for that purpose. There appears to be some friends of the Orange Institution disposed to advise against any display on the approaching interesting occasion. We can fully appreciate the kind feelings which have prompted a Farnham and a Verner to recommend this course; and whilst we may entertain different views on the subject, we are not ungrateful for their intentions.[67]

63 Robert Hedges Eyre (1770–1840) of Macroom Castle was, by 1828, one of the three deputy Grand Masters of the Grand Lodge of Ireland. This position gave him responsibility for southern Orangemen. **64** *NG*, 5 July 1845. **65** *LJ*, 1 July 1845. **66** *DEM*, 9 July 1845. **67** *NG*, 2 July 1845.

The *Journal* did however recognize the need for good behaviour:

> Much depends on the conduct of the brethren on the forthcoming anniversary. Strict order and sobriety must be observed. Let every man act as if the character of the institution depended on his conduct. Let the masters of lodges use their powerful influence, and enforce, by severest penalties, proper decorum. The eyes of the empire will be upon you, Orangemen of Antrim! Celebrate the glorious achievement of the Boyne, so as to prove yourselves truly worthy of the liberty it conferred.[68]

This viewpoint, in effect, summed up the feelings of many Orangemen who desired to officially march again after thirteen years of government suppression but who were wary against causing any trouble or any offence that might cause the government to re-enact the Party Processions Act. Fermanagh MP Mervyn Edward Archdall, nephew of the Orange extremist Mervyn Archdall,[69] reluctantly agreed to head a parade at Enniskillen but demanded sobriety and best behaviour from his brethren.[70] It was considered that peaceful overtures offered by O'Connell, who was still campaigning for repeal, and his lieutenant Thomas Steele, a Protestant landlord from Clare, who was engaged in a 'tour of Ulster', were part of an overall Catholic plan to bring the Order into disrepute with the government. If such a plan was in place, Orangemen were determined not to fall into this trap.

With the advice of Verner and Roden in the minds of rank-and-file Orangemen, most processions on the Twelfth passed off relatively peacefully. Large crowds turned up in Portadown (30,000), Monaghan (30,000) and Rathfriland (15,000) and smaller assemblages occurred in Belfast, Dungannon, Newtownards, Coleraine, Lurgan, Tandragee, Magherafelt, Markethill, Richhill, Moy, Killyman, Tynan, Loughgall, Stewartstown, Ballinahinch, Enniskillen, Pettigo and Shrinrone, King's County.[71] Turnout in terms of numbers was strong, with the correspondent of the *Belfast Newsletter* enthusing that 'about eight hundred Orangemen are now in the town of Newtownards; and I dare say that before our next twelfth, our numbers will be 2,000'.[72] The paper went on to predict that:

68 Ibid. **69** Mervyn Archdall (1763–1839) of Castle Archdale was a war veteran who had lost an arm in the Egyptian campaign. He served as MP for Fermanagh from 1802 to 1834, was grand master, 1818–22, and was described by ministers as being among the 'violent ultras'. Stephen Farrell, *The history of parliament*, https://www.historyofparliamentonline.org/volume/1820–1832/member/archdall-mervyn–1763–1839, accessed 5 September 2019. **70** *DEM*, 11 July 1845. **71** *BN*, 18 July 1845. **72** *BN*, 16 July 1845.

> If the remark of the sage woman lately, that all failures in the potato fields began with the cessation of the July procession, be deemed true, there will, this year, be no scant or want among these delights of every man's table, for certainly the 'walking' appears to have been pretty universal. We understand that one effect of the demonstrations has been, to bring vast accessions to lodges in many districts. The whole display, we are told, seems to have awakened a rather general desire for membership.[73]

The one black mark of the day from the point of view of gaining respectability was the death of a Catholic, John Boyle, in Armagh city, who was fatally wounded by a shot during a riot involving around 300 Orangemen who had been met by a barrage of stones thrown by Catholics as they attempted to march towards Irish Street.[74] Aside from this, it appeared to most observers that common sense had prevailed. Although most of the better classes had not gotten involved, their pleas had largely been listened to ensuring that, apart from Armagh, general peace prevailed.

JAMES WATSON

The parades of 1845 could have passed into comparative insignificance had it not been for one action of the government. This action would provide a further impetus to the already growing swell of support for an overall reformation of the Orange Order. The parade at Lisburn had been led on horseback by magistrate James Watson and had proceeded with 70–80 lodges to Derriaghy, outside Belfast. This in itself should not have been a problem as the event passed off quietly; but Watson had signed the resolutions of the Lisburn Orangemen, one of which resolved that 'we deem it essential to take immediate steps to re-organize the Orange institution of this county'.[75] As a gentleman in a private capacity this was perfectly acceptable; as a magistrate and deputy lieutenant of County Antrim, it was not, at least not in the eyes of the government, which had little desire for anything that might lead to a full-scale revival of the Order. As part of the government 'clean up' of the magistracy designed to ensure an impartial system of justice in the previous decade, public displays of support for Orangeism were considered dismissible offences. Verner and Blacker had already been removed for this very reason as had Tyrone grand master Joseph Greer, and

73 *BN*, 18 July 1845. 74 Réamonn Ó Muirí, 'Orangemen, Repealers and the shooting of John Boyle in Armagh, 12 July 1845', *Seanchas Ardmhaca*, 11:2 (1985), pp 435–529. 75 *NG*, 13 August 1845.

Watson was not about to escape this fate. Dublin Castle took almost immediate action and informed Watson that he was to be removed from both of his positions. A letter of dismissal informed Watson that magistrates were expected to discourage processions and that 'in allowing the act to expire which prohibited Party processions in Ireland Her Majesty reposed a willing confidence in the loyalty and good sense of Her Majesty's subjects'.[76] This 'loyalty and good sense' had not been applied by Watson as far as the government was concerned. In the House of Lords, the marquis of Londonderry pleaded with the government to consider 'whether it would be wise and just to punish the venerable gentleman; he had been mistaken, but', he added prophetically, 'it would do mischief in that part of the country if anything were done against him'.[77] These pleas fell on deaf ears.

As foretold by Londonderry, a furious reaction was immediately unleashed in support of Watson from among the Protestants of Ulster. The *Protestant Journal* was to the forefront of this anger:

> We thank you, Sir Robert [Peel], for dismissing Mr Watson – 'it has nerved our arms, it has fired our blood'; henceforth Episcopalian, Presbyterian, and Methodist, will band together, forgetful of non-essential differences, and fight over again the old battles of Protestant ascendancy [...] The Orangemen of Ulster are sober, patient, and enduring; but when the time of trial comes – when their feelings are despised – their loyalty accounted treason – their devotedness a crime – then is the time for action – that is the moment for rousing the giant energies of their unconquered hearts [...] There are other magistrates in Ulster situated as Mr Watson – men who feel proud that they are connected with the Orange Institution [...] to these gentlemen we would say, fling your commissions to the winds – tell the rulers in Downing Street that you are not to be cramped in the exercise of your liberties, and that you will hold no situation which would prevent you from the conscientious discharge of your duties.[78]

In support of Watson, the Armagh County Grand Lodge wrote:

> that instead of being an 'expiring or insignificant faction', we can, on any constitutional emergency (if called on) bring into the field 200,000 good Orangemen and true – and like the old Volunteers of Ulster, armed and equipped at their own expense – who, with such a leader at their head as you, Sir, would sustain our own integrity, and preserve Ireland to the British Crown.[79]

76 PRONI, Copy of letter from E. Lucas Dublin Castle, D714/7/3. **77** *Hansard, HL debate, 18 July 1845, vol. 82, cc 651–6.* **78** *NG*, 13 August 1845. **79** *BN*, 2 September 1845.

A groundswell of support for Watson quickly gathered strength with a reported crowd of around 30–50,000, including Verner and the marquis of Downshire, assembling in Lisburn to attend a 'Great Protest' meeting. Very quickly it was evident that the meeting had been backboned by Orangemen. A large number of lodges made their presence felt by marching 'through the town in regular procession to the meeting, headed by Mr Thomas Irwin, grand secretary of the county, who was accompanied by a number of friends on horseback. The effect was most imposing'.[80] The effect may have been imposing but it was not to everyone's taste. Arthur Hill, the third marquess of Downshire, had died in April and had been succeeded by his son, also named Arthur. Politically, the Downshire interest was conservative. At the same time, Arthur senior had voted for Catholic emancipation and was by no means a Protestant ultra. Although he had been involved in the Hillsborough meeting in 1834 (held on his own estate), he was 'very wary of Orange loyalism, preferring co-operation with elite English Conservatives; he only contemplated using plebeian loyalism as a last resort if support from England failed'.[81] No supporter of Orangeism, Downshire was caught in a difficult situation and had to play a careful game so as not to offend the Orangemen while maintaining his English alliances. Thus, the Orange nature of the meeting had to be addressed by the new marquis following his father's line:

> I have now only to say that I am sorry to see that the Orangemen have met this day wearing the insignia of their lodges – for this is not an Orange meeting – and I think, therefore, that they were badly advised in doing so, because I believe it will have the effect of getting some of their friends into a scrape however, that will depend upon their conduct; and I call on you all to return, when this meeting is over, to your homes peacefully and quietly without offending your Roman Catholic countrymen (cheers). I should consider that if any ill will arose out of this day's proceedings – if blood was shed – or if anything unpleasant occurred, that I myself was to blame for it; and I therefore implore of you to be peaceful, orderly, and quiet, after the termination of this meeting (cries of we will).[82]

The crowd indeed did disperse peacefully, but it was essential that control be maintained as rallies continued throughout Ulster. A demonstration in Belfast organized by the Belfast Protestant Operative Association was also attended by Verner along with Roden. But even an ultra like Verner expressed similar caution to Downshire stating that:

80 *BN*, 22 August 1845. **81** Blackstock, 'The trajectories of loyalty and loyalism in Ireland', pp 103–24. **82** *NG*, 23 August 1845.

> He did not wish to be supposed to be an advocate for Orange processions – on the contrary, he had expressed his disapprobation frequently. Unless they should be conducted in the way in which he would wish to see them conducted, and as he had sometimes seen them when there was a large turn-out of respectability – he thought it would be better to abstain from them altogether. He thought they might use better means than mere display to advocate their cause.[83]

If protest at the treatment of Watson was to be effective, sheer weight of numbers was required at demonstrations. However, these potentially disruptive numbers needed controlling by the better classes as suggested by Verner. At this point, few elites were willing to wholeheartedly lend support to the Order. The powerful Lord Enniskillen maintained a distance from the Orange demonstration in the town on 12 August, which was attended by a reported 16–17,000 Orangemen. Also absent were the earl of Erne and the marquis of Ely, although the duchess of Enniskillen was present along with many wives of the absent elites. This would indicate that although these men were not ready to attend such meetings, they were happy to have their wives represent their names. This was a way of demonstrating support of their house while steering clear of government sanction.

Not off put by this possible sanction was Edward Archdall of Riversdale, JP, and deputy lieutenant of County Fermanagh (father of MP Mervyn Edward Archdall), or the son of Ely, George Loftus, who took time to address the crowd. He was followed by barrister Samuel Yates Johnston of Snow-Hill, Lisbellaw, who stated that 'this principal object of this day's meeting is to call into renewed existence that institution to which you formerly belonged, and of which you will again be shortly members'.[84] The Order needed to be reformed because:

> Of the present distracted state of this country [...], the length to which concession to popery has been carried, and the significant hint which has been thrown out that it would be carried still further, render it necessary that the Orangemen of Ireland should be re-organized (cheers). We have this day made a beginning, and I trust it is only the beginning of a more united combination and exertion than we have had.[85]

The abstentionist policy of the elites was not wholly welcomed however. Their absence was condemned by the Monaghan grand master Arthur Holmes who

83 *NG*, 10 September 1845. **84** Ibid. **85** Ibid.

resolved from the platform, 'that deeply regretting the absence of many of the aristocracy, who should in our opinion identify themselves with us in the great constitutional movement this day, we pledge ourselves to support at an election none who do not come forward and join our loyal and venerated institution'.[86] Holmes did understand their thinking nonetheless and:

> Regretted that the aristocracy of the country and some of the Grand Masters were prevented by events within the last few weeks from joining them in their demonstration of that day. He must deprecate the acts of the Government that took from the people those who would lead them to do good, thus leaving them, if they had no other leaders, to their own passions, that might tend to evil (hear, hear).[87]

It was considered by many within the Orange camp that the absence of a gentry figure at the procession in Armagh had been the reason for the lack of control that had led to Boyle's death. Holmes regretted the absence of 'their natural leaders' and called on the earl of Enniskillen to become grand master of a new Grand Lodge of Ireland.[88]

The desire to have Enniskillen as grand master made perfect sense for those on the platform and those among the crowd. The third earl of Enniskillen (William Willoughby Cole) was the dominant figurehead in Fermanagh. He had served as Fermanagh MP from 1831 to 1840, opposing the government policy of reform and Catholic relief. Steeped in the Orange tradition, his father, the second earl, had been an active yeomanry leader in 1798 and later became grand master of the Grand Lodge of Ireland. In 1840, upon his father's death, Cole entered the House of Lords, and inherited his father's titles along with the Florence Court estate. Cole had served as deputy grand master until 1836 and was considered a champion of the Protestant cause. Well-travelled, well connected, and part of the Anglo-Irish aristocracy, Cole was an immensely powerful figure not just within Ulster but within the United Kingdom as a whole. For a revival to succeed, it was vital that Cole should re-embrace the Order.

In fact, Fermanagh was an unusual case 'even in Ulster for the dominance of its leading landed proprietors'.[89] In addition to Enniskillen, the Archdall, Loftus (Ely), Brooke, Lowry-Corry (Belmore) and Creighton (Erne) families had all been active members of the Order prior to its dissolution. More unusually, political representation of Enniskillen borough and Fermanagh county remained solely within this circle of ultra-Tory families until the 1880s.[90] Fermanagh

86 *FJ*, 13 August 1845. **87** Ibid. **88** Ibid. **89** Peter Jupp, *The history of parliament*, https://www.historyofparliamentonline.org/volume/1820–1832/constituencies/co-fermanagh, accessed 9 September 2019. **90** Ibid.

essentially remained under the political control of this landed aristocracy for most of the century with no opportunity, in contrast the rest of the province, for the up-and-coming business classes to break the monopoly. It was inevitable that Fermanagh would prove to be the centre of the Orange Order revival as it contained these 'natural leaders' that the likes of Holmes called for.

As the meeting reached its conclusion, it was resolved 'as the only means of safety left to us in these perilous times, to re-organize the system of Orangeism'.[91] The treatment of Watson by the government was enough proof in the eyes of many Protestants that Orangeism stood as their only bastion in the battle for their own very survival. The dominant question remained, however, as to whether the likes of Enniskillen would re-join.

THE RIBBON THREAT

The times could indeed be considered 'perilous' by many Protestants. As well as the fear of O'Connell and his repeal movement, and the supposed treachery of Peel, Ribbon activities during the previous months had reached a new level. In February, resident magistrate Captain McLeod had been murdered in north Leitrim, allegedly by Ribbonmen. This was followed by the shooting dead of fellow magistrate R.B. Booth in Cavan in June. That Booth was murdered in broad daylight in front of his wife and children added to the horror and outrage. Although Booth was the deputy grand master of the Cavan Grand Lodge, the reasoning behind his murder is hard to fathom as he owned a mere 250 acres of land on which no tenants resided. The murder had the effect of spreading widespread alarm among an already fearful Protestant community and a crowd of 2,500 mostly armed Protestants attended the funeral of Booth. The alarm was further heightened by reports that 500 armed Ribbonmen had taken over the village of Killeshandra. As only fourteen police constables were based in the village, 'the lives of about 400 Protestants in Killeshandra, depended for eight hours on the forbearance of many hundred armed Ribbonmen, or of their chiefs'.[92] Although the Ribbonmen withdrew without incident, the *DEM* warned that 'at no point since '98 was the country so convulsed as at present. We appear to be on the verge of a sanguinary insurrection, and the symptoms of a malignant civil war are showing themselves with an impatience which hardly submits to a restraint'.[93] The situation moved Farnham to write on behalf of thirty-eight Cavan magistrates that:

91 *NG*, 16 August 1845. **92** *DEM*, 30 June 1845. **93** Ibid.

> The Protestants of the lower orders, who are ardent and energetic people, witnessing the atrocious crimes which have been committed of late (in almost all of which they have certainly been the victims), and that the perpetrators have all escaped with impunity, have most generally imbibed the idea that they are not adequately protected by the government, and that they must look to themselves alone for the protection of their lives and properties; in such a state of mind may any unforeseen accident, but, above all, any repetition of the outrages committed by the miscreants, by whom there is too much reason to believe we are surrounded, may lead to the most disastrous consequences.[94]

These feelings were repeated at a 'great county meeting' in early July attended by a reported crowd of 10,000 in Cavan town including Farnham, Enniskillen and several high clergymen. Many Catholics also attended and a union of all denominations was formed to raise a reward fund and find Booth's murderers. But for large numbers of Protestants, especially from among the lower classes who felt utterly unprotected, the Orange Order was the only body seemingly capable of challenging the danger posed by the Ribbonmen.

THE ROAD TO REUNION

The enthusiasm of the lower classes for a full-scale Order revival was clear. It was further stoked by Edward Archdall's removal from his position by the government for his appearance at Enniskillen. Curiously, the only other magistrate to attend the meeting, James Lendrum, escaped punishment. His patron, the earl of Erne, succeeded in convincing the government that he had only been present in order 'to keep the peace' in his capacity as a magistrate.[95] In the same way as Enniskillen's wife and Ely's son attended, Lendrum most likely attended as an agent of Erne. *The Nation* would later describe Enniskillen as 'cunning' and Erne as 'crafty' for these actions, but they could be considered justifiable as they could not yet lend total public support to the Orange revival.[96]

This removal of Archdall saw a dinner held in Enniskillen in honour of both himself and Watson. Once more gentry ambivalence was evident as the influential Sir Arthur Brinsley Brooke of the Colebrook estate, himself a high Orangeman, questioned the right of the August assembly.[97] Brooke, MP for Fermanagh, had voted in favour of the Order's termination in 1836, and was

94 *LJ*, 1 July 1845. **95** *The Nation*, 6 September 1845. **96** Ibid. **97** *NG*, 6 September 1845.

clearly hesitant in seeking its revival. Indeed, Brooke did not attend the dinner, nor did Roden, Verner, Erne or Farnham.[98] More surprisingly, Archdall himself was not present, citing ill-health. Enniskillen did see fit to attend, and chaired the meeting, but not in an Orange capacity. Yet again it appeared as if the elites were undecided as to the proper route to pursue.

Not so easily deterred was the *Protestant Journal*, which was vigorous in asserting that 'the time has come when the Protestants of Ireland must be roused from the lethargy in which they have so long lain; and what was so well calculated to effect this purpose, as the recollection of the glories of the Boyne and Aughrim'.[99] Spurred on by militant rhetoric such as this, the desire to re-construct the Order gained increasing strength. Orangemen in Fermanagh had already met on 29 July to establish a County Grand Lodge and appoint a County grand master. The nominee, Samuel Yates Johnston, agreed to take the position but only if the officers from the pre-1836 Order did not accept first. The thought of this though was contentious to many members who had remained loyal despite the Order's dissolution. Mattison emphasizes that, 'below the surface, palpable hostility and suspicion among many within the lower orders and, to an extent, within the middle class was directed towards their social betters who had so easily abandoned them in 1836'.[100] Such feeling was emphasized by Mr Alexander, Enniskillen district secretary, who:

> Was not against a resuscitation of the late Grand Lodge of Ireland, but he would never advocate a revival of the Grand Lodge of Ireland through and by the men who had betrayed them. The Grand Lodge had forsaken them in their day of peril, and left them to stand alone in the breach [...] let Ulster be the rallying ground and rendezvous for all (cheers). The Ulster lodge had nobly stood – not in the days when Orangeism shone in its resplendent glory; but when the horizon was dark and cloudy (cheers).[101]

Alexander was adamant that the officers of the 1836 Order be made firstly affiliate to the Grand Lodge of Ulster before they could form a new Grand Lodge of Ireland. Once they did this, the Grand Lodge of Ulster would then become the Grand Lodge of Ireland. Should they refuse to do this, then Alexander was content to remain loyal to the existing Ulster governing body. This attitude was shared by many members who felt bitter at the 'betrayal' of 1836. It was to ensure that the path to reformation was far from smooth.

98 *FJ*, 30 October 1845. **99** *NG*, 16 July 1845. **100** Mattison, '"From Dolly's Brae to Westminster"', p. 9. **101** *DEM*, 1 August 1845.

DISPUTE

To satisfy the growing desire to officially re-form, it was obvious that a new Grand Lodge of Ireland had to be established. But for the elites, this could only be done on a strictly legal basis. The existing Grand Lodge of Ulster, at this stage representative of most Orangemen, agreed that a closed meeting be held in Enniskillen on 27 August. The Grand Lodge of Ulster proceeded to send representatives to this meeting, which was held in the town hall. Among the objects of the assembly was to be 'a proposal from the officers and members of the Grand Orange Lodge of Ulster to the nobility and gentry of Ireland, who were supposed to be warm in the good old cause, to meet them, in order to consult together as to the best means to be adopted for carrying out and completing the organization of the Protestants of Ireland'.[102] That the proposal was addressed to 'the nobility and gentry of Ireland' indicates that the Grand Lodge of Ulster was bereft of this class. This Grand Lodge was organized and officered by the middle and lower classes. By sending representatives, the Grand Lodge of Ulster was willing to let itself be superseded by a new Grand Lodge of Ireland, which could be considered a major sacrifice. The Ulster representatives were 'authorized to place at the disposal of the Enniskillen meeting the several offices held under your [Grand Lodge of Ulster] authority, and in fact, your entire organization, embracing about 30,000 Orangemen of Ulster and Connaught'.[103] They were, in effect, willing to surrender the authority of the Grand Lodge of Ulster to a new Grand Lodge of Ireland.

Representing the Enniskillen delegation were Verner, Farnham, Colonel Hugh Barton of Pettigo, Henry Johnston, Revd George Welsh, Yates Johnston, Edward Atthill JP, the earl of Enniskillen and Brooke.[104] It needs to be stated that this group did not yet represent the Fermanagh Orangemen who had met on 29 July. They had not yet succeeded in enticing the earl of Enniskillen into taking office as their grand master and remained somewhat in limbo. Despite this, a Fermanagh group professing loyalty to Ulster did attend the meeting. Also present was a delegation from the Grand Lodge of Monaghan. Monaghan had not affiliated with Ulster as a result of a row over the issuing of warrants and favoured the Enniskillen delegation.[105] In Monaghan's view, the warrants issued by Ulster could not possibly be legal as its Grand Lodge was an illegal body, therefore a distance was maintained.[106] A clergy deputation, which adopted a mainly neutral stance, completed the groupings present.

102 *The Spectator*, 11 October 1845. **103** Ibid. **104** Wright, *Two lands on one soil*, p. 270. **105** *The Warder*, 30 August 1845. **106** *NS*, 27 September 1845.

The members of the Grand Lodge of Ulster would not receive the reception they expected from their Enniskillen hosts. Reporting back to the Grand Lodge of Ulster, their representatives complained that, 'we naturally looked for the co-operation of the leaders of the Protestants of Ireland [the Enniskillen delegation]: but we have to regret that we were met with opposition from a quarter which we did not expect'.[107] The meeting was held a mere fifteen days after the Enniskillen Twelfth gathering, and those that had stayed away from the platform were still seemingly unwilling to fully commit to a full revival. The reluctance of those among the elites including, most notably, the earl of Enniskillen to involve themselves caused great annoyance among the Ulster delegation who also complained that:

> Private conferences were held, to some of which, with a want of confidence, we were not invited; and to one in particular, held at Mr W.A. Dane's office, Enniskillen, to which we were invited, we were refused admission; of this we have especially to complain. The result was, that your grand secretary, by whom the meeting was convened, was displaced, and a nominee [Dane] of Lord Enniskillen's placed in the office.[108]

Further surprises awaited the Grand Lodge representatives, one of which was the debate over the actual name the new Order would be called as an inoffensive title was considered necessary by the Enniskillen delegates. The possible removal of the word 'Orange' from the title was mooted. 'As if any other than Orange could be adopted by the men of Ulster!' fumed the Ulster delegation.[109] In addition to this insult, it was hinted that oaths, secret passwords and signs were to be abolished. Thoroughly dissatisfied with the day's proceedings, the Grand Lodge representatives refused at this point to hand control to the fledgling Enniskillen central body.

Enniskillen and his faction were faced with a major problem. While the earl and his fellow elites welcomed a revival of the Order, it could not be run on its previous principles. In its previous lives, the Order had been targeted by successive governments and political opponents for its use of secret oaths, rituals and passwords. For the elites, such as Enniskillen, this element had to be abolished. For the Grand Lodge of Ulster, however, it had to remain. Few elites had involved themselves with the Ulster body, its revival had been powered by the middle classes who were much closer to ground level and the 'ordinary'

107 *The Spectator*, 11 October 1845. **108** Ibid. William Auchinleck Dane was the Sheriff of Fermanagh. **109** Ibid.

membership. As previously discussed (chapter one), grass-root membership placed great importance on the element of secrecy and were unwilling to give it up. Thus, given the mainly plebeian composition of the Grand Lodge of Ulster membership, the clash with Enniskillen over this issue was inevitable.

Another problem was the age-old issue of controlling the lesser classes. The events of the previous months – Maynooth, Watson, Ribbon violence, and government concessions to Catholics – had polarized and pushed many Orangemen towards extremism. The *Northern Whig* explained that 'they are in a state of unwonted excitement: they are exasperated against not only the Government, but [also] the more moderate Orangemen; and their councils will be characterized by intemperance, to the serious prejudice of the public interests, and the endangering of the public peace'.[110] The paper summed up that 'the members of the old Grand Lodge of Ireland were not sufficiently staunch – not reckless enough – to suit the temper of the men who are now stepping to the front'.[111] The elites had already been threatened with the loss of votes, while general deference continued to wane. Maintaining a moderate position within a leadership position would be a difficult task given the increasingly frenzied political and social climate.

A meeting, held by the Antrim Grand Lodge in Ballymena in September, criticized the projected Enniskillen confederation and declared that the Grand Lodge of Ulster to be 'steadily proceeding to a fixed determination to maintain *Orangeism in all its integrity*'.[112] While welcoming the proposed Protestant confederation, Antrim condemned the Enniskillen faction 'as having a tendency to supersede the Orange Institution as originally constituted'.[113] In the view of many members, the Order could only be revived in its original format. Any compromises, such as renaming the institution, would be considered a betrayal and would not be tolerated. Such division prompted the *Freeman's Journal* to gleefully declare that:

> The Orange confederation is now divided – torn asunder by jealous hate – and the petty bickering of interested individuals. The grand lodge of Monaghan had adopted a system of its own, Enniskillen has followed its example, and has also formed a separate lodge for the organization of Fermanagh. But there is a quarrel between the grand lodge of Ulster [Coleraine] and the Antrim lodge [Belfast], which probably will, sooner or later, lead to the disorganization of the whole body.[114]

110 *NW*, 5 August 1845. **111** Ibid. **112** *DEM*, 24 September 1845. **113** *BCC*, 22 September 1845. **114** *FJ*, 20 September 1845.

The *Journal* claimed that Coleraine and Belfast were at loggerheads due to Belfast's desire to be the seat of the Grand Lodge of Ulster. There is no further evidence to back this claim however. Mischief making on the part of this Catholic publication is most likely. Nonetheless, there seemed to be a distinct possibility of a number of separate independent Grand Lodges coming into opposition. The authoritative *Dublin Evening Mail* was confounded by the attitude of what it considered 'some few rash and over-zealous men' belonging to the Grand Lodge of Ulster. The paper rightly recognized the dangers of a split being 'a most unsafe and ruinous proceeding to the cause'.[115] The *Waterford Mail* seemed to best sum up the rather confused situation:

> the Grand Lodge of Ulster has issued its constitution; and the Grand Lodge of Fermanagh (though locally comprised in the provincial denomination) has issued another. The former is, or professes to be, a rigid revival of the old Orange system: the latter proposes to itself the new functions of a Protestant Confederation retaining the name of Orange but purified of every technical objection which rendered its predecessor objectionable to the law.[116]

Backing the Fermanagh system (to which the Enniskillen delegates now belonged) and pointing to the recent re-constitution of the Cork County Grand Lodge, which adopted its 'new' structure, the paper warned 'discord or division now would be ruin irretrievable'.[117] Brooke had also rather oddly conveyed in public that his Tory friends in parliament were of the opinion that the Order was little more than a 'senseless mob', an opinion that he seemed in agreement with.[118] This was not at all well received in Orange circles and a stream of condemnation poured into the letters column of the *DEM*, condemnation to which Sir Arthur readily replied. Sheriff of Fermanagh, William Auchinleck Dane, in particular, challenged Brooke and denounced him as one 'expectant of a peerage'.[119] There may have been a deeper reason for this public spat. Brooke had suffered in the past from electoral alliances conducted between the earls of Enniskillen and Belmore, which had resulted in his electoral defeat. Most likely, there was little love lost between Enniskillen and Brooke. It is possible that Dane, tightly wound under Enniskillen's patronage, was answering Brooke on behalf of his benefactor. Even though Brooke was part of the Enniskillen committee, he evidently had no issue in making his sentiments known. This public 'washing of dirty laundry' did not help the Enniskillen case and reflected the continuing tension surrounding the Order's reformation.

115 Ibid. **116** *TC*, 3 October 1845. **117** Ibid. **118** *DEM*, 19 September 1845. **119** *FJ*, 20 September 1845.

Nonetheless, work continued in a bid to capitalize on the newly awakened interest in the Order. The seemingly blasphemous idea of a possible re-naming of the Order was part of an overall recognition by the earl of Enniskillen, in particular, that the Order could not be reformed along the same lines as it previously had been. The earl had employed a lawyer, Mr Joseph Napier, QC, to ensure that the regulations proposed by the Enniskillen confederation were legal. The work carried out by Napier was sanctioned at a meeting in Enniskillen on 10 October as 'the committee reported that they had agreed to a certain system of laws and ordnances, which, having been laid before eminent counsel, are pronounced to be perfectly legal'.[120] Although members were not happy with the public leaking of the complaints of the Ulster delegation, 'there was a oneness of feeling evinced by all the speakers in favour of a union with the Grand Lodge of Ulster, and of forgiving and forgetting past differences'.[121] This apparent thaw in attitudes came as a relief to the *DEM* who demanded that they 'hear no more bickering between Mr. A., and Mr. B., the Grand Lodge of Antrim, or of Ulster, and the Orangemen of Fermanagh [...] you have one common cause – you cannot afford such misgivings and misconceptions'.[122] Yet despite these pleas division continued, with the Grand Lodge of Ulster showing little inclination for a union.

Such reluctance prompted the Grand Lodge of Ulster to issue a newspaper address 'to the Protestants of Ireland' listing the crisis facing Protestantism. It asked 'Why, then, keep aloof from us; come forward like men, and aide us in the stand we are making. Peruse our rules, our regulations, our qualifications, and if you can join us and become one with us in our noble brotherhood'.[123] This address drew a furious response from the *Belfast Protestant Journal*, which demanded to know by what authority did the '*pseudo* Grand Lodge of Ulster' publish the address.[124] The issue of leadership social class seemed the main bugbear of the *Journal*. It lambasted the publication of the address by 'a number of gentlemen of whom nobody knows anything', and asked 'will they be allowed to exalt themselves to a place to which they are not entitled, either by rank nor wealth, by talent or by years of long-tried work?'.[125] As far as the *Journal* was concerned, the Grand Lodge of Ulster was not a legitimate body because first it was illegal, and second, because its leaders did not come from the elite classes. It was considered those that came from outside this class did not have the education, the wealth, the judgement, or the skills to assume such positions.

120 *BN*, 14 October 1845. **121** Ibid. **122** *DEM*, 13 October 1845. **123** *DEM*, 3 November 1845. **124** *BPJ*, 8 November 1845. **125** Ibid.

Therefore, the *Journal* and many of the upper classes had little time for the upstart Grand Lodge of Ulster and its leadership.

Such criticism was readily answered. In writing to the *Sentinel*, a former officer of the Grand Lodge under the pseudonym 'Vigilax' reminded the *Journal* that Ulster had re-organized 'at a period when the Orangemen of Ireland were deserted by their leaders, and left without one to countenance or support them [...] none were found to assist them; all looked on with indifference at the passing events'.[126] 'Vigilax' conceded that 'we may not have the "wealth or the rank" of the land at our back', but stressed that it was they who 'continued to assemble in their lodge rooms and never to this moment abandoned their meetings. These are men of "tried worth"'.[127] A fair point was being made. It cannot be overlooked that the elites had indeed abandoned the Orange Order and left the masses to their own devices. It is not remarkable that a new Grand Lodge of Ulster emerged under the organization and leadership of the lesser classes. These lesser classes were willing to hand control to Enniskillen and his fellow elites but it is understandable that they were not willing to accept the toned down Orangeism proposed by their 'natural leaders'. As the winter months of 1845 drew in, there seemed little chance of a newly reconstituted national Orange Order coming into being.

One county that did take decisive action was Cavan. The influence of Farnham loomed large over the county, which made it difficult for its Orangemen to favour a union with Ulster. An initial meeting held in December, with Somerset Richard Maxwell (the future 8th Baron Farnham) in the chair, pledged to buy copies of the rules and regulations drawn up by Enniskillen, and distribute them to the county gentry.[128] This was an action that sought to encourage the return of the gentry, which again indicates a lack of interest on their part. The Orangemen of Cavan, just like the rest of Ulster, were of a lower-class nature. It would be assumed that their natural tendency would be with the Grand Lodge of Ulster. Yet, because of the Farnham dominance over the county, his influence determined that an alliance with Enniskillen would be the dictated chosen path. By early 1846, only four counties had taken this route however – Fermanagh, Cavan, Monaghan and Cork. Cork, far removed from the complexities of Ulster, can be considered as being out of the ordinary regarding its revival. Monaghan allied with Enniskillen mainly because it did not recognize the warrants of the Grand Lodge of Ulster. Fermanagh and Cavan, on the other hand, were dominated by the Enniskillen and Farnham elites respectively. Thus, they had little choice but to follow their leaders. But the problem was that the elites throughout the rest of Ulster did not take an active role in reviving the Order. For

126 *L Sen*, 15 November 1845. **127** Ibid. **128** *DEM*, 12 December 1845.

instance, Tanderagee's Lord Mandeville was the chief landowner in north Armagh but he did not get overly involved despite his Orange background. The key Orange leader in the county was Verner, who despite being an MP, did not own enough land to be considered among the wealthy elite of the county. Similarly, large landholders such as Downshire, Londonderry and Abercorn did not drive for revival in their respective counties. Therefore, the Grand Lodge of Ulster continued ably without opposition or interference from the majority of the elite class. This, of course, was to the disadvantage of those desirous of a new Grand Lodge of Ireland.

The reconstitution of the Cavan Grand Lodge saw Farnham become the County Cavan grand master. He took the role apparently 'after months of anxious consideration' on the condition that the lower classes behaved appropriately.[129] It was imperative for the Enniskillen faction that violence and disruption could not occur during Orange activity. After all, there was little use in reconstituting the Order to remain within the law if its members broke the law in clashing with Catholics or the police. Farnham explained that he had been deterred previously by 'the very abuses which were manifest – the drunkenness, the excesses, the bitter party spirit of individual Orangemen – the sad results occurring in parts of Ulster, from processional displays and insult, all chronicled by its enemies, and mourned over by its friends'.[130] Over the following months, regarding proposed processions in the county on 12 July, he warned that:

> The eyes of both friends and foes will be directed towards you in the coming month; and you will bear with me while I earnestly entreat you to abstain from every public display of a professional nature under the very peculiar circumstances of our county. I know I am drawing deeply on your self-denial in making a request, compliance with which may be though to afford a triumph to the Ribbonman and Repealer, but allow me to say that far greater will be the triumph of your enemies, if they can make (as I know will be their aim) such public displays of your Protestantism conductive to disorder and dangerous to the public peace. That such, at the present juncture would be the result of the public celebration of the Orange anniversaries in Cavan, I can have no doubt. It is, therefore, my bounden duty, as your sincere friend, as one holding the commission of the peace, solemnly to urge upon you the necessity of exercising the act of self-denial which I now advise – which indeed, as your grand master, I demand, as due to the well being of our cause, and to the peace of our county.[131]

129 *BPJ*, 14 March 1846. **130** Ibid. **131** *ECEP*, 2 July 1846.

The difficulty in exercising control over the rank and file was evident however as 'immense gatherings' took place throughout the county especially in Arva, Bailieborough and Cootehill 'in defiance of the advice of the grand master'. The *Anglo-Celt* highlighted the composition of these processions and commented that, 'some years ago many of the first names in Cavan would have been found at the head of these processions. Their absence on this occasion is abundantly significative [*sic*] of the decline of party spirit'.[132] This would indicate that the better classes of Cavan were not yet ready to join with the Orangemen despite the distribution of the Enniskillen rules. In any event, the lower classes of the county seemed willing to continue their Orange activities despite what the *Anglo-Celt* might have thought. A reported clash between Orangemen and Ribbonmen on 12 August at Ballyhaise was only prevented by the exertions of Farnham and Colonel Saunderson, of Castle Saunderson, on one side, and Revd Dr Browne, bishop of Kilmore, and O'Connell's lieutenant, Thomas Steele, on the other.[133] Clearly, public Orange activity still remained the preserve of the Protestant lower classes. The difficulties in controlling this faction would remain a serious issue for the likes of Farnham.

Throughout Ulster Orangemen marched in greater numbers than the previous year. The Fermanagh Grand Lodge refused to sanction any procession on the Twelfth (a Sunday) or on the following day. But they did tentatively allow that 'on the 13th each district may act according to their own discretion but that any brothers walking in procession must carefully abstain from carrying arms of any description as they would thereby render the meeting illegal'.[134] The *Protestant Journal* regretted that:

> Some of the most esteemed friends of the Orange Institution have thought fit to denounce public processions as being unnecessary, and injurious. We do not for one moment question the motives of these men; but we cannot discover the force or tendency of their argument. We do not look upon Orange processions as idle pageantries and unmeaning shows. No, they are exhibitions of principle; manifestations of gratitude for past deliverances.[135]

But as far as Enniskillen was concerned, great care had to be taken to ensure that the peace was not broken. Where the influential elites were in charge, this was much more likely to be maintained. At Lowtherstown, under the sanction of Enniskillen, 25,000 Fermanagh Orangemen assembled in a field provided by Edward Atthill of Ederney. Atthill himself was present, as was his patron, Captain

132 *AC*, 17 July 1846. **133** *AC*, 14 August 1846. **134** PRONI, Minute book of the County Fermanagh Loyal Grand Orange Lodge, D1402/1/1. **135** *NG*, 15 July 1846.

William Irvine, and several carriages of representatives from Castle Archdale. Other processions in the county saw 5,000 in attendance at Derrygonnelly and 2,000 at Brookeborough.[136] In Monaghan, Orangemen met at Tydavnet, where leaders were refreshed at the residence of Mr Skelton, the united body (2,000) then proceeded to Fort Johnston, the residence of the county grand master Samuel Yates Johnston. Here they were 'warmly welcomed and entertained, several barrels of ale having been broached for the occasion, and the leaders of the party partook of lunch at Fort Johnston House'.[137] Under the watchful eye of the likes of Yates Johnston and Atthill, the processions organized by the elite classes passed off peacefully.

The Grand Lodge of Ulster, of course, did not possess the same level of influence and control over its members. Twenty-seven lodges marched through Belfast, 30,000 attended at Clogher, while 15,000 took part in a procession through Armagh. An attendance of 60,000 was anticipated in Lisburn, while other parades took place throughout the province in Ballymena, Newry, Seaforde, Dungannon, Benburb, Clogher, St Johnston, Claudy, Keady, Newtownards, Guildford, Bangor, Ballinderry, Hillsborough, Coleraine, Cookstown, Tanderagee, Rathfriland and Downpatrick. Some minor clashes with Catholics occurred in Newry and Lurgan, while windows were broken in a chapel near Muckno, County Monaghan, by marchers 'with the usual decorations and music'.[138] No clash occurred at Muckno even though 'the area is inhabited almost entirely by Roman Catholics', but Catholics near Portadown attacked a procession with stones, which resulted in a riot 'in which those engaged on each side suffered considerable personal injury'.[139] A more serious clash took place in Keady 'by reason of the combatants being mostly armed', but overall the day could be considered a success as far as the Grand Lodge of Ulster was concerned. That is, if a lack of fatalities could be considered something of a dubious benchmark.[140]

The internal quarrels in Ulster proved somewhat confusing for the Dublin membership. 'A member of Schomberg Orange Lodge' summed up this uncertainty by asking the *Warder* for clarification on the state of affairs. He summarized that 'a great number are in favour of the Ulster, and others of the Enniskillen movement; but in consequence of being in ignorance of the existence of either, further than newspaper reports, we are in an awkward position and know not how to proceed'.[141] The mixed messages coming from Ulster and Enniskillen clearly were divisive for the organization in Dublin. The Order in Dublin had remained active during the years of dissolution with a Grand Lodge being re-established in the city in October 1843 in response to the dangers posed

136 *ECEP*, 16 July 1846. **137** *ECEP*, 16 July 1846. **138** PRONI, files of reports relating to Orange processions, MIC 371/4. **139** Ibid. **140** Ibid. **141** *The Warder*, 4 April 1846.

by O'Connell's repeal agitation. This Dublin Grand Lodge later reported that 'the Orangemen found that for personal safety, and the preservation of their religion and freedom of conscience that they should again unite. Several private lodges in Dublin and elsewhere never ceased in holding their meetings but they still laboured under many difficulties'.[142] Although a partial reunification did happen with six lodges being represented by the County Grand Lodge by February 1844, Dublin lodges remained split by internal matters.[143] Some of these lodges met at Radley's Rooms in the city and, with Farnham, Dane and Yates Johnston in attendance, re-organized under Fermanagh rules.[144] Unsurprisingly, the newly reconstituted Grand Lodge of Dublin was not representative of all city members. At a November meeting of the eight Dublin lodges who had sided with Ulster, it was resolved that 'we the undersigned Orangemen of Dublin beg to protest against the misrepresentation of our feelings and sentiments at the meeting in Enniskillen in August last for the purpose of forming a Grand Orange Lodge for Ireland by persons who attended there professing to represent the Orangemen of Dublin'.[145] This faction also declared that 'the Grand Lodge of Ulster possess our fullest confidence. We admire the principles upon which they have acted and are acting. And we respectfully beg to suggest that no movement in Orangeism will be effective if not based upon the principles upon which they have been guided'.[146] The feelings of these Dublin Orangemen reaffirmed the reluctance of many to move away from the traditional path of Orangeism. This reluctance remained seemingly ingrained in the Ulster faction who again rejected an appeal from Enniskillen for unity. Attending a meeting of Dublin's Cumberland True Blues, a deputation of the Grand Lodge of Ulster reaffirmed that 'it was impossible for them to take part in, in as much as the intended Grand Lodge of Ireland was not to be based on the good old Orange system handed down to us by our forefathers'. While a union was desirable, 'they would not, even to bring about this desirable object, consent to abandon the great fundamental principles of the Institution'.[147] The influence of Tresham Gregg was likely a factor in the intransigent mindset of the Dublin working classes. Gregg recognized that the better classes 'do not choose to countenance a movement that they have not themselves originated. Perhaps they do not think it proper that the masses should move without them; and perhaps they imagine that there cannot be a display of Protestant feeling and Protestant power, of which they are not at the head and

142 PRONI, Dublin minute books October 1846, MIC 201/2. **143** J.H. Hill, 'The 1847 general election in Dublin city' in Allan Blackstock and Eoin Magennis (eds), *Politics and political culture in Britain and Ireland, 1750–1850: essays in tribute to Peter Jupp* (Belfast, 2007), pp 41–64. **144** *The Statesman*, 9 December 1845. **145** PRONI, Minute book of Hardcourt Orange Lodge, Dublin and Grand Lodge of Ireland, 1844–9, MIC 201/1. **146** PRONI, Minute book of Hardcourt Orange Lodge, Dublin and Grand Lodge of Ireland, 1844–9, MIC 201/1. **147** *BPJ*, 17 October 1846.

front. If they do, brethren, we think them wrong'.[148] Gregg was the very type of figure that the upper classes feared. They frowned at his influence over the working classes and the popularity of his apocalyptic message among a community that had little else to cling to during this particularly bleak time. Any combination between Gregg and his lower-class following with the elitist Grand Lodge of Ireland was unlikely at this stage. This Dublin split was reflective of the attitudes that was preventing a proper revival of a Grand Lodge of Ireland.

Nevertheless, attempts continued to restore a body of central national authority. Deputations from all the Ulster counties and from Dublin were present at a meeting in Enniskillen Town Hall on 3 August 1846, having been invited by circular and public advertisement. These 'deputations made statements concerning the organization and numbers of their respective counties, which seemed so satisfactory as to determine the meeting at once to proceed to the formation of a Grand Lodge for Ireland'.[149] The issue was, however, that the deputations were all Enniskillen loyalists. The Grand Lodge of Ulster did not send a delegation. Ignoring this detail, those present voted for the Grand Lodge of Ireland to be reformed after ten years of official non-existence. But the election of its officers betrayed the shallow nature of this new Grand Lodge of Ireland. Naturally the earl of Enniskillen was the grand master, but of the eleven deputy Grand Masters none came from outside of the Enniskillen clique. Watson, Blacker, Archdall, Barton, Yates Johnston and Lendrum were joined as deputy Grand Masters by Henry Kingsmill of Dublin, Henry Richardson, JP, of Fermanagh, Sir Charles Coote from Cavan, William Beers from Down and Antrim's William Eaton Caldbeck. No representative from the Grand Lodge of Ulster, in their absence, was given a position. Equally glaring was the fact that only nineteen officers overall were elected, such was the scarcity of numbers in attendance. Thus, although officially reformed, and perfectly legal, the new Grand Lodge of Ireland was at this point little more than an upper-class skeleton body. Representative of only four counties, the new Grand Lodge of Ireland was some distance from reclaiming its previous position of unquestioned authority.

Immediately, the Grand Lodge of Ulster stated its determination 'to stand by themselves and not join with the Orangemen connected with the Grand Lodge of Ireland'.[150] Likewise, at a meeting in Coleraine in April 1847, it again declared that 'whilst we would strongly advise that a band of union should once again prevail amongst all Orangemen, we could not recommend that any dissolution of the Grand Lodge of Ulster should take place, and thus the Orangemen of Ulster be left without a rallying point, if it ever should unhappily occur that the Grand Lodge of Ireland should be declared dissolved'.[151] The bitterness of the

148 *AC*, 19 June 1846. **149** *DEM*, 5 August 1846. **150** *AG*, 11 August 1846. **151** Grand Orange

'abandonment' of 1836 obviously remained firmly in the minds of the Ulster faction and its memory ensured an entrenched position. At this stage, the Grand Lodge of Ulster, consisting of 240 lodges, claimed that three-quarters of all Irish Orangemen were affiliated to it. Consequently, it was still very much the driving force behind grass-roots Orangeism throughout the country. This was exemplified by the Killylea district of Armagh who fretted that 'the proper spirit and original intention of Orangeism has been lost sight of in the absence of a Grand Lodge'.[152] It resolved therefore to place itself under the 'care and protection' of the Grand Lodge of Ulster rather than under the parallel new Grand Lodge of Ireland. It was obvious that the Enniskillen Orange faction still had some way to go in creating an all-inclusive Grand Lodge of Ireland.

EVENTUAL REUNION?

Further intransigence was evident at the Grand Lodge of Ulster meeting, attended by delegations from a reported 500 lodges, in November 1847. The chair repudiated reports 'which have been circulated in reference to a junction with the Grand Lodge of Ireland, and are fully determined that no agreement with that body shall ever take place without a special meeting being summoned to consider the subject, and due notice given to that effect'.[153] Problems remained with Black Orders who had little inclination to cede control to a suppressive Grand Lodge of Ireland. Indeed, some took the step of forming their own independent leadership.[154] Nonetheless, talks did continue albeit at a slow pace. The Grand Lodge of Ireland seemed in no great hurry to bring Ulster under its wing. It did not meet again until November 1846, then not until the following May. This lack of urgency hardly inspired confidence among the lower-classes. Additionally, proceedings of these meeting were kept secret and therefore not reported upon in the press. With the lower classes being kept in the dark, it is little wonder that the process of unification was slow and cumbersome.

* * *

It mattered little to the rank-and-file membership whether they were affiliated to a Grand Lodge of Ulster or to a Grand Lodge of Ireland. The bickering of the upper classes and the subsequent slow pace of an ultimate final revival was

Lodge of Ireland, Grand Lodge of Ulster half-yearly meeting, April 1847. Archives box 2, shelf B1. **152** *ECEP*, 13 May 1847. **153** *BCC*, 8 November 1847. **154** Mattison, '"From Dolly's Brae to Westminster"', pp 35–6.

considered unfortunate but not fatal to the prospects of the core members of the Orange Order. Too many threats existed that were considered to endanger the future of Protestantism in Ireland. These were threats which undeniably had to be countered as far as its members were concerned. Catholic menace and government betrayal, joined with the need to be part of the wider Protestant family, ensured that the rebirth of the Orange Order would be inevitable.

CHAPTER THREE

Famine and unrest

By 1845, THE GRAND LODGE of Ulster was returning to its former strength and the Grand Lodge of Ireland was tentatively laying foundations for its revival. It surely seemed that the way was clear for Orangeism to regain its previous strength and popularity given the continuing apprehension over Catholic political mobilization and secret society activity. Although the government had suppressed O'Connell's campaign for repeal, the issue had not gone away as the Liberator sought to re-invigorate his crusade. Protestant fears were not eased by the fall of Peel's Tory government in 1846; although its leader was mistrusted it was still the preferred party of extreme Protestants. Its replacement was by a new Whig administration that was considered unlikely to have the best interests of the Established Church, or indeed the Protestant ascendancy, at heart given its reform measures of the 1830s. Furthermore, O'Connell had been quick to renew his alliance with his former allies joining with them for a short period in 1846. With these considerations in mind, it seemed that conditions were in place that could only further popularize Orangeism. However, it was not to be man-made hostility that would cause the most anxiety among both the Catholics and Protestants of Ireland over the course of the next five years. Famine and disease would now vie with Catholic demands in the occupying thoughts of Irish Protestants. However, old grievances did not fade because of famine. Running parallel to the devastation caused by food scarcity were two campaigns that took on a national face – the demand for tenant right and a renewed drive for repeal. The campaign for tenant right was supported by many Protestants and Orangemen, repeal was flirted with by a small few. Both of these issues would ultimately bring confusion and some degree of division to the newly reborn Orange Order.

ONSET OF FAMINE

Food shortage and famine was not a new phenomenon in Ireland or even indeed in Europe. In the previous decades there had been several periods of crop failure that led to almost regular comment and speculation regarding future season prospects. It is calculated by Christine Kinealy that between 1800 and 1850 eight subsistence crisis and three famines struck the country.[1] The worst of these, occurring in 1800–1 and in 1817–19, had claimed between 40,000 and 60,000 lives. Therefore, while 1845 had certainly seen a degree of potato crop failure, it was considered that this was merely just another in a series of irregular harvests. The serious nature of the wind-spread *phytophthora infestans* was not yet recognized at this point. Although the main potato crop had been largely harvested by September when the first signs of blight appeared, it was ominously reported that 'in the counties both of Derry and Donegal, the disease in question has made its appearance with a suddenness and a violence that in many districts have created no slight uneasiness'.[2] This 'uneasiness', however, was a relatively familiar feeling in agricultural circles, and in any case the oat and wheat harvests had been good. Optimism was exemplified by Verner who reported to the House of Commons in April 1846 that 'in his part of the country [north Armagh], after having made every possible inquiry, he found the produce of the last harvest so fair, that there was at least an average crop for consumption. The tenantry unanimously stated that since the war [with Napoleon] they did not recollect so good a season for paying rents; and that at present there was a great quantity of grain in the country'.[3] By August however, fungus had set in the potato crop and many areas of Ulster were feeling the early effects of what was at this stage already a nationwide epidemic. It was soon reported in Cootehill that 'the prevalent disease in the potato crop has made fearful strides in this neighbourhood, and in the adjacent portions of the county of Monaghan', a report that was replicated throughout much of the province.[4] The fall of the Peel government had inadvertently worsened the situation as the new Whig administration had no desire to follow Peel's lead by involving itself in the natural mechanisms of market economics. Instead, it adopted a *laissez faire* attitude of non-interference in the selling of grain that priced it beyond the reach of the lower classes. By December of 1846 the effects of potato blight and the lack of a substitute source of nutrition were such that the Lurgan poorhouse, as an example, was full to its capacity of 800, and 'frightful mortality' was reported within it by the following February.[5] The poorhouse system was enacted in 1838 by a Whig government incapable of seeing Ireland as distinct from the rest of Britain in its economic, geographical and social circumstances. Workhouses were basic in the extreme and certainly incapable of coping with the influx of people that the food shortage of the Famine brought about. For most people, entering the local workhouse was their

1 Christine Kinealy, 'Introduction' in Christine Kinealy and Trevor Parkhill (eds), *The Famine in Ulster, the regional impact* (Belfast, 1995), pp 1–14. 2 *DEM*, 20 October 1845. 3 *Hansard, HC debate, 17 April 1846, vol. 85, cc 703–86.* 4 *AC*, 21 August 1846. 5 *BN*, 12 February 1847.

last resort as conditions were bleak, families were torn apart according to their gender, and discipline was harsh. As conditions worsened, with starvation and overcrowding resulting in the spread of disease, the *Londonderry Journal* reported that in the Armagh Fever Hospital 'typhus fever of the most malignant character is still on the increase, attacking all classes, ages, and sexes, and with every variety of combination, that with dysentery, however, being most prevalent'.[6] Indeed, prominent Whig Lord Lurgan perished from typhus within months, a demonstration that even the upper classes were not immune to the effects of the Famine.[7] But even the loss of a peer was not sufficient to convince some among this class of the severity of the situation. While Verner may have been correct in his assessment of the crop situation in north Armagh, he may well have also been expressing the feeling of many of the elite classes in Ulster who adopted a policy of almost denial regarding the severity of the Famine in the province.

EXEMPTION OF ULSTER?

A number of ultra Protestants took the view that the Famine was 'a retributive punishment, the direct act of an angry God against a sinful nation' in which Catholics predominated.[8] For other ultras, the feeling was that God's anger had been invoked as they had not done enough to convert what were considered the Catholic heathens; now His vengeance was directed at themselves. On a more worldly level, among many of the better off it was a popular thought that admission of the severity of the Famine in Ulster would bring disgrace to themselves and their province. The 'superiority' of Protestantism was best demonstrated in Ulster and to admit that areas of the province were being hit in the same way as the Catholic-dominated south of Ireland would dismiss the notion that Ulster Protestants were God's 'chosen people'. It would also contradict the idea that Ulster, with its Protestant work ethic, was vastly superior to the rest of Ireland in a moral, economic and production sense. Therefore, it could not possibly be as badly affected as the 'uncivilized' and backward Atlantic seaboard in particular. It is no coincidence that the Poor Law Unions of Belfast, Newtownards and Antrim did not offer outdoor relief – the only Unions in Ireland which did not. O'Connell's *Vindicator* newspaper bitterly pointed out that 'the grand jury in Down was determined to show, for Ulster's honour, that hunger had not visited it'.[9] In addition to pride was the financial cost. The public works scheme set up by the government in August 1846 was financed by a public

6 *LJ*, 14 April 1847. **7** *BN*, 4 May 1847. **8** Peter Gray, 'National humiliation and the Great Hunger: fast and famine in 1847', *Irish Historical Studies*, 22:126 (November, 2000), pp 193–216. **9** 'Famine in

cess and landlords were expected to contribute their share, a burden that was often not well received. This approach by many of the landholders in the province has led to a general consideration that the Famine quite simply did not affect Ulster as badly as the rest of the country. Recent historical work by Kinealy, however, has sought to challenge this view. Trevor McCavery, in his study of County Down, has pointed to considerable distress in Ballymacarrett, Banbridge and in the south of the county. Such a finding is at odds with Reverend Abraham Dawson's *Annals of Christ Church*, written in the 1850s, dismissing any notion that east Ulster was subjected to the ravishes of the Famine.[10] In fact, the workhouse in Newtownards soon exceeded its capacity of 600, while by early 1848 there were almost 1,500 occupants of the Banbridge workhouse.[11] In reality, as David Miller has argued, 'in the pre-Famine decades the contraction of rural weaving and spinning had created in Ulster an impoverished Protestant underclass whose members' vulnerability to the crisis of 1845–52 can be compared with that of Catholic cottiers and labourers in the south and west'.[12] This vulnerability was compounded by soaring inflation as the price of potatoes and oatmeal sharply rose.[13] Interviewed by the Devon Commission (a government commissioned report on the state of the land) in 1845, the Presbyterian minister Reverend Daniel Gunn Brown noted the decline in living standards in south Armagh:

> I have been ten years in the parish of Newtownhamilton, and upon my first visitation of the parishioners, I noticed meat in the farmers houses – a pig hanging up in the chimney; but for the past two years, except in the houses of the more wealthy farmers, I have scarcely seen meal or meat, and it is evident from the deterioration of their dress, observable upon coming out of their places of worship, that they are rapidly getting worse.

Brown also confirmed that the small tenantry and labouring class were 'much worse'.[14] A similar assertion was forthcoming from Presbyterian minister Fletcher Blakely of Comber parish who lamented that 'all the farmers I am acquainted with, what I may call the large farmers, and the small farmers, are in much worse condition than formerly'.[15] A memorial sent to Dublin Castle seeking the

Ulster' in John Killen (ed.), *The Famine decade, contemporary accounts, 1841–51* (Belfast, 1995), pp 60–1. **10** Sean Farrell, 'Providence, progress and silence: writing the Irish Famine in mid-Victorian Belfast', *The Canadian Journal of Irish Studies*, 36:2 (Fall/Autumn, 2010), pp 100–13. **11** Trevor McCavery, 'The Famine in County Down' in Kinealy and Parkhill (eds), *The Famine in Ulster*, pp 99–127. **12** David W. Miller, 'Irish Presbyterians and the Great Famine' in J.H. Hill and Colm Lennon (eds), *Luxury and austerity: Historical Studies,* 21 (Dublin, 1999), pp 165–81. **13** Liam Kennedy and Peter M. Solar, 'The rural economy, 1780–1914' in Liam Kennedy and Phillip Ollerenshaw (eds), *Ulster since 1600 politics, economy and society* (Oxford, 2013), pp 160–76. **14** *The Devon Commission, part I*, p. 405. **15** *The*

erection of a police station in Tynan pointed to trouble caused by 'a considerable body of unemployed labourers', and further explained that 'considerable destitution prevails in the district, particularly at the outskirts of it, which are inhabited in a great degree, by a cottier population'.[16] The worsening situation of all classes was replicated throughout much of Ulster highlighting that even without Famine, many people were facing a dire situation.

LANDLORD ASSISTANCE

Some of the chief landholders, the marquis of Londonderry in particular, provided little aid. Charles William Stewart Vane, the third marquis of Londonderry, had not endeared himself to his Newtownards tenantry in 1845 by threatening that any of them participating in the July Orange procession 'would subject himself to his marked disapprobation'.[17] This would indicate that the relationship between Londonderry and his tenants was fragile, and the fact that his tenants marched in spite of his directive hints at a lack of deference on their part. Londonderry's refusal to provide aid to his tenantry highlights how the disrupted relationship between landlord and tenant had not been repaired on many estates. The resistance of Londonderry to the idea of setting up relief committees was indicative of the feelings of many of his class. As pointed out by Kinealy, 'a general consensus was that poverty was the fault of the individual and caused by moral failure'. Thus, 'many poor were deemed "undeserving" of assistance' and philanthropy was only bestowed to those considered to be deserving and able to help themselves.[18] Unfortunately, one of the impacts of the introduction of the Poor Laws was that the private philanthropy engaged in by the elite classes had dropped off to a great degree.[19] Many landlords now chose to place the burden of poor relief onto the relevant central committees brought into existence in 1838. Londonderry donated scantily to distress funds and refused to reduce the rent on his estates either in County Down or in County Antrim. Placing the blame on his tenantry, and highlighting their failure to embrace the new agricultural methods being introduced by land agents as part of estate improvement schemes, he declared that 'it can only be the supine and inert, who have neglected to profit by instruction and example that can be suffering, in any serious degree, under the failure of the potato'.[20] Indeed, Londonderry spent a

Devon Commission, part I, p. 509. **16** NAI: Outrage Reports, Co. Armagh (1847) 33/2. **17** *DEM*, 9 July 1845. **18** Christine Kinealy, *Charity and the Great Hunger in Ireland: the kindness of strangers* (Manchester, 2013), p. 2. **19** Mel Cousins, 'Philanthropy and poor relief before the Poor Law, 1801–30' in Laurence M. Geary and Oonagh Walsh (eds), *Philanthropy in nineteenth-century Ireland* (Dublin, 2015), pp 23–37. **20** *AC*, 4 December 1846.

reputed £150,000 on improving his rarely used Newtownards Mount Stewart mansion. Similarly, his wife, who did, it must be said, control most of the family money, built the folly Garron Tower at Carnlough rather than distributing worthwhile relief to their needy tenantry.[21] To their credit, several landlords did play their part in providing aid, but a co-ordinated plan was difficult to implement. In Fermanagh, Sir Arthur Brooke seemed to recognize the extent of the crisis but possibly not the condition of his tenantry on the Colebrooke estate when he addressed them in January of 1847:

> It is with anxious solicitude for the prospects of the next harvest that I have witnessed the almost total neglect of agricultural labour, which so generally and frightfully prevails around us, and I fear through most parts of Ireland at this season. I, therefore feel it is one of the most important duties which devolves upon me as your landlord, to again warn you, of the fearful consequences of this short sighted, destructive and impoverishing system, and to urge upon you, most strenuously, the necessity of arousing yourselves, and exerting all your energies in preparing your land for your spring crops, and by putting in the seed, by laying up manure, ploughing, trenching, etc, etc, and thereby providing by every means in your power against a continuance of that awful calamity, with which it has pleased the Almighty, in his wisdom to afflict our land.[22]

Instead of continuing to grow blight affected potatoes, Brooke advocated instead the growing of beans, which really did sum up his non-practical solution. In his defence, Brooke did at least make some attempt to form a relief committee but was hampered by a general disinterest shown by the landed classes. The Brookeborough Relief Committee resolved to adopt the voluntary system by 'supplying food to the destitute and employment to the able-bodied, and it was arranged for communications with the several landlords holding property in the district'. Unfortunately for Brooke, and more so for his tenantry, little response was forthcoming other than a £10 donation from the earl of Belmore. Dungannon's earl of Ranfurley offered to double the amount of whatever subscription the tenantry on his property raised, which would most likely have amounted to very little. The *Dublin Evening Post* bemoaned that, 'this is the whole extent of the co-operation afforded to that high-spirited and benevolent gentleman, Sir Arthur Brooke, in his attempt to provide for the destitute in five electoral divisions containing a population of about 12,000 souls!'.[23] It must be

21 Christine Kinealy, 'Introduction' in Kinealy and Parkhill (eds), *The Famine in Ulster*, pp 1–14. **22** *ECEP*, 11 January 1847. **23** *AC*, 4 June 1847.

noted that other landlords did assume responsibility and take action accordingly. Government outdoor public works had been a failure as a severe winter in 1846, coupled with bureaucracy and corruption, had led to their discontinuation and replacement, albeit briefly, with soup kitchens. In Armagh, Sir James Stronge supplied tenantry with soup free to the 'really destitute' while Roden set up a 'cook shop' for the sale of food at cost price and called on the gentry of Ireland to do the same. The 'cook shop' was able to sell 'one pound and a half of excellent rice and meal porridge, seasoned, for one penny; one quart of soup for one penny; twelve ounces of potato cake for one penny'.[24] The Belfast General Relief Fund was well supported by many of the city's elites and raised over £7,000 for distribution controversially throughout the country rather than the city during its short existence.[25] Lord and Lady Farnham also set up a soup kitchen with his Lordship reportedly 'thinning his fine head of deer for this benevolent purpose'.[26] The 3rd earl of Caledon followed in the generous footsteps of his philanthropist father by reducing rents and the price of coal while distributing meal 'at a modest price'.[27] In the winter of 1847 the earls of Enniskillen and Erne brought food down the Ulster Canal to feed their tenantry, while William Jones of Liscoole allowed his tenants to hold back their rent and save their grain.[28] In Donegal, Lord George Hill defied government regulations and sold Indian meal below cost price to his tenants while Colonel Connolly reduced the rent on his Ballyshannon estate by 25 per cent.[29] Rents were also reduced by many landlords of the smaller variety in a bid to ease the crisis; for example, Sir George Molyneaux of Castledillon, County Armagh, reduced rents by as much as 20 per cent on smaller holdings as did John Ynyr Burgess and Mr Robert Evans in Dungannon. Similar reductions were granted on Mr Hornby's property in Drumkeen, County Armagh, and by Marcus Synott of Newtownhamilton.[30] These actions by some of the more benevolent landlords were vital especially in the face of the underwhelming government response and, to be fair, did produce some limited relief for the tenantry of Ulster.

TENANT RIGHT

However, despite these efforts on the part of some landlords, land-related discontent rather than a shortage of food emerged as an issue among many

24 *BN*, 1 January 1847. **25** Farrell, *Providence, progress and silence: writing the Irish Famine in mid-Victorian Belfast*, pp 100–13. **26** *DEP*, 9 January 1847. **27** Noel Kissane, *The Irish Famine, a documentary history* (Dublin, 1995), p. 138. **28** Neil McAtamney, 'The Great Famine in County Fermanagh', *The Clogher Record*, 15:1 (1994), pp 76–89. **29** Anthony Begley and Sionbhe Lally, 'The Famine in County Donegal' in Kinealy and Parkhill (eds), *The Famine in Ulster*, pp 77–98. **30** *BN*, 13

tenants. A greater issue than simple temporary rent reduction emerged as a major grievance among the tenantry of Ireland. The level of security enjoyed by tenants had been steadily declining since the beginning of the century. But while there had been sporadic tenant protest, it had been uncoordinated and of a localized nature. However, continuing economic decline and the onset of the Famine would serve to bring organized, united protest to the fore.

Disaffection over security on the land manifested itself throughout 1847 and 1848 and culminated in the formation of the Ulster Tenant Right Association. This association paralleled the footsteps of the Cork Tenant Right League, which had been formed in January 1847. Set up by radical County Down landlord William Sharman Crawford, the Ulster Tenant Right Association sought, among other things, more security for tenants on the land and the legalization of the Ulster Custom. Since 1835, Sharman Crawford, as MP for Rochdale, had introduced a number of unsuccessful bills to parliament seeking a resolution to the tenant-right issue. His introduction of the Tenants (Ireland) bill in 1847 was the first time an attempt had been made to legalize the Ulster Custom. This custom, which had no legal standing, was long established in parts of the province and allowed for compensation to be paid to outgoing tenants for improvements they had made to the land during their tenure. Although the significance of the Ulster Custom is probably overstated, this compensation, usually paid for by the incoming tenant, played a part in facilitating the emigration that had prevailed to a great degree in Ulster over the previous one hundred years. It also provided tenants with the incentive to improve the land while they resided there. From a tenant point of view, the legalization of the Ulster Custom had taken on a greater urgency following the report of the Devon Commission, which condemned the practice.[31] Although many Ulster landlords had hitherto not interfered with the custom, it was coming under increased scrutiny from some more 'progressive' landlords who considered it a hindrance to the re-invigoration of their estates as they sought to maximize profitability. The extraction of maximum profit from the land was the central recommendation of the Devon Commission, not the well-being of tenants. Already, the granting of short-term leases had eroded the sense of security allowed by the longer leases that had been frequently issued in the early part of the century. The knock-on effect of granting shorter leases, or indeed no leases at all, was to reduce the financial benefits of the Ulster Custom to tenants.

The Famine dramatically stressed the need for compensation to be paid to outgoing tenants. The repeal of the Corn Laws in 1846 removed the protection

November 1846. **31** Thomas P. O'Neill, 'The land question, 1830–1850', *Studies: An Irish Quarterly Review*, 44:175 (Autumn, 1955), pp 325–36.

that Irish-grown wheat had previously enjoyed. By importing foreign produce, prime minister Peel sought to lower the price of corn thereby making bread more affordable to the needy. This he succeeded in doing, but his actions caused a sharp decline in the incomes of tenant farmers. Already severely impacted by the decline of the linen industry, tenant farmers felt stretched to breaking point. In this predicament, a reduction in rent was urgently needed but little flexibility was forthcoming from the majority of landlords. Further down the social scale, many landlords took advantage of the destitution of landless labourers and began the clearance of minute unviable holdings. Evictions increased considerably as tenants fell behind in their rents. Although southern Ireland suffered a much higher rate of evictions than Ulster, Bardon highlights regular evictions in Antrim, Monaghan and Armagh.[32] Those evicted received no payment compensation as they were in payment arrears and, in any case, they were not being replaced by incoming tenants. This ominous situation fuelled the drive for a legal recognition of the Ulster Custom and a reduction in rents as quickly as possible.

While Sharman Crawford's bill was defeated, it prompted the government to provide greater attention to the issue of tenant right. The Somerville bill of 1848 proposed to recognize that improvements made on a farm entitled the outgoing tenant to compensation but only if they had been carried out in the previous twenty-one years. This was unacceptable to many long-term Ulster tenants, as was the fact that no legal recognition was to be given to the Ulster Custom. In any case, the Somerville bill, which was of little or no benefit to the tenants, was ultimately dropped. The passing of the Encumbered Estates Act the following year only served to highlight the insecurity of tenants. This act provided bankrupt landlords with a simplified route to sell their estates. But it failed to protect the rights of tenants as many new buyers were land speculators, unconcerned with the rights of the tenantry they inherited.[33] The act and the failed Somerville bill marked the first instances of government interference in the land issues of Ireland. However, these parliamentary actions were of little benefit to the tenantry. In the light of such an impotent government response, it was surely inevitable that coordinated popular protest should mushroom. It remained to be seen whether coordinated protest would bring all denominations together as a united front.

As the Ulster Custom existed mainly only in the north of the country, the Ulster tenants had potentially more to lose than their southern counterparts. This ensured initially a more focused campaign in the north of the country. Sharman Crawford was joined by the Presbyterian editor of the *Londonderry Journal*, Dr James McKnight, by Catholic bishop Dr Edward Maginn, and by large numbers

32 Bardon, *A history of Ulster*, p. 312. **33** Thomas P. O'Neill, 'From Famine to near Famine, 1845–1879', *Studia Hibernica*, 1 (1961), pp 161–71.

of Presbyterians and their clergy. Presbyterian clergy, in particular, were eager to disrupt the monopoly that landlords, who were overwhelmingly members of the Established Church, held on the land. While the majority of Presbyterians were firmly in the unionist camp, Andrew Holmes points out that they were not necessarily politically conservative and that 'many remained ardent political liberals and supported a wide range of reform measures, including tenant right'.[34] Although many Presbyterians were advocates of Henry Cooke's Trinitarian scriptural theology, this did not mean absolute obedience to his social and political conservatism. Landlords could indeed be challenged, as a core aspect of evangelical Presbyterianism sought a return to what Holmes terms 'Covenanter politics' – a return to the 'golden age' of seventeenth-century religious purity and political principle.[35] McKnight's argument considered that the descendants of landlords had merely received large tracts of wilderness from the Crown for their services during the 1600s. It had been the tenantry, through the generations, that had made the improvements on the land not the landlords, many of whom had been absentee. Therefore, in his opinion, they were entitled to more security on the land than that allowed to them.[36] With the backing of large sections of the Catholic and Presbyterian clergy the Ulster Tenant Right Association quickly gained momentum. An early Tenant Right meeting held at Ballybay attracted an estimated audience of between 1,500 and 2,000, with police noting that 'considerable excitement prevails' around the issue.[37] The *Anglo-Celt* reported that the audience 'consisted of Roman Catholics, Presbyterians, and Protestants, Orangemen and Repealers'.[38] Meetings followed in Cookstown and Carrickmacross.[39] Excitement continued to grow as shown by a meeting in Lurgan that was attended 'by 6,000 and chaired by James Browne Esq, Donaclooney House. Revd Mr Miller, Revd James Moorehead (Presbyterian) and Revd Bernard O'Loughlin put forward motions rejecting Sir William Somerville's bill'.[40] Again, the meeting passed off peacefully as 'it was attended by a number of influential persons'.[41] A crowd of 10,000 subsequently attended a meeting in Dungannon addressed by Sharman Crawford who reminded the assembly of the resolutions passed at the Dungannon Convention of 1782 regarding basic freedom and civil rights.[42] These meetings and sentiments were

34 Andrew Holmes, 'Millennialism and prophecy in Ulster Presbyterianism' in Crawford Gribben and Timothy C.F. Stunt (eds), *Prisoners of hope? Aspects of evangelical millennialism in Britain and Ireland, 1800–1880* (Milton Keynes, 2004), pp 150–76. **35** Andrew Holmes, 'Covenanter politics: evangelicalism, political liberalism and Ulster Presbyterians, 1798–1914', *English Historical Review*, 125:513 (2010), pp 340–69. **36** Paul Bew and Frank Wright, 'The agrarian opposition in Ulster politics, 1848–87' in Samuel Clark and J.S. Donnelly Jr (eds), *Irish peasants: violence and political unrest, 1780–1914* (Dublin, 1983), pp 192–229. **37** NAI: Outrage Reports, Co. Monaghan (1848) 23/19. **38** *AC*, 14 January 1848. **39** *BOU*, 15 February 1848. **40** *LJ*, 5 April 1848. **41** NAI: Outrage Reports, Co. Armagh (1848) 82/2. **42** *LJ*, 7 June 1848.

echoed around the province during the early months of 1848 and gained much popular support.

The formation of this body and its composition with so many Presbyterians and Catholics involved made it a worry for the landed aristocracy who dominated the top ranks of the Grand Lodge of Ireland. The *Londonderry Standard*, which supported tenant right, explained its case that 'the chief reliance of the landlord faction is upon the Orangemen, whom they imagine they can first cajole out of their own rights as Ulster tenants, and then employ them as a sort of a "Swiss" legion for destroying the rights of all their Protestant, and other neighbours without distinction'.[43] But now, as suggested by Blackstock, 'clearly economic issues threatened to disrupt class and creed unity'.[44] The relationship of deference between landlords and their tenants had remained unsteady partly due to the recession of the previous thirty years and the modernization of estates. As earlier discussed, some tenant resentment lingered due to upper-class withdrawal from the Order in 1836. A bigger problem was that the Grand Lodge of Ulster at this stage was by far the biggest Orange association and had not yet reconciled wholly with the Grand Lodge of Ireland. Orangemen seeking tenant right were much more likely to be affiliated with the Grand Lodge of Ulster which was, of course, lacking in elite class leadership. It had already shown that it would not be forced to do what the elites demanded. The Grand Lodge of Ireland therefore had to tread a delicate path. It could simply not afford to allow its desire for Orange unity to be stalled over the issue of tenant right. Worse still was the possibility of a cross-religious alliance with Catholics. The 'Coleraine correspondent' of the *Dublin Evening Packet* was dismayed by the introduction of such an issue into the minds of Orangemen, writing that 'I regret that a political question, as the "tenant's claim of right" should have been thrust upon those parties who have hitherto avoided any identity with abstract questions of agitation [...] this, I, understand, was got up by the itinerant "tenant right" doctor, who had not ceased, by every stratagem, to organize the assembly'. The reporter went on to allege that McKnight:

> caused his reporter to attend meetings of different lodges; and as an Orangeman, of course this person, greatly to the annoyance of his brethren, proposed resolutions in favour of this scheme of his employer, advocating the imaginary right, and thus, in many instances, pledging the members of the lodges to adopt the doctrine (no matter what it might be) of the doctor.[45]

43 *LS*, 16 June 1848. **44** Blackstock, 'The trajectories of loyalty and loyalism in Ireland', pp 103–24. **45** *DEP*, 15 July 1848.

The 'Coleraine correspondent' was greatly underestimating the resolve of the tenantry. To term the issue as 'an abstract question of agitation' showed a complete lack of understanding. Tenant right was certainly not an abstract issue, while to claim that the tenantry had hitherto not been involved in agitation was simply wrong. To blame McKnight for arousing the tenantry was greatly deflecting the issue. This would be the line that opponents would depend upon throughout the tenant right campaign. It would be in their best interests to discredit McKnight and his allies at every opportunity.

On the other hand, it was in the propagandist interests of McKnight to claim a widespread Protestant and Orange membership. The *Standard*, which admittedly had links with McKnight, was happy to report that a toast was raised to 'Sharman Crawford and tenant right' at a meeting of the masters and officers of the Churchill district in Fermanagh.[46] Such reports simply had to be countered by the landed classes. A wild claim at the Dungannon meeting that nine-tenths of Orangemen were advocates of tenant right invoked outrage in the area and did result in venomous counter argument. A 'Dungannon Orangeman' writing to the *Tyrone Constitution* was quick to state 'that the tenant right agitation is *not* sympathized with by the Orangemen *of this district*'. Continuing, the writer clarified that 'I, in common with many other Dungannon Orangemen, of whose sentiments I am aware, strongly repudiate the language of Dr McKnight. I disclaim him as the exponent of my feelings, or of the loyal body with whom in the present crisis I feel it an honour to be connected'.[47] It needs to be recognized, however, that the author of such a letter would not belong to the lower classes, and, it has to be doubtful whether such feeling was indicative of popular feeling in the area. As if to prove this, a certain urgency was felt by the predominant Knox family of the town who returned to the Orange fold in response to the brewing discontent in the area.[48] With marching season imminent, and with it a platform for large assemblages of tenant Orangemen, McKnight's claim would shortly be put to the test.

If the leaders of the Ulster Tenant Right Association had hoped to convince Orangemen on 12 July to join with them, they were sorely mistaken. The Association had its biggest success at Garvagh, County Derry, where the traditional Twelfth celebration was turned into a demonstration in favour of tenant right by the Orangemen. North Derry was to prove the most fertile recruiting ground for the association among Orangemen which is unsurprising as this was Grand Lodge of Ulster heartland. The Kilrea district had already issued a declaration that re-affirmed its 'unalterable attachment' to the Queen but which

46 *LS*, 25 February 1848. **47** *TC*, 9 June 1848. **48** Blackstock, 'The trajectories of loyalty and loyalism in Ireland', pp 103–24.

also declared 'our total want of confidence in Her Majesty's present ministers, and [we] look with disgust and abhorrence on the bill of Sir Wm Sommerville now before parliament [...] which we affirm, will, if unhappily passed into a law, confiscate the tenant's property, and hand it over to the landlords'.[49] McKnight, in attendance, was placed in a chair by the Garvagh and Kilrea Orangemen and carried in triumph through the town. McKnight's attendance had been well publicized, with placards and notices freely circulated. The result was a reported crowd of 20,000 including Orange lodges from Aghadoey as well as the aforementioned lodges from Garvagh and Kilrea, which added to a total of twenty-four lodges. McKnight was allowed on the platform along with district master David Smith who repudiated charges connecting the association with repeal, and subsequently asked 'when did the Orangemen give room to anyone to suspect their loyalty?'. Smith went on to stress that the object of the meeting 'was to ask their gracious Sovereign to prevent the landlords from robbing the tenant-farmers of their just rights'.[50] But, ominously for the association, some Orangemen refused to enter the field claiming that while they supported the idea of tenant right, the Twelfth was not the day on which to agitate for it. The *Standard* lambasted what it considered an 'intentional dodge' of the landlords, which ensured that:

> when other means failed, the Orangemen were induced to forego their adherence to their own rights by promises that, on any other day, that they would not only be allowed, but encouraged to declare for tenant right, provided only that the Twelfth July should not be so desecrated, as the aristocratic tools in question affected to deem it.[51]

Outside of McKnight's north Derry hub, this compliance with the alleged landlord directive seemed to prevail among Orangemen. In other areas downright hostility was evident. In Dungannon an attempt was made to raise a tenant right flag but it was pulled down after about a minute with 'strong intimation given to the parties not to attempt displaying it a second time'. In Carrickfergus 'one of the speakers was interrupted by a person asking "Is tenant right to be the law of the land?" The culprit was immediately grasped by the neck and taken out of the meeting' despite protesting that he was 'as good a Protestant as any of them'.[52] A similar abrupt fate befell a member of the crowd in Dromore who loudly asked the marquis of Downshire, who was seated on the platform, if he would 'reduce the rents and pay the poor-rates for us?'[53] On the whole however, most parades passed without any interruptions from Orangemen who may have been swayed

49 *LS*, 16 June 1848. **50** *LS*, 14 July 1848. **51** *LS*, 21 July 1848. **52** *LJ*, 19 July 1848. **53** *NW*,

by McKnight and his Association. In fact, the coming together of the Protestant social classes on the day seemed to galvanize their relationship. This moved Sharman Crawford to:

> Regret to observe that proceedings have taken place on the 12th of July which leave me small grounds of hope that the Protestant mind will be brought to the views which I have suggested. The old 'No Popery' cry seems to have been successfully raised by those who desire to uphold their own interests by sacrificing the interests of the people and the welfare of the state. A union had commenced between Catholics and Protestants, for the redress of one important grievance. This union, if continued, would have been irresistible; therefore it must be dissevered, and the Orangemen are now stimulated and caressed by those who had before deserted them. Every topic to excite man against man is now again being raised, even by those who ought to be the ministers of 'peace and good-will towards men'; and thus the Orangemen are deluded into the suicidal course of becoming the forgers of their own chains.[54]

The *Standard* had hoped throughout the campaign that:

> if the Orangemen, as a body, have only the spirit to act independently of that aristocratic leadership, whereby they have hitherto been too often only first misled, and then deliberately betrayed, they have it fully in their power to settle two questions at once, namely the power of landlord oppression, whereby in a few years the poorer classes among their own order will be totally exterminated, if an effectual check is not put to the present system.[55]

However, the ability to act independently proved a bridge too far for most Orangemen. For these tenants, it would thus seem apparent that commonality of religion and the traditional fear of Catholicism was of greater importance than improving their security and position on the land.

The Ulster Tenant Right Association did continue with its activities but largely without the physical support of Orangemen. Although the *Sentinel* reported that 1,500 'loyal Orangemen and Protestants of all denominations' attended a demonstration in Garvagh on 14 August, the association was by now on the wane.[56] It was hampered by its lack of a conclusive definition of 'tenant right', while it also faced competition and bitter denunciation from the rival Antrim and Down Tenant Right Association who were led by the influential Presbyterian

15 July 1848. **54** *BN*, 21 July 1848. **55** *LS*, 16 June 1848. **56** *NELA*, 15 August 1848.

minister Henry Montgomery. Montgomery had in fact, despite his differences with Cooke, actually sided with his nemesis on the issue of land reform.[57] Ulster Presbyterians in the Whig camp, including Montgomery, on this particular issue were focussed on the idea that land reform should be carried out by 'good' landlords and that the existing status quo be left untouched. By 1850 the Ulster Tenant Right Association had been amalgamated into a national association, the Irish Tenant League, which attempted to join north and south, Catholic and Protestant, into one movement. Irish liberal MPs who had formed the new Irish Independent Party joined with the Irish Tenant League and for a while it seemed that this coalition could enforce real change having adopted the 3 Fs (fair rent, free sale and fixity of tenure) as their rallying cry. By now however, the brief flirtation of some Orangemen had ended as they had been well and truly brought into line by their leadership. The Presbyterian Revd John Rogers, a significant player in the movement, at a Wexford meeting explained the problem as far as he was concerned – 'I will tell you who the Orangemen of the North are – landlords and agents in one extreme – bailiffs and the tag-rag and bob-tail of society, which landlordism and Church of Englandism, may be able to buy for Orange purposes, and a miserable bargain they have'.[58] Nonetheless, miserable as the bargain may have been, the precarious Ulster landlord–tenant alliance held firm.

A contributing factor to this may have been a wave of 'no popery' that swept mainland Britain in 1851, caused by the Pope's assigning English territorial titles to Catholic bishops. An outraged prime minister Russell responded by passing the Ecclesiastical Titles Act that forbade Catholic clerics to assume such titles and banned the wearing of religious habits.[59] Irish protest manifested itself in the formation of a Catholic Defence Association, which included several MPs. In tandem with the Irish Independent Party, they pledged to oppose any party who did not repeal the Ecclesiastical Titles Act. Immediately, this brought a sectarian element to the IIP which was still demanding the '3 Fs'.[60] The problem was that the sectarian issue held little appeal to the Presbyterians of Ulster. This was evident in the general election of 1852. Although 48 IIP candidates were elected in the south, in Ulster none were, not even Sharman Crawford. The only 'popular' candidate returned was William Kirk in the Newry borough albeit as a Whig candidate. To vote for a party with such an obvious Catholic agenda was too much for many Ulster voters.

Additionally, it is probable that, in contrast with southern Ireland, Ulster landlords still controlled their tenants' vote. While O'Connell had broken landlord electoral dominance in the south during his emancipation campaign over twenty

57 O'Neill, 'From Famine to near Famine, 1845–79', pp 161–71. **58** *DD*, 28 September 1850. **59** F.S.L. Lyons, *Ireland since the Famine* (London, 1971), pp 116–18. **60** Ibid.

years previously, his lack of success in Ulster guaranteed that landlord–tenant electoral unity had not been impacted significantly. The eventual reparation of relations between the Grand Lodge of Ulster and the Grand Lodge of Ireland ensured that the threats of the previous decade from Orangemen to withhold their votes had generally passed by 1852. The power of such 'pacts' between landlord and tenant practically made certain the failure of McKnight and Sharman Crawford. In any case, the Irish Independent Party would soon lose momentum as prime minister Lord Aberdeen enticed key members John Sadleir and William Keogh with the offer of positions within his government. This and a subsequent rise in agriculture prices saw a general decline in interest.[61] By 1858, the party had ceased to exist. The Irish Tenant League struggled on but as a semblance of agricultural prosperity improved tenant conditions, it soon also disintegrated. The land question did not re-emerge in any meaningful way until the 1870s. When it did resurface it was at a much more powerful level than previously. However, interested Orangemen (mostly concentrated in Fermanagh) were once again strongly warned against any fraternization with what was considered part of a greater Catholic agenda by the Grand Lodge of Ireland.

THE ESCAPE VALVE OF EMIGRATION

Much has been written regarding emigration from southern Ireland during the Famine years. While the level of Ulster emigration did not reach the heights of the 'southern' exodus, considerable numbers of both Catholics and Protestants left the province. It was reported that 'from every part of Ulster, the middling and small classes are leaving in hundreds for the purpose of seeking a future home on the other side of the Atlantic [...] we have been informed that within the last three weeks fully fifteen hundred persons have embarked at Portrush, the steamers, on arriving there, being scarcely able to take all the passengers offering'.[62] William McClure, secretary of the Presbyterian Colonial Mission, explained that:

> being of an independent spirit and enterprising character, and many of them possessing a little means, the members of our church are emigrating in numbers proportionally far greater than those of any other denomination. In a single parish, containing formerly 6,000 souls, the Protestant population of 600, has within the last eighteen months, been diminished by emigration, to 280.[63]

61 Timothy W. Guinnane and Ronald I. Miller, 'Bonds without bondsmen: tenant right in nineteenth century Ireland', *Journal of Economic History*, 56:1 (March, 1996), pp 113–42. **62** 'Emigration of farmers from Ulster', *Belfast Newsletter*, Tuesday, 6 April 1847; CMSIED 800243. **63** *BN*, 15 August 1848.

Meanwhile, the *Monaghan Standard* reported that 'in one small congregation or cure, where the number of Episcopalian Protestants was 1,600, a number exceeding 240 left this year for the Americas. This far exceeds the decimation of the population'.[64] While Catholic emigration was a relatively recent phenomenon, the links established with the 'new world' had already been long established by Ulster Presbyterians seeking economic opportunity in particular. Catholic emigrants, many of whom were Irish speaking, faced an uncertain future upon emigration. A hostile Protestant North America or indeed mainland Britain did not provide a welcome arena for poverty-stricken Catholics. Conversely, Protestant emigrants did not face such hostility. To begin with, the Protestant emigrant generally came from a slightly higher social stratum than his or her southern Catholic counterpart. This removed some of the social stigma faced on arrival and the struggle for basic survival that extreme poverty brought. For Orangemen, this advantage was greatly supplemented by the number of Orange lodges already in existence especially in colonial Canada. This network made it much easier to integrate and create a new beginning. The Order, in the words of Don MacRaild, provided a 'simple framework of emotional ties and physical ties that transcended place and space'.[65] Kerby A. Miller points out that 'in Canada, the Orange Order provided a fraternal network and patronage system which ensured loyal Irish Protestants they could find security, community, and opportunity overseas'.[66] This web allowed for a rapid movement in social mobility with Orangemen rising to social and political prominence especially in Toronto, 'the Belfast of Canada'. The city already held a pronounced British and Protestant identity, which allowed Ulster Protestants to adapt and quickly come to dominate the municipal corporation and police force especially.[67] Almost inevitably, tensions from home crossed the Atlantic as emigrants continued to clash in a new arena. New Brunswick saw clashes between Orange and Green at Boyne commemorations in 1847 and 1849 following the murder of a Mr Clark Leonard by 'an Irish mob' at the St Pierre races allegedly for having 'entertained a number of Orangemen at breakfast some time before'. In reporting the incident, the *Newsletter* was forced to lament that 'Montreal continues to be disgraced by savage feuds between the Ribbondmen [*sic*] and the Orangemen'.[68] Such clashes would continue in Canada until the closing decades of the century and also in the United States. But in the context of the United States, although the *Protestant Journal* dreamily predicted that 'the hands that bore the Orange standard in the

64 *BN*, 12 December 1848. **65** Donald M. MacRaild, 'Wherever Orange is worn: Orangeism and Irish migration in the 19th and 20th centuries', *Canadian Journal of Irish Studies*, 28/29:1 (Fall, 2002–Spring, 2003), pp 98–117. **66** Miller, *Emigrants and exiles*, p. 191. **67** Michael Cottrell, 'Green and Orange in mid-nineteenth-century Toronto: the Guy Fawkes' Day episode of 1864', *Canadian Journal of Irish Studies*, 19:1 (July, 1993), pp 12–21. **68** *BN*, 18 September 1846.

green vales of Ulster may plant it by the banks of the Ohio and Mississippi, and the rose of Orange and the lily of Nassau may blossom as fair by the waters of Lake Erie as on the banks of Lough Neagh', the reality was rather different.[69] While Canada 'offered Orangemen a home of rich potential', to a large extent the advantages of Orange membership were not replicated in the United States as the Order did not enjoy the same level of support – nativist groups such as the American Protection Association, the Order of United Americans, and the Order of the Star Spangled Banner already provided a strong anti-Catholic platform.[70] Orangemen allied to such groups clashed with Catholics most notably in Philadelphia in May 1844 where sixteen people lost their lives. But although joining these groups helped distinguish Irish Protestants from Irish Catholics, they did not offer the same social network or employment advantages that the Orange Order did in Canada. Indeed, Miller argues that 'in contrast to Irish Catholic immigrants, Protestant migrants from Ulster generally lacked large, cohesive, and supportive working-class ethnic communities and sub-cultures in mid- and late nineteenth-century America'.[71] Although sizable numbers of Catholics certainly did emigrate to Canada, the vast majority chose the eastern coast of the United States. This ensured, by sheer weight of numbers, which were gladly embraced by the Democrat Party, a dominant position among ethnic emigrant groups. For most Protestants there was little to attract them to the eastern seaboard other than its facility as a point of entry; those that did choose the United States frequently pushed westwards towards the Frontier often as a result of religious schism within their own Church. Mainly for this reason, Canada remained the destination of choice for the Protestant emigrants of the Famine. Although it is calculated that Protestants only accounted for around 10 per cent of Irish emigrants during the Famine years,[72] this would still amount to a considerable figure, perhaps as high as 150,000 Protestants leaving the country. Many of these brought their Orange traditions overseas with them, ensuring a flourishing Order in British colonies, particularly Canada.

THE TOLL OF THE FAMINE

For those who remained in Ireland however, the Famine and its by-product disease was of key importance to all factions. The Orange Order was certainly affected by the severity of the situation which, of course, made no distinction in claiming its victims. This was demonstrated when Stewart Betty, an Enniskillen

69 *BPJ*, 17 July 1847. **70** MacRaild, 'Wherever Orange is worn', pp 98–117. **71** Kerby A. Miller, Bruce D. Bolling and Liam Kennedy, 'The Famine scars: William Murphy's Ulster and American odyssey', *Éire-Ireland* (Spring–Summer, 2001), pp 98–123. **72** Kevin Kenny, *The American Irish, a history* (Harlow,

poorhouse guardian and deputy master of Loyal Orange Lodge 642 for fourteen years, succumbed to fever aged just 43. The funeral of William Nevin shortly afterwards in Saul, County Down, demonstrated the downward spiral faced by many Orangemen. The ritual of the Orange funeral was carried out at Nevin's interment, which was:

> attended by a large procession of Orangemen. The deceased had been latterly, until his health failed, porter in the workhouse, a situation which reduced circumstances obliged him to accept. He was First Lieutenant in the Down yeomanry, and his sword and sash were placed on the coffin. There were seventeen lodges at the funeral, and several thousand persons.[73]

The fact that Nevin had achieved such a position of prominence within the yeomanry would suggest a better class background, as would the huge attendance at his funeral. Yet, he had been reduced to the indignity of employment in the workhouse, which aptly demonstrates the crisis in which many Orangemen found themselves. An increased need for unity was recognized to be of principal importance by the Grand Lodge of Ulster. It expressed its desire to make 'the Orange Institution a *benevolent* as well as a *defensive* one, as far as possible, by raising an Orange fund that would enable them to provide for the widows of their poorer brethren, and to obtain the means of instruction for the orphan children of Orangemen, and also to relieve those brethren who might be suffering from persecution or distress'.[74] This lead was followed by the Omagh district who pledged that 'we will use every exertion, as a united association, to alleviate the distress of our poorer brethren, by procuring them employment, so far as in our power, and, consequently, preserving them from the danger of famine'.[75] The scale of the crisis in Monaghan was such that the Clones district acknowledged 'about two hundred of our members, with their respective families [are] in a most deplorable condition [...] but are bearing up under all their melancholy afflictions and privations with meekness and charitable forbearance'. The district pledged 'to use our utmost exertions, as far as our power lies, to alleviate their present state of destitution'.[76] A similar promise was forthcoming from the district of Ballybay and Castleblayney, while donations were also offered by the rank and file despite their diminished circumstances. The Belfast Twelfth procession of 1847 saw every participant Orangeman subscribe six pence towards the fever hospital.[77] Such contributions allowed the Belfast district treasurer to forward £13 1*s.* to the *Belfast Commercial Chronicle*'s fund to clothe the poor.[78]

2000), p. 98. **73** *BCC*, 29 March 1847. **74** *BPJ*, 17 October 1846. **75** *TC*, 6 November 1846. **76** *NS*, 20 February 1847. **77** *NG*, 17 July 1847. **78** *BCC*, 31 July 1847.

This fund, one of many established in the city, was 'to be applied in the purchase of cheap clothing for the destitute when discharged from the hospitals'.[79] The donation from the Orangemen allowed Dr Anderson, the hospital's chief surgeon, to spend £8 10*s.* 3*d.* on 24 shirts at 1*s.* 8*d.* each, 30 petticoats at 1*s.* 8*d.* each, 29 shifts at 1*s.* 3*d.* each and 24 bed-gowns at 1*s.* 10*d.* each.[80] In order to avoid pawning, each item of clothing bore the stamp of the hospital, highlighting the dismal situation of those availing of such donations. Private charity was a key component in the attempt to reduce the effects of Famine and co-existed with the less than generous government charitable measures. The Orange Order as an institution, despite the earlier appeal from the Grand Lodge of Ulster, did not provide official donations but it is clear that some individuals and individual lodges played their part in contributing to private funds. Their charitable donations were not confined to alleviating immediate Famine suffering however. Religious conversion was still considered key, possibly even more so than previously given the widely held belief that the Famine was Divine retribution for the failure to convert the Catholic 'heathens'. The sum of 10*s.* 6*d.* was bestowed by Schomberg Lodge no. 486 to the Revd William Johnston 'in aid of the Connaught Mission of the General Assembly of the Presbyterian Church' rather than to more immediate short-term Famine relief. Such missions 'were primarily interested in reviving lapsed Protestants, but they also supported Irish schools which had been founded in Mayo, and they gave help to the small Synod of Munster as it sought to sustain itself'.[81] These attempts by the Presbyterian Church and its driving force, Revd John Edgar, to infiltrate Connaught were controversial and led to allegations of proselytization; nonetheless, general subscriptions to the Connaught Fund were high as were subscriptions to educational bodies. The idea of self-improvement through education in particular as a way of lifting oneself above poverty was one that predominated, although once again overall motives were controversial. The sum of £3 3*s.* was donated to the Down and Connor and Dromore Education Society by Belfast's Eldon Lodge[82] while Revd Theophilus Campbell, treasurer of the Down and Connor and Dromore Church Education Society, received donations of £1 10*s.* from Eldon Orange lodge (no. 7) and £1 1*s.* from Verner Orange lodge (no. 853) towards the support of Trinity Church schools.[83] A donation of £2 2*s.* 6*d.* was gratefully received by the committee of the Church Education Society from the Royal Nassau Orange Lodge 670.[84] Such generosity was also received by the Protestant Orphan Society of Downpatrick who delighted in seeing 'the Orange lodges in this neighbourhood subscribing to this excellent society; and although

79 *BN*, 27 July 1847. **80** *BCC*, 2 August 1847. **81** Bowen, *The Protestant crusade in Ireland 1800–70*, p. 33. **82** *BN*, 11 January 1850. *BPJ*, 23 June 1849. **83** *BN*, 23 January 1849. **84** *DEM*, 4 April 1849.

the sum given by each individual society is not very large, it shows the Orangemen feel in their hearts the value of an institution such as this, and especially when they know Orangemen founded it'.[85] While donations from Orange lodges may not always have been very large, they did continue throughout the course of the Famine and demonstrate that despite the reduced circumstances of many individual members the charitable aspect of the Order did persist during this particularly difficult period. However, more than simple charitable donation was needed. In cancelling its February meeting in 1847, the Grand Lodge of Ulster recognized 'the paramount necessity which exists for everyone to be at his post, in their several localities at this awful crisis'.[86] By March, plague had broken out in Belfast and by the summer months typhus was endemic throughout the province. This 'fatal and contagious epidemic now so fearfully prevalent in this country' claimed the life of a young Orangeman named McKenna from Aughnacloy whose funeral was attended by a large gathering of Orangemen surely apprehensive of their own futures.[87] It was soon reported that in Belfast:

> All the fever hospitals are as full as full can be, and very many unfortunate people are necessarily refused admission at the doors of each. On Monday last the Barrack Street Hospital was opened, and was in a very few hours filled, there being about two hundred patients within its walls. The Frederick Street Hospital contains between four and five hundred people, double as many as it ought to have […] the entire number in the three institutions in town, the Workhouse, Barrack Street, and Frederick Street Hospitals, is little under 1,100 individuals, and from all we can learn there are at least an equal number lying in the garrets, on clay floors, and in humble hovels, in the most crowded neighbourhoods, for whom no provision can be made.[88]

THE PROPRIETY OF MARCHING

The severity of the crisis led many higher Orangemen to consider that marching during the summer season was simply inappropriate. In responding to an invitation from County Down's grand master William Beers, the Revd J.R. Moore replied that:

> If I thought I could be the means of strengthening my brethren in any way in their duty of God or man, I would gladly hoist the purple and orange

85 *BPJ*, 11 August 1849. **86** *ECEP*, 11 January 1847. **87** *AG*, 4 May 1847. **88** *DEM*, 2 June 1847.

> but I do firmly believe in my heart that it is desirable for all party processions to cease and when sickness, in short, pestilence and famine is throughout the length and breadth of the land, we are more than ever called upon to humble ourselves before God instead of stirring up angry feelings in our neighbourhood. I hope you will not be offended with me, for saying I hope very few people will walk on the 12th.[89]

Monaghan Orangemen were addressed by their grand master, H.G. Johnston, who wrote that:

> In the midst of famine and pestilence which has fallen upon our country, in the midst of your lamentations for the death of many a worthy though humble member, who has fallen a victim to this fearful visitation, I raise my voice as your friend and brother. At this hour of tribulation, I would deem any outward display unseemly, indiscreet, and ill-timed. It would be unseemly to behold a political flag, even though one of our own loved colour, waving over a famine-stricken land, where hundreds are dying of starvation, where fever racks the brain and the graveyards are teeming with the early dead. It would be indiscreet to hear the sounds of joy and musical instruments, and political exultation, in a land whose people are existing on public charity, and it would be ill-timed to see a procession marching in review past the soup kitchens to which our poor countrymen are obliged to resort for sustenance. There is scarce among you that has not some dear friend to mourn after.[90]

The staunchly Orange Revd Hartley Hodson felt unable to preach as normal to the brethren of the Belfast and Lisburn districts and asked them to refrain from marching. Hodson promised 'to preach to the men of the Lisburn district, *provided they leave their colours and music at home*; not otherwise' and asked:

> How many, alas, of your flags have but too recently enwrapped the dead? Suffer then the days of their mourning to be ended before you drag them forth to help in an *untimely* mirth. What one of your lodges is unbroken by death, unstriken [*sic*] by disease, unreached by affliction? Nay – where is *the house* that has escaped? If there are any such to be found; if there are in the mercy of God, a few whom his destroying angel has passed by, let these favoured ones rather 'weep with them that weep', than selfishly rejoice with music and banner amid 'lamentation, mourning and woe'.[91]

89 PRONI, Letter book for Earl Annesley's affairs, D1854/6/3. **90** *AC*, 2 July 1847. **91** *FJ*, 28 June 1847.

This plea, however, was to fall on deaf ears. The independence that local lodges clung to was evident, 'when after a long discussion, it was determined by a majority, that the lodges should walk in procession with all their insignia, colours, etc., on Monday next, the anniversary of the Battle of Aughrim'.[92] Police reported that Hodson and James Watson of Brookhill 'did everything in their power to prevent any display, but without effect'.[93] Once again, the desires of the lower classes were acted upon without conforming to traditional deferential protocol.

Throughout Ulster, restraint was continuously called for, despite the likelihood that such pleas could well be ignored by a membership anxious to parade. The threat of Divine retribution was stressed by Newry district, which asked its members not to march:

> Owing to the present awful state of visitation of Divine Providence on our beloved country, we deem it our duty rather to humble ourselves than express our feelings of rejoicing on the approaching anniversary of our deliverance from Popish tyranny by any public demonstration; and we earnestly entreat all sincere supporters of our glorious institution to faithfully consider their responsibility should they indulge in any other feeling but that now expressed.[94]

The *Belfast Newsletter* echoed this sentiment in pleading: 'let it not be remembered that this season, at least, is not a fitting one for any display of a triumphant character. While the afflicting dispensations of Providence are thickening about us like a cloud, it is surely no time to further provoke His wrath by thoughtless displays of party feeling'.[95] The *Chronicle* pointed out that:

> the land is groaning under the most afflictive dispensation with which it has ever pleased God to visit it – in every town and village and clutter of cottages, death is busy with its victims, and shall we hear, as though in wilful mockery of these solemn judgements, the air ringing with merry music, and the voice of triumph and jubilee, when thousands of our fellow creatures are perishing to disease and want?[96]

The sentiments of the newspapers were indicative of the general feeling that the Famine was without question the absolute and exclusive work of God. This was widely agreed upon yet some extremists persisted in the belief that Protestantism (and Orangeism by connection) was immune from Divine wrath. The *Armagh Guardian* furiously turned on Hodson 'for having drawn a dark picture of Ireland', and questioned whether he meant 'to infer that the Orange processions

92 NAI: Outrage Reports, Co. Antrim (1847) 82/1. **93** Ibid. **94** *DEM*, 9 July 1847. **95** *BN*, 29 June 1847. **96** *FJ*, 28 June 1847.

have any connexion with its cause? Or that the system itself is such to excite the displeasure of Heaven?'[97] This debate summed up the quandary faced by many Orangemen convinced they were God's chosen people yet confused that His afflictions were directed at them as well as what they considered the 'Papish heathens'. For instance, Dartree Lodge labelled the Famine 'a just retribution coming from the hand of a long-suffering God'. This retribution, in its opinion, was triggered by Protestants not standing up to Catholic idolatry and for not defending the constitution.[98] The Grand Lodge of Ireland had little doubt that the Famine was caused by the continuance of apparent government favour towards the Catholic religion. This line was evident the following year in a strongly worded rebuff address to the Repeal Association as the Grand Lodge made it clear that Catholicism 'and the national support of it, in addition to the most natural evils which spring therefrom, has most certainly called down the plagues of heaven on our ill-fated country'.[99] To understand such unquestioning belief in the highest power, Gray points out that it 'is necessary to recognize the extent to which a Christian – and more particularly a Protestant evangelical – world-view permeated early Victorian British society'.[100] Scientific reasoning did not enter this world-view, with its religious fervour greatly renewed by the Second Reformation. Already, a national day of penance and remorse had taken place on 24 March prior to which the Revd Thomas Hanley had warned that 'He is angry and He has manifested His anger by laying bare His arm [...] Famine, disease, and death are the consequence'.[101] With such a feeling of doom prevalent, 'all the Protestant houses of public worship were crowded during Divine service, as on the Sabbath with the most numerous and, to all appearance, devout congregations'.[102] The penance was also observed by the Catholic Church, which led the *DEM* to laud the coming together of the Churches in a common cause.[103] Yet, despite such piety, the Famine and plague continued. Johnston highlighted a practical danger in pointing out that:

> the spread of fever is rapid, and contagion exists almost everywhere. It would be therefore highly injurious and very dangerous to assemble together large masses of people, amongst whom one person infected though at the time unconscious of the infection, may spread the malady amongst hundreds, by which we may lose the very best and most useful members of our society.[104]

97 *AG*, 6 July 1847. **98** *NS*, 27 February 1847. **99** *Refusal of the Orangemen of Dublin to fraternise with Repealers, or join in the present revolutionary movement* (Dublin, 1848), p. 8. **100** Gray, 'National humiliation and the Great Hunger: fast and famine in 1847', pp 193–216. **101** 'A sermon, Reverend Thomas Hanley' in Killen (ed.), *The Famine decade, contemporary accounts, 1841–51*, pp 129–31. **102** *BN*, 26 March 1847. **103** Gray, 'National humiliation and the Great Hunger: fast and famine in 1847', pp 193–216. **104** *AC*, 2 July 1847.

On a practical level, the need to preserve and use money wisely was a concern for Hodson who advised brethren that 'this is not a time for expending your money in vain. What can you now spare from the pressing wants of your families? If *anything*, it is claimed by the wants of your famishing neighbours. One procession costs the district of Belfast alone a sum of *thirteen hundred pounds!*'[105] This sum may seem exaggerated but the previous year the admittedly anti-Orange *Banner of Ulster* had questioned the economic folly of parading on the Twelfth. It speculated that:

> there can be no doubt that 80 to 100,000 will lose a day's wages in this proceeding through Ulster. If we assume one hundred thousand as the number, and take their wages at an average of only one shilling, which must be below the truth, as many of them are artizans, and their expenditure at another shilling each, we have an outlay of *ten thousand pounds*.[106]

The *Banner* continued its condemnation of such excess by observing that 'some Orange lodges in Belfast have paid "twenty pounds" for new flags. We had occasion, lately, to ask from "the brethren" some assistance to their neighbours in Ballymacarrett, who were reduced to starvation; and from all working classes – Orange and Repeal, purple or green – the value of one flag or half a flag was not received'.[107] Economic concerns were of lesser interest to O'Connell's *Vindicator*, which had an altogether different take on the approaching processions. Calling them 'the Famine shows of the Twelfth', the paper suggested that 'the fever-hospitals, the soup kitchens, and the asylums of the province, were to send forward their array of meagre skeletons, to shout "the glorious, pious, and immortal memory" that has left them without even the necessities of life'. It predicted that 'those long trains of animated corpses, moving, or rather crawling, to party tunes, will be eloquent evidence of what "party" has done. The processions should rendezvous at graveyards, that they may inter such as happen to drop by the way'.[108] Perhaps with such mockery in mind but more likely because of the impracticalities involved, celebrations were greatly scaled back throughout the province. No parade took place in Londonderry although bells rung throughout the day, nor did any occur in Newry where lodges simply dined together instead. The *Newry Telegraph* was happy to announce that:

> in our town, at least, this commemorative period had passed by in peace and harmony. Everything induced us to believe such would have been the case. The lesson of last year, taught to both Orangemen and Roman

105 *FJ*, 28 June 1847. **106** *BOU*, 10 July 1846. **107** Ibid. **108** *TC*, 16 July 1847.

> Catholics; the National calamities, of which our town has also so largely partaken; our over-filled hospitals; out thinned population; our crowded graveyards; and our pauperized condition formed, we thought, sufficient ground for this supposition.[109]

In Enniskillen, the *Chronicle* reported that 'the brethren did not make any public display, not for want of loyalty, but taking into consideration the present distressed state of the town. The members of the different lodges dined together in the Town Hall in the evening'.[110] However, this lead was not followed everywhere and a large number of parades did occur throughout Ulster. In the earl of Enniskillen's home town, it was natural that the Grand Lodge of Ireland would hold sway over the town's Orangemen. But with most Orangemen aligned with the rival Grand Lodge of Ulster, the obedience shown in Enniskillen was not evident in much of the rest of the province. The schism between the competing Grand Lodges was still in place during the 1847 marching season. With the Grand Lodge of Ulster offering little sense of direction regarding marching, its members were free to act as they chose.

Many chose not to march. In Belfast, despite the wishes of Hodson, around 3,000 Orangemen marched to the field at Ballyleeson although numbers were less than other years as 'perhaps one half of the members did not turn out on this occasion'.[111] The *Mail* recounted how, 'in consequence of the prevalence of fever, no music was played until the processions had got without the town and the same consideration towards the sick was observed in returning through Belfast [...] a drunken man could not be seen amongst them'.[112] Twenty-four lodges assembled in Banbridge although police considered that 'the number of Orangemen were very few compared with the assemblages of former years, while 5–6,000 Orangemen from Lurgan and Portadown met and marched into Lurgan.[113] Parades took place in Tyrone at Moy, Caledon, Dungannon and Middleton, while Armagh's Tanderagee district met the Newry district at Pontzpass. Some 1,000 Lisburn Orangemen followed the advice of Hodson, who did indeed preach, as 'one by one the lodges entered the town in solemn silence, and, but for the waving of flag and hearty look, one might have thought they were gathering to mourn rather than to rejoice [...] it was indeed a noble sight to know that those silent drums and that stilly march were a token of humiliation beneath the hand of God'.[114] A similar scene was evident in Randalstown, while several thousand spectators watched the sham fight at Scarva, County Armagh.[115] In general, the day passed off peacefully although some trouble occurred in Newry

109 *ECEP*, 18 July 1847. **110** *ECEP*, 15 July 1847. **111** *BN*, 13 July 1847. **112** *NG*, 17 July 1847. **113** NAI: Outrage Reports, Co. Down (1847) 179/8. **114** *DCJ*, 24 July 1847. **115** *BN*, 16 July 1847.

as Orangemen returning from Pontzpass clashed with Catholics prompting the *Newry Telegraph* to ask, 'are not such doings heart-sickening to every right thinking man?'[116] This tone was echoed by the *Newsletter* who re-iterated that 'this is not a season for displays of such a kind. If each man had walked with a Bible in his hand, and not have carried any other emblem of his Protestantism, it would have had a much more imposing and becoming effect at this time, when the judgements of God are abroad in the earth. It should have been kept as a day of humiliation, and not as a holiday, or day of amusement'.[117] The *Londonderry Journal* opined that 'objectionable as those processions are under ordinary circumstances, they seem to be peculiarly so at the present time, when the general suffering which has been experienced ought to have subdued or softened down those angry animosities in which they originate'.[118] On the other hand, the *Tyrone Constitution*, although not in favour of the processions, did reason that Orangemen 'were determined to convince the public, and to prove to their maligners, that they were not the recipients of state charity, or the emaciated skeletons which had been pictured [by the *Vindicator*] but that they were men of nerve and sinew, prepared to uphold the time-honoured constitution of their land, and to remember with gratitude its deliverance from thraldom'.[119] Therefore, despite how objectionable some may have found the processions, they did demonstrate that at this stage of the Famine, the will still existed among many Orangemen to continue with their activities and demonstrate their continuing loyalty and togetherness, despite the hardships that many were enduring.

THE WORKHOUSE

Irrespective of what some elites may have wanted to believe, it is clear that Protestants were as badly affected as Catholics by 'God's wrath'. The first 440 entrants to Lisnaskea workhouse, for example, were divided almost evenly between the religious denominations according to John Cunningham's study of Fermanagh.[120] Ballyshannon workhouse was forced into buying increased amounts of new Bibles and prayer books, such was the influx of needy Protestants. The Protestant Shankhill graveyard was reported to be full to its capacity such were the numbers dying daily.[121] The overflow of paupers in the workhouses of counties Down and Antrim, numerically dominated by Protestants, would also indicate the extent of the suffering of Protestant communities. The lifeblood of these people,

116 *NT*, 14 July 1847. **117** *BN*, 13 July 1847. **118** *LJ*, 14 July 1847. **119** *TC*, 16 July 1847. **120** John Cunningham, 'The Famine in County Fermanagh' in Kinealy and Parkhill (eds), *The Famine in Ulster*, pp 129–45. **121** Gerard McAtasney and Christine Kinealy, 'The great hunger in Belfast' in Crowley, Murphy and Smyth (eds), *Atlas of the Great Irish Famine* (Cork, 2012), pp 434–9.

namely the linen industry, had already been severely hit at various times since the beginning of the century, now it was under attack again as flax prices were driven upwards as the blight attacked this essential crop. While the price of flax soared, the wages of weavers remained low. This was pointed out in parliament by Verner when he dismissed the 'notion that in the north of Ireland the people could support themselves by means of the linen trade'. In fact, according to Verner, only 2*s.* was paid for a web of sixty-four or sixty-five yards which gave 'some idea of the earnings that could be derived by this branch of industry'.[122] In addition to this, Kinealy points out that 'a feature of the domestic textile industry was the fact that it was underpinned – and sustained – by the availability of nutritious and readily available food, in the form of the potato.[123] It is obvious therefore that the potato blight wreaked havoc with the linen industry and drastically weakened one of the central survival modes of Protestant Ulster. Yet whether continuing to work within a greatly decimated linen industry or on the work-schemes of the Poor Law Unions, it does appear that most men were able to keep out of the workhouse. By 1848, children made up over half of the workhouse population while it is acknowledged that there was 'a preponderance [a ratio of almost 3:1] of females among the adult population in the workhouses of Ulster'.[124] It has to be acknowledged that workhouse assistance was directed at those most vulnerable and unable to help themselves – usually in society these tend to be women and children. Nonetheless, despite the fact that the majority of entrants to the poorhouses were women, children and the elderly, and although only the utterly destitute entered, the place and importance of Orange life for those within the walls of the poorhouse was not extinguished. To an extent this was facilitated by some Poor Law guardians who themselves publicly continued with their Orange activities. A complaint was brought against the officials of Newtown-Limavady workhouse by its Catholic chaplain, Fr Bernard O'Neill, who alleged that boys and girls from the workhouse were allowed to witness and indeed join in an Orange procession on 12 July 1847. O'Neill also alleged that boys had worn Orange emblems during the day. Despite the protests of the Presbyterian minister, the Reverend George Steen, who countered that 'it had always been the practice, in former years, to allow the children to see the procession', the Poor Law Commission Office in Dublin found that 'it seems sufficiently clear [...] that the children were taken to see this procession as an amusement to which they were annually treated' but 'it was an indiscretion [...] that should not be repeated in any future years'. The matron and schoolmaster were 'severely reprimanded'

122 *Hansard, HC debate, 19 February 1847, vol. 90, cc 251–93.* **123** Christine Kinealy, *Hidden Famine: hunger, poverty and sectarianism in Belfast* (London, 2000), p. 39. **124** Trevor Parkhill, 'The Famine in County Londonderry', in Kinealy and Parkhill (eds), *The Famine in Ulster*, pp 147–68.

and reminded to, 'on all occasions, studiously refrain from doing or permitting anything calculated to perpetuate or awaken religious animosities'.[125] Two years later, officers of the Cootehill Union faced an enquiry into their conduct on the Twelfth of July. It was found that all charges were unsubstantiated other than one against a clerk, Mr Graham, for attending the local procession. Yet little sanction was forthcoming as:

> the commissioners intimated to Mr Graham, that his having done so was unwise in a public functionary; but that as he acted without knowing that it was against the wishes of the commissioners, that not having given directions on the subject, that they would merely intimate that he should in future guard against taking part in party demonstrations.[126]

With such ambiguous central instruction, it is quite likely that such occurrences continued. Indeed, the *Freeman's Journal* bemoaned that 'there cannot be a doubt but that the cabals of some workhouses have been justly regarded by the paupers as little better than a new species of Orange lodges'.[127] Such feeling continued to be borne out as witnessed in the case of a memorial from Courtenay Orange Lodge, Ballymena, which asked the Board of Guardians to grant the Twelfth of July 1849 as a holiday to Protestant inmates. This was a request that the Guardians considered 'just and fair' although they themselves did not have the authority to judge on the matter.[128] In Ballymoney, poorhouse children singing Orange songs at a wedding invoked the ire of local Catholic clergymen who complained strongly to the Board of Guardians.[129] That instances such as these occurred within the squalor and misery of the poorhouse is indicative of the strength and depth of lower-class Orangeism. Similarly, it would seem that men were able to maintain their Orange activities and beliefs in their everyday lives despite the increasing destitution. Indeed, Belfast mill workers who had been threatened with dismissal if they missed work to attend the Twelfth in 1846 felt sufficiently confident to ignore the directive of the mill owners despite the catastrophic consequences that would surely have followed dismissal.[130] The mill owners notice had an ominous tone: 'we the undersigned mill owners and others, employing the working classes, have resolved, that any of our workers, joining in, or accompanying any processions, on Monday next, will be turned out of our employment and not taken in again by any of the parties whose names are attached to this document'.[131] The threat was ignored as 'the parties thus addressed felt too strongly on the subject for this document to produce the

125 *DEM*, 6 October 1847. **126** *BN*, 25 September 1849. **127** *FJ*, 22 September 1849. **128** PRONI, Poor Law minute books, BG/4/A/2. **129** PRONI, Poor Law minute books, BG/5/A/5. **130** *LJ*, 15 July 1846. **131** Ibid.

desired effect'. The following year, 'a similar species of tyranny was enacted, not so openly, but with more Jesuitical cunning', according to the *Protestant Journal*.[132] The paper reported that two members of the Belfast district band were refused permission to take the day off work, while one 'respectable' painter dismissed an employee for taking part in a procession. Condemning 'liberal' mill owners, the *Journal* expressed concern for the rights of the working man opining that 'respect and attention are all that can be expected by an employer. Abject servility no honest mind can demand, no independent spirit can brook'.[133] Yet the musings of an extremist newspaper suddenly 'adopting' the working classes for its own agenda were of little use to mill workers facing an uncertain future. Thus, it can be tentatively concluded that the desire to keep parading was such that threats from employers could not dampen the will of such Orangemen to continue their normal activities. The requests of the better classes were rejected. The ravages of starvation and disease could not halt their march. Similarly, the misery of the poorhouse could not quell the strength of Orange feeling among its inmates. Clearly, the lower classes were not prepared to abandon Orangeism despite the severity of the Famine.

GENERAL ELECTIONS

The continuance of such activities or indeed any great show of Orange strength was not, for once, required at the countrywide elections that took place the following month. Previous election contests had frequently turned violent as Orangemen had physically made their presence felt at election centres. The elections of 1847, however, saw little of the disruption that marred previous contests as few county constituencies actually went to the poll. In fact, the majority of outgoing MPs retained their seats without contest as no challengers emerged. According to Brian Walker, little mention of the Famine was made by these MPs in the build up to the election. Only Brooke, sitting MP for Fermanagh, had the previous year 'announced to his tenantry immediate reduction of all rents, the supply of meal, free or at reduced prices, and the provision of employment'.[134] Other than this, the issue of famine aid was largely ignored by the candidates. Seemingly more pressing was the ongoing need to block apparent government favouritism shown towards Catholics. The Grand Lodge of Ireland felt compelled to issue a newspaper address 'to the Protestant electors of Great Britain' pleading for renewed assistance in the ongoing struggle

132 *BPJ*, 17 July 1847. **133** Ibid. **134** Brian Walker, 'Politics, elections and catastrophe: the general election of 1847', *Irish Political Studies*, 22:1 (2007), pp 1–34.

against mushrooming Papist strength.[135] Some Orangemen did use the contest to voice their fears over government-backed Catholic incursion to those candidates running. On the morning of the Lisburn borough election, 'a deputation from the Orangemen of Lisburn, headed by Revd Hartley Hodson, T.F. Caldbeck Esq., and Doctor Innes, waited upon Sir Horace [Seymour, the outgoing MP] to know his intentions, in the event of any attempt being made to renew the [Party] processions act'. Seymour had controversially voted in favour of the increased Maynooth endowment in the belief that educated Catholics were less dangerous than uneducated Catholics. The deputation demanded no repeat of such a vote forcing Seymour to rather hurriedly concur to their wishes. Continuing to desperately court favour, Seymour 'then denounced the policy which had permitted turbulent, disaffected, mobs to meet and walk in procession unmolested, whilst the loyal commemorations of events to which this Protestant country owed all its religious and political blessings were most unjustly prevented'.[136] It did seem to some Protestants that the gatherings of Catholic groups such as Ribbonmen did not attract the same judicial sanction as gatherings of Orangemen. The law certainly did appear lax in its dealings with Ribbonmen. In one example, a party of thirty Ribbonmen was apprehended marching towards Downpatrick the previous February. The party had a drum and a fife and was firing shots. Despite this, 'one person only was made amendable, he was tried and acquitted, a doubt being suggested that the offence of unlawful assembly had been committed'.[137] Orangemen could not see the difference between a Catholic procession and a Protestant procession, yet in their eyes it seemed that Catholic gatherings rarely suffered the sanction of the law in the way they did. In this vein, the somewhat browbeaten Seymour pledged to 'oppose "tooth and nail" any attempt to put down processions, and to grant further concessions to popery'.[138] Evidently, Seymour had no desire to face the cries from the crowd of 'rogue, ruffian and rascal' endured by Lord Castlereagh at the County Down count due to his approval of the Maynooth grant. Fortunately for Castlereagh his seat was uncontested, nevertheless his victory speech could not be heard above the uproar.[139] Such disapproval and disruption again demonstrate that traditional lower-class deference was flexible and conditional. Although most of the lower classes did not actually possess the vote, they still turned up in large numbers at election contests to make their feelings known. Despite his high social position, Castlereagh was not obviously immune to his tenants' displeasure. Although Dublin city was firmly in Tory hands, guarantees of this nature were also sought by Dublin Orangemen, who had incidentally moved by this stage

135 *DEM*, 26 July 1847. **136** *BPJ*, 7 August 1847. **137** PRONI, files of reports relating to Orange processions, MIC/371/4. **138** *BN*, 6 August 1847. **139** *BN*, 10 August 1847.

closer to joining the Grand Lodge of Ireland following meetings in Coleraine and Belfast in the previous months. A meeting was held at 5 College Street 'for the purpose of taking into their consideration the most necessary, prudent, and admirable course to be adopted by them with regard to the election of honest and faithful men to be their future representatives in parliament'.[140] Although letters of invitation were sent to the sitting MPs, W.H. Gregory and Edward Grogan, neither attended citing election commitments as an excuse. The well-attended meeting of 'respectable Orangemen' had instead to be satisfied by letters of apology from both men. The burning question regarding the endowment by the state of Catholic priests moved Grogan to stress his opposition to this and outline his plans to make 'a determined stand against any further government concessions to, or encouragement of, Papish tenets and doctrines'. Gregory's stance was moderate in comparison, stating that, 'I shall always be an advocate for civil and religious liberty', although with an eye on his listenership he did highlight that he would continue to maintain and support 'the interests of our Protestant religion'.[141] This end assurance did little to convince the better classes of Dublin Orangemen who subsequently resolved to vote for Grogan but to deny Gregory their vote.

At the other end of the class spectrum, these issues of further government concessions to Catholics were a constant sore for Tresham Gregg. Gregg used the build up to the election to lash both Gregory and Grogan as they had, in his opinion, done little to help the working-class Protestants of the city.[142] Gregory, in particular, was castigated by Gregg for his apparent support for Peel's policies. Although the proposed running of hard-line Protestant and Orangeman W.B. Ferrand from Yorkshire fell through, the influence of Gregg on hard-line Orangemen was such that Gregory lost his seat to Repeal candidate John Reynolds in what was a major surprise. Reynolds had only stood at the last minute and his election shocked even his fellow Repealers. The *DEM* summed up that 'Mr Tresham Gregg's friends gave their second vote to the Repealer, to put out Mr Gregory for supposed liberality and pro-Catholic tendencies'.[143] Evidently, Gregg was prepared to cause the loss a safe Protestant seat in the interests of the Protestant working classes. The better classes of Orangemen, who were unhappy with Gregory's seemingly lukewarm attitude to the defence of the Protestant Church, followed this lead. The election of Reynolds saw no Orange disaffection surface and, on the whole, the elections of 1847 passed without any incident of note with the *Anglo-Celt* being happy to over optimistically report that 'party spirit has vanished'.[144]

140 PRONI, Minute book of Hardcourt Orange Lodge, Dublin and Grand Lodge of Ireland, 1844–49, MIC 201/1. **141** Ibid. **142** Hill, 'The 1847 general election in Dublin city', pp 41–64. **143** *DEM*, 9 August 1847. **144** *AC*, 13 August 1847.

A FALSE LULL?

One of the principal reasons that little attention had been devoted to the famine situation during the 1847 election campaign was that a feeling prevailed that its worst days had passed. Indeed, government relief had been wound up at this stage. But worrying was the report from the *Londonderry Journal* from later in the same month in which it regretted 'to state that the warm weather, succeeding the late rains, has brought out the potato rot in many fields in this neighbourhood, where it must have been previously lurking. The stalks have become blackened, and the smell proceeding from them at night is most offensive'.[145] In any case, few potatoes had been planted by a tenantry that had been preoccupied in attempting to find paid work. Along with this threat to the small crop of 1847 came a potentially bigger menace to the Protestant ascendancy in Ireland, a danger which would spread fear and paranoia throughout Protestant Ulster – the real peril of another Republican uprising.

* * *

Although not as devastating as in some southern and western areas, the Famine ravaged parts of Ulster to dramatic effect. Those affected were not greatly helped by their landlords and many chose emigration or were forced to the poorhouse. But the rights and wrongs of assembling during this time of God's apparent vengeance were largely overridden as Orangemen clung to their days of parading as one of the few lights that remained during this dark time. That they were able to muster the strength to do so would hint at a resilience amid unprecedented calamity. This, once again, summed up the centrality of Orangeism to a vast number of Protestants.

145 *LJ*, 18 August 1847.

CHAPTER FOUR

Overtures from Young Ireland

DESPITE THE ENORMITY of a nationwide famine, political matters remained very much in the public domain. For the middle and upper classes not afflicted by starvation, disease or emigration, political life continued much as before. Irish MPs in Westminster voiced their anger at the lukewarm initiatives put into practice by a government seemingly becoming more disinterested in the Irish situation as the months passed. But the O'Connellite faction of Irish politics still saw fit to press its claims for repeal despite the anguished state of the country. From this faction emerged a disaffected, radical group, determined to take their cause to a new level, beyond anything their former leader could have envisioned. Part of the agenda of both factions involved the wooing of Orangemen amid a greater overall courtship of Protestants. How the Orangemen reacted to the approaches of O'Connell's Repealers on one hand, and the increasingly revolutionary 'Young Irelanders' on the other, will form the basis of this chapter.

A NEW LORD LIEUTENANT

In praising the appointment of Lord Clarendon as successor to the deceased Lord Bessborough as lord lieutenant of famine-stricken Ireland, London's *Morning Chronicle* rather naively ventured that the new governor of Ireland held a distinct advantage over his predecessors because 'calamity has almost annihilated the distinction between the Orange and the Green'.[1] Nonetheless, despite these confident sentiments, Clarendon was not overly anxious to accept the position. The position of lord lieutenant was not greatly sought after in the corridors of Westminster and had stunted many a political career, such were the political, religious and social complexities of Ireland. This seemed to be a country which, in the context of the British Empire, could almost be paralleled to the nightmare colony of the Roman Empire that was Judaea. Yet it must have seemed to political observers, at least from the distance of mainland Britain, that despite the ongoing Famine and the underwhelming government response to it, religious

1 *CE*, 26 May 1847.

division and sectarian conflict had lessened. This, if true, would certainly be a blessing to the new appointee. The Party Processions Act had not needed to be renewed due to the thus far largely peaceful nature of processions, which augured well for a less turbulent future. However, if the reluctant Clarendon was under any impression that his job would be less taxing than what his predecessors had experienced, he was to be gravely mistaken.

A RENEWED CAMPAIGN FOR REPEAL

Following the signing of the Litchfield House Compact the political alliance between the Whigs and Daniel O'Connell had prevailed throughout the 1830s. In return for a role in government and the continuation of its reform policy O'Connell had agreed to put his repeal campaign on hold. This action thereby removed, at least temporarily, a source of serious unrest in Ireland and the accompanying danger that the re-mobilization of the Catholic multitudes could potentially bring. Inevitably, the influence of O'Connell within government circles came to an end with his discontent at the slow pace of Whig reform, and with the eventual return of the Tories to power in 1841. O'Connell then turned his attention back to the repeal campaign, which he hoped would be successful through the use of the pressure tactics that had gained Catholic emancipation in 1829. The difference this time was that while Catholic emancipation had many advocates among liberal Protestants throughout Britain and Ireland, a repeal of the union most assuredly did not. There seems to have been little likelihood that repeal would ever have been granted by either political camp. When the Tory government clamped down on O'Connell in 1843 with its outlawing of the planned Clontarf 'monster meeting', the limitations of peaceful protest and public pressure were dramatically exposed. O'Connell did remain in the public eye, especially with his triumphant release from prison the following year where he had been held on trumped-up conspiracy charges. But his repeal campaign in its present guise of peaceful pressurization, although not recognized immediately, realistically had little place left to go.

THE 'FIGHT' FOR ULSTER

Nevertheless, despite the apparent bankruptcy of O'Connell's peaceful pressure tactics, repeal agitation did continue up to and even after his death in 1847. The problem had been that throughout O'Connell's campaigns few Ulster Protestants could be convinced to join his cause. Attempts at gathering support during the previous two decades by John Lawless, Marcus Costello, O'Connell himself and Thomas Steele had all been miserable failures as Orangemen provided violent opposition. Undeterred, many Repealers held on to the notion that if Protestants could be simply enlightened to the perceived advantages of repeal they would willingly join or at least support the campaign. While there had been little in the way of organized action in Ulster twenty years previously during the campaign for Catholic emancipation, a different picture emerged during the 1840s. Repeal clubs had been formed in Ulster throughout the decade, notably in Dungannon, which claimed a membership of almost 1,000, and in Belfast where five clubs existed. Indeed, Hirst points out that 'a firm consistent base of support' existed in the city with 2,000 people per week attending repeal meetings.[2] These almost exclusively Catholic Repealers of Belfast were especially vigorous and actively attempted to 'convert' Orangemen to their cause. Such an 'Appeal to the Orangemen of Ulster from the Belfast Repeal Association' pointed out that:

> William was a repealer having repealed the union between Spain and the Low Countries, as was Luther who had resisted Roman interference […] You who have been born and bred Irishmen, ought as little to be Englishmen in your country as William of Orange was a Spaniard in Flanders, or Martin Luther an Italian in Germany. If you followed the example of either of these great men, you ought to be Irishmen for Ireland first, and then Orangemen for the rest of mankind.[3]

This appeal was angrily rejected by the ultra-Protestant press and by Orangemen incredulous that any comparison could be made between the aims of Repealers and William of Orange and Martin Luther – two of the figures upon which Ulster Protestantism was built. Yet again, it was made abundantly clear that Protestant Ulster had no intention of being swayed towards any notion of repeal. Despite such rejection, repeal campaigners continued their efforts to make inroads in Ulster, but these exertions merely had the effect of further enraging Orangemen. Despite this, the subsequent formation of a Loyal Anti-Repeal Association was not wholly welcomed by rank-and-file Orangemen. Some distrust (considered jealously by the correspondent of the *Newry Telegraph*) was voiced, forcing the Association to publicly express its admiration of Orangeism. It appealed to Orangemen to join, 'reserving, however, their own distinctive features as a loyal society, and the privilege of acting at all times in unison with the leaders of their own body'.[4] But for many Orangemen, an association lacking a physical

2 Catherine Hirst, *Religion, politics, and violence in nineteenth-century Belfast: the Pound and Sandy Row* (Dublin, 2002), pp 51–2. **3** *FJ*, 15 July 1848. **4** *DEP*, 25 April 1848.

presence was worthless. After all, Catholic emancipation had been granted in the face of such toothless organizations of passive resistance. Thus, the use of violence was considered legitimate by many of the lower classes especially, and was an ominous presence in the face of repeal campaigners. This threat of Orange violence continued as the year progressed, as was evidenced in Cavan town when placards erected by the Repeal Association advertised a meeting to be addressed by members of the Dublin branch. With rumours abounding, 'vast' numbers of Orangemen entered from the Ballyhaise direction and lined the streets. Upon the arrival of the Dublin coach, 'a rush was made to it, anticipating the appearance of the promised deputation' but they were not on board much to the disappointment of the uncompromising Orange multitudes. Such an episode rather sums up the enthusiastic but somewhat haphazard activities of the Repeal Association and the feelings of Orangemen in Ulster against it. Indeed, in the words of the *Londonderry Journal*, 'the extraordinary efforts made by the Repeal Party in this province have just the effect of confirming and inflaming the spirit of the Orangemen'.[5]

THE PROTESTANT REPEAL ASSOCIATION

It would be quite wrong however to suggest that all Protestants were opposed to breaking with the union. This was especially evident in Dublin where a number of liberal Protestants who backed the idea of repeal had founded a Protestant Repeal Association. At a meeting held in the Music Hall, where 'there was a large attendance of the lower classes', a membership of 1,500 was claimed including some 100 Orangemen. The committee promised that 'they would have 300 Orangemen, in costume, upon the platform next night'. Among those enrolled on the night was prominent Orangeman and editor of the *Drogheda Conservative* newspaper Mr Phillip Coulter.[6] An address read to the Protestants of Ulster attempted to sway Orangemen by playing the tenant right card, the solving of the land problem being part of the Repeal Association's overall agenda. This, of course, made it easy for scaremongering landlords to link both associations much to the detriment of the completely separate Tenant Right Association. The address read 'let each hamlet and town in Orange Ulster have its Protestant Repeal Association, and place itself in communication with the central body at Dublin. Believe us, brethren, if this be done, your rights are sacred; and if your tenant right be taken from you, it will be that it may be restored under our local legislature'.[7] The extreme Protestant press scorned that the promised 300 Repeal

5 *LJ*, 31 May 1848. **6** *DEM*, 31 May 1848. **7** *BN*, 2 June 1848.

Orangemen were '*non est inventus*' [he is not found],[8] but at a subsequent meeting held on 12 July to deliberately coincide with a *soirée* organized by the Dublin Orange Institution, many on the platform were seen to be wearing scarves and badges of the Orange Institution.[9] Mr Daniel Sullivan, taking the chair, produced an Orange lily and 'suggested it should no longer be viewed as a symbol of discord, but one of unity'.[10] Membership, it was claimed, had increased to 3,000 at this stage although it was counter claimed, possibly justifiably, that the Protestant Repeal Association had swollen meeting numbers with 'counterfeit Orangemen' dressed in full regalia.[11] Again present was Coulter who said he was 'a Protestant Freeman of the town of Drogheda, and an Orangeman. He referred to the manner in which Orangemen had been treated by government in times past, and said that they were now called on to come forward in aid of a government which would crush them tomorrow if it suited their purpose'.[12] Quite simply, many Protestants had lost faith in Westminster and the way they had been treated by successive governments. For some Protestants, the option of a Dublin parliament could scarcely be any worse than perceived continued suppression from London. The enrolment of Coulter indicated some uncertainty among Orangemen and small numbers did join the Protestant Repeal Association, branches of which were also set up in Belfast, Lurgan and Drogheda. This radical change in opinion was explained by Mr Glew, an Orangeman who had in the past been active in the Dublin institution. Glew described how:

> The change in his opinions was the result of his having examined the arguments on both sides without party feeling. He had felt determined not to be prevented from joining the movement for national independence, simply because it might have originated by those differing from him in religious persuasion. He was, however, determined to guard his Protestant rights, so far as they were consistent with truth and justice; and although he was unfavourable to republican principles, he could not but admire the manly spirit and noble bearing of the martyred John Mitchel.[13]

Following a 'tour' of Ulster, Reverend John Dunmore Lang, senior member of the Presbyterian Church, was convinced that he had seen enough evidence of the joining of Catholic and Protestant tenant farmers to announce that, 'I am, therefore, decidedly of opinion that the age of Orangeism is past in Ireland, and that it will no longer be practicable in that country, as it was in times past, to array large masses of Catholics against Protestants, or of Protestants against

8 *The law dictionary*, thelawdictionary.org/non-est-inventus, Accessed 20 October 2019. **9** *PW*, 30 June 1848. **10** Christine Kinealy, *Repeal and revolution: 1848 in Ireland* (Manchester, 2009), p. 185. **11** Richard Davis, *The Young Ireland movement* (Dublin, 1987), p. 228. **12** *LJ*, 19 July 1848. **13** *DEM*,

Catholics, for selfish purposes and objects of any political party whatsoever'. Dunmore Lang, touring from Australia, agreed that the interests of the people 'have not been promoted by the Legislative Union with Great Britain'.[14] But extreme warnings were issued to the Orange membership not to fall for any repeal rhetoric. By now, the Dublin lodges had fully joined with the Grand Lodge of Ireland having received their new warrants from Samuel Yates Johnson the previous November. The Schomberg Lodge quickly issued a reply to the advances of 'the Committee of Trades' in Dublin which made it clear that:

> One thing we are determined on, and we may as well let you know it in time, that no matter how England or her rulers may feel towards us, the Orangemen of Ireland – the mighty and magnanimous band of Irish Protestants – will, with the help of God, preserve this land from the domination and ascendancy of your seditious faction. The spirit of Protestants slumbereth [*sic*] not.

The Repealers' optimism that Orangemen would join their cause was met firmly by Orange leadership. At a meeting of fifteen lodges in Whitefriars Hall in the company of the earl of Enniskillen, the newly formed Grand Lodge of Dublin resolved that 'in consequence of the false and malicious assertion repeatedly made by Repealers, etc., that we would join in the reckless proceedings […] we shall not, however remotely be identified or connected with any treasonable or seditious movement'.[15] Speaking at the aforementioned July *soirée*, one Brother Babington assured 'those misled individuals that they, the Orangemen of Dublin, neither recognized them as Orangemen or true Protestants'.[16] The Luther Orange Lodge of Dublin warned young Protestants that 'men calling themselves Protestants, seek to induce you, by high flown and bombastic language, to join the popish millions of Ireland […] they calumniate the Protestants of Ireland by falsehoods of the highest magnitudes. They are sending their spies throughout the country, to allure some of you to ruin'.[17] Traditional Protestant suspicion of Romanism was close to the surface as the Grand Lodge of Ireland warned Protestant Repealers that 'those whom you have fraternized with hate you in reality, and you would be the first victims of your own duplicity and guilt. Papists are consistent when engaged in any work, no matter how vile. Their church will sanction their treason'.[18] The central Orange Institution further added that 'the heart sickens at this, but is relieved by the thought that the whole world looks

14 July 1848. **14** John Dunmore Lang, *Repeal or revolution; or, a glimpse of the Irish future: in a letter to the Right Honourable Lord John Russell* (Dublin, 1848). **15** *DEP*, 25 April 1848. **16** *DEM*, 14 July 1848. **17** *NG*, 15 July 1848. **18** *DEP*, 13 April 1848.

upon you as outcasts from your brethren, as a disgrace to your profession, and as Papists as heart'.[19] Whatever about some members fraternizing with the Tenant Right Association, there could be absolutely no crossover between Orangemen and Repealers as far as most Orangemen were concerned. Thus, the penalties were extreme for Orangemen who joined the Repeal Association. The Co. Antrim Orange Lodge, at a meeting held in Belfast, resolved 'that the attention of all Orangemen in this county be called to the warning now given, that if any of them, under the misguided and rash politicians, shall be misled to fraternize with Repealers, whether Popish or Protestant, they shall be summarily expelled [from] this institution'.[20] These warnings were replicated around the country. Despite the dismissal by magistrate R.M. Dolling of rumours that some Orangemen in Lower Iveagh 'had turned Repealers', ten members within the county were expelled for unspecified reasons for periods of one year to life and it was reported that sixteen other northern Orangemen were expelled for joining the Repeal Association in July.[21] One disenchanted grand master wrote to the *Freeman's Journal* to inform it that 'twenty-nine persons were expelled from lodges in the Belfast district alone for holding Repeal opinions, viz., five from lodge 245; one from lodge 54; one from lodge 633; one from lodge 215; seventeen from lodge 241; two from lodge 666; one from lodge 182; one from lodge 636'.[22] Among those expelled were medical doctors J.W. Beck and William Seeds, which would tend to suggest that those likely to be tempted by Repeal overtures came from the middling to better classes – the educated with a tendency towards more independent and reasoned thinking.[23] But overall, the directives issued by Orange leadership against joining any repeal association were generally adhered to and there is little evidence of any real Orange involvement. While some Orangemen may have passed a mild interest in the notion of repeal, the vast majority were all too aware of an even more dangerous threat that had built momentum over the previous five years. This threat was spearheaded by a group labelled Young Ireland by contemporary commentators.

YOUNG IRELAND

Since the early part of the decade the limitations of peaceful protest had come under attack from both radical and moderate former supporters of O'Connell. These included Thomas Davis, Charles Gavan Duffy, James Fintan Lalor,

19 *Refusal of the Orangemen of Dublin to fraternise with Repealers, or to join in the present revolutionary movement*, p. 10. **20** *The Nation*, 1 July 1848. **21** *NW*, 13 July 1848. **22** *The Nation*, 8 July 1848. Kinealy, *Repeal and revolution: 1848 in Ireland*, p. 185. **23** Grand Orange Lodge of Ireland, Half-yearly meeting of the Grand Lodge of Ireland, 14–20 November 1848. One expelled member, John Porter, was

Thomas Francis Meagher, John Blake Dillon, William Smith O'Brien, Thomas Martin and John Mitchel, all of whom grew increasingly impatient with the cautious approach of their leader. In addition to concern at the seeming redundancy of O'Connell's protest policy, the possible place of religion in a post-Repeal Ireland proved to be a major source of irritation for this increasingly radical faction. They did welcome the government's Irish University Act, which provided for secular university education in its new Queen's Colleges in Belfast, Cork and Galway, as an opportunity for religious denominations to mix and familiarize themselves with the 'other'. On the contrary, O'Connell and the Catholic hierarchy with which he was closely aligned roundly condemned these 'Godless Colleges' and demanded a fully Catholic university. In a numerically Catholic dominated country, O'Connell's close ties with the Catholic Church were intolerable to the Young Irelanders who 'were appalled at the vista of a Catholic ascendency replacing a Protestant one'. For Young Ireland, 'confessional religion was a private matter and that the public religion they espoused – nationalism – was the only true faith'.[24] Also infuriating for this branch of Repealers were O'Connell's approaches to Sharman Crawford's liberal federalists, and more damningly to the newly returned Whig government. This pointed to a repeat of a suspension of Irish protest and a return to the contentious patronage that he and his family had availed of during their previous alliance of 1835–40. For the Young Irelanders, as educated members of the middle classes although varying in their political ideology, a different line of thought was promoted and passed through literature and their newly founded *Nation* newspaper. These romantic non-sectarian nationalist idealists broke from the Repeal Association by refusing to dismiss the possibility of an armed uprising along the lines of the 1798 rebellion, following an ultimatum from O'Connell. This is not to say that armed rebellion was their preferred methodology, far from it in fact (Duffy and Smith O'Brien were cautious in the extreme), but every possible option had to be left open as far as the group was concerned, thus O'Connell's stipulation had to be rejected. In common with the United Irishmen of the 1790s, the religious affiliation of the leadership was mixed; Davis and Smith O'Brien being members of the Established Church, Mitchel and Martin Presbyterian, while the others were Catholic. The parting of these Protestants from the O'Connellite camp was evidence in the minds of some among the Protestant press of the perceived Catholic agenda of the Repeal Association and served as a strong warning not to

later allowed by the Grand Lodge to seek re-admittance to his lodge having 'expressed his deep contrition for the error of which he had been guilty'. PRONI D2966/16/1 Printed volume containing the reports of the proceedings of the Grand Lodge of Ireland 1849–60. **24** Thomas Bartlett, *Ireland: a history* (Cambridge, 2010), pp 277–8.

fall for the overtures of this apparently treacherous Catholic organization. The *Cork Constitution* cited the forced departure of Smith O'Brien from the mainstream Repeal Association as proof that O'Connell, despite his outer façade, had little interest in fair treatment for Protestants. It knowingly lectured that:

> for months past it has been obvious that the presence of the 'Protestant Billy' was anything but acceptable, and now the ['Conciliation] Hall' has become 'too hot' for him. Would that every Protestant were made to feel the folly of trusting a faction who are 'liberal' only on the lip; but there are Protestants whom naught but personal penalty will suffice to teach.[25]

Nonetheless, as with their revolutionary predecessors – the United Irishmen – this mixed group, although very much in the minority, hoped that all the religious factions could come together and create a non-sectarian Ireland free from British interference. Now however, exactly fifty years on, a very different arena was in place for these Young Irelanders to contend with.

The rising of 1798 had enjoyed strong Presbyterian support, particularly in counties Antrim and Down; by 1848, however, the republican ideals of many Presbyterians had been long since eroded. The rebellion had been severely crushed, and many Presbyterians adopted a 'heads down' attitude in its aftermath. While the passing of the Act of Union in 1801 had been widely opposed initially, many Ulster Presbyterian merchants had benefitted by the transforming of east Ulster into an economic powerhouse and had no desire now to break from Britain. The constricting test oaths that had been removed following the granting of Catholic emancipation had greatly benefitted Presbyterians. The abolition of these oaths facilitated Presbyterian upward social movement, and removed many of the restrictions imposed on the 'dissenting' branch of Protestantism. Added to this was the sectarian nature of the rebellion and the atrocities carried out by Catholics in the south of Ireland, especially in Wexford, which were not in keeping with the ideals of its leaders. Suspicion and mistrust of Catholics was fuelled throughout the 1830s, in particular, with the preaching of the Presbyterian Revd Henry Cooke who called for a closer alliance with the Established Church and unity against Romanism. While many Presbyterians clung to their liberal beliefs and did not by any means uniformly follow Cooke, their desire to remain within the Union was clear. Indeed, Holmes points out that by this stage many Presbyterians were 'part of a broader Protestant popular culture that was inherently anti-Catholic', while Miller adds that 'a combination of socio-economic, religious, and political factors (not least of which was mass

25 *C Con*, 30 July 1846.

emigration by disaffected Presbyterians) had virtually eradicated among Northern Protestants the ecumenical radicalism of the United Irishman'.[26] Thus, a number of factors had, by the 1840s, combined to ensure that few Ulster Presbyterians or indeed Church of Irelanders had any desire to lend support to any type of uprising. In fact, the reverse was true; any uprising would now be vigorously opposed.

APPEALS TO ORANGEMEN

It was into this pitted arena that the Young Irelanders, or Confederates as their more radical members were termed, attempted to muster support. Confederate or Drennan Clubs, as they were also known, were formed in Belfast while national leaders attended meetings in Newry and Belfast throughout November 1847 in a bid to convince Orangemen and the general Protestant population that their interests coincided. In a series of three meetings held in Belfast, Smith O'Brien, a County Clare Protestant and landlord, acknowledged that 'repeal had been hitherto looked upon as an almost exclusively Catholic movement', but he now contended that 'the Protestants had just as great an interest in the right to conduct their own affairs as any of their fellow Catholic citizens'. He pointed to the Dungannon Convention of 1782 from which middle-class Protestants had forced government reform ultimately resulting in the formation of a Dublin parliament. Highlighting general Ulster Protestant opposition towards the Act of Union, he recalled thirty-two Orange lodges in Antrim and Down that had come together in 1800 to declare that 'they were determined strenuously to persevere in declaring that the Legislative Union must have the effect of bringing inevitable ruin upon the peace, prosperity and happiness of the kingdom'. He put it to Orangemen 'whether they had, since that period – in their experience of 47 years – occasion to change the opinion so expressed?'[27] Such appeals to Orangemen were one of the main reasons for this incursion north. However, the three meetings held in Belfast descended into chaos as not Orangemen but followers of O'Connell, by now deceased, attended and continually disrupted these meetings rendering them almost farcical. Meagher later admitted at a meeting in Newry that 'they were not prepared – he wished to God they had been – for the effective demonstration of which they had been made the victims'. But he did counter by declaring that 'this would not deter them from making a further experiment in that locality'.[28] Nonetheless, the difficulties in convincing

26 Andrew R. Holmes, *The shaping of Ulster Presbyterian belief and practice, 1770–1840* (Oxford, 2006), p. 97. Miller et al., 'The Famine scars: William Murphy's Ulster and American odyssey', pp 98–123. **27** *BN*, 23 November 1847. **28** *BN*, 26 November 1847.

Protestants to the merits of repeal were greatly increased by opposition from within the majority mainstream repeal 'Old Ireland' Party, which had clung firmly to the non-violent ethos of O'Connell. The rather loose confederation of Young Irelanders was also predisposed to internal dispute and was unable to define any clear policy outside of its 'national movement' policy. For instance, the issue of tenant right was barely given the attention it deserved. If the purpose was to court Protestants, a concerted and highly visible tenant right campaign should have been mounted by Young Ireland. But although *The Nation* called for fixity of tenure and Dillon had written articles on the subject,[29] Young Ireland policy on tenant right was lacklustre and imprecise. Michael Doheny did address a tenant right meeting organized at the symbolic Shane's Hill in County Down where Catholics and Protestants had previously joined together to oppose high potato prices. His message hoped to revive this spirit of united lower-class protest and sell his agenda to Protestants tenant farmers. But rather than directly address the issue of tenant right, he instead relayed the message that 'if the Queen told him to take it [repeal] he would not do so, unless he had the support of the Protestants of Ulster'. But the issue of repeal was not what the meeting had been called for. The appeal was rejected empathically by 4,000 Orangemen assembled in nearby Gilford, where drums were beaten 'to the music of old Orange tunes', and an effigy of the radical John Mitchel burned and thrown into a nearby river.[30] Ó Luain points out that Young Ireland 'only came late to the growing demand for tenant right in Ulster'. Labelling their involvement 'opportunistic', he argues that 'their main objective in speaking at tenant right rallies remained the promotion of repeal rather than a genuine desire to marry the land and national questions as Lalor envisaged'.[31] This was evident at Shane's Hill. The fact was that Young Ireland hoped to form an alliance with landlords. Therefore, they could not, on the other hand, oppose these same landlords and support tenant right.[32] This most likely explains the rather lukewarm response of the organization towards the issue of tenant right. By attempting to ally with the landlord class, Young Ireland destroyed any likelihood of gaining lower-class Protestant support. As it transpired, no support was forthcoming from the landlords of Ireland. A golden opportunity to gain cross community, and possibly Orange, support in Ulster was lost. This particular flawed policy of Young Ireland really was indictive of its overall inability to come up with a feasible national objective.

29 O'Neill, 'The land question, 1830–1850', pp 325–36. **30** *BPJ*, 27 May 1848. **31** Kerron Ó Luain, '"Calculated to excite the minds of the public": south Ulster and the Young Ireland rebellion 1848', *The Irish story online*, http://www.theirishstory.com/2018/06/21/calculated-to-excite-the-minds-of-the-public-south-ulster-and-the-young-ireland-rebellion–1848/#.XcnZwzP7TIU, accessed 11 November 2019. **32** O'Neill, 'The land question, 1830–1850', pp 325–36.

Undeterred by this failure, the early months of 1848 saw a renewed vigour among the Young Irelanders even though the discontented ultra-revolutionary Mitchel had seen fit to depart from the organization. In the lead up to St Patrick's Day 1848, coloured placards were placed around Belfast with the heading, borrowed from Davis's *Nation* ballad, that 'Orange and Green will carry the day'. These placards called for 'an aggregate meeting of the citizens of Belfast' to take place on 17 March in the Theatre Royal at 12 noon 'for the purpose of presenting a congratulatory address to the French people and of taking means to obtain an immediate repeal of the legislative union'.[33] Speculation abounded that a new unity had been born between both repeal factions, but this was unlikely especially given the nature of the 'Old Ireland' disruption of their rival's November meetings. The meeting called by the Young Ireland faction, however, did not take place as they were refused the use of the Theatre Royal by its owner, Mr Pearson, who had not been aware of its intended use. Nevertheless, the call was considered a great insult by many Orangemen (as was the use of the colour orange on the placards) who were in turn called by a counter-placard to assemble at McClean's Fields south of Donegall Square 'in order to repudiate the foul aspersion cast upon your loyalty'. The placard called on the Orangemen 'to be well armed' and to 'come with powder dry'.[34] This particular placard caused a great sensation and apprehension but it was considered to be merely 'a despicable rouse of the Repealers' by the Orange hierarchy. This was strongly denied by the Young Irelanders who in turn claimed that the police, in a bid to stir up trouble, had in fact erected these placards.[35] Whatever the truth, a subsequent official placard issued by William Madden, district secretary, called on Orangemen to 'give heed to no such advice. Be only guided by the orders of your district lodge. Hold yourselves in readiness to aid the authorities if called upon, but do not disgrace yourselves or your society, by becoming part of an illegal assembly'.[36] The latter advice seems to have been heeded as the city remained peaceful during the day and overnight. Further afield, an intended demonstration in Derry was forbidden by magistrates while planned demonstrations in Cookstown, Omagh and Dungannon did not take place. Trouble did occur in Downpatrick following a repeal meeting at the racecourse, and also in Ballinahinch, while a rumoured repeal meeting in Coleraine did not take place as Coleraine Orangemen had vowed to 'prevent, to the utmost of their power, all illegal and insurrectionary movements'.[37] Madden made it clear 'that the loyal Orangemen of Belfast view with marked indignation any attempt made, on the part of the Repealers, to shake the Protestant spirit and institutions of this country by effecting what they

33 *BN*, 17 March 1848. **34** *BN*, 21 March 1848. **35** Ibid. **36** *BN*, 17 March 1848. **37** *BN*, 21 March 1848.

term a repeal of the Union'.[38] Meanwhile, Aughnacloy Orangemen were stunned to read in the *Armagh Guardian* that they had apparently warmly received Smith O'Brien and Meagher and had welcomed them with orange and green flags. This allegation, most likely mischief making by the Young Irelanders, was quickly refuted by the *Constitution*.[39] Despite the best efforts of the Young Irelanders, who, it must be said, made a much stronger effort to engage with Ulster Protestants than the 'Old Irelanders', it was patently obvious that Protestant Ulster had no intention of being swayed towards any notion of repeal.

INTERNATIONAL CONTEXT

This general Protestant opposition was further fuelled by events in Europe and in mainland Britain. The spring of 1848 had seen rebellion and revolt in Paris, Vienna, Budapest and Berlin as people en masse rebelled successfully (at least initially) against the oppressive *ancien régime*. Added to European insurrection was the re-emergence of the Chartist movement in Britain. This had been an 1830s movement of the working classes that sought political reform, suffrage for men, and the right to secret ballot. The rebirth of this movement was a worry for the ascendant Protestant upper classes who had most to lose by a lower-class rebellion or lower-class suffrage. This concern permeated the minds of the Protestant elites in Ireland who worried that while Chartists had so far confined their protest to petitions and peaceful meetings, the potential of violence was present. To alarmist Protestants, it must have seemed that Young Ireland was part of a European-wide coalition intent on toppling the old Church and state ascendancy. In contrast with the dismissal by O'Connell of Chartism, links with Young Ireland had been established. Indeed, there had been combined Chartist and Young Ireland meetings held in the north of England throughout the spring of 1848. As events transpired, these links came to nothing as the Chartists were unable to make any inroads in their own campaign and were in no position to assist the Young Irelanders. Nevertheless, Martin called on Orangemen to look to events in France for guidance rather than to their clergy and put it to them, 'If you can induce your clergymen to lay aside their sectarian spectacles, and come out from the mists of bigotry, and read the New Testament in the clear light of simple truth, they will tell you that "liberty, equality and fraternity" is the doctrine of Christ and His Apostles'.[40] The events in Europe prompted, for the first time, some Young Irelanders to think that an Irish republic rather than a mere Dublin parliament within the Union was an achievable target. These

38 *BPJ*, 18 March 1848. **39** *TC*, 26 May 1848. **40** *AC*, 24 March 1848.

European events convinced Mitchel, in particular, that the time was right for a rebellion in Ireland. Impatient with their comrades in Young Ireland, Mitchel and Martin split from the group and initially called for a rising on St Patrick's Day. This call went unheeded but, in calling for a national guard to be organized, Mitchel called out to Orangemen by stating that he would rather see 5,000 Orange yeomen on his side than 50,000 Frenchmen. Mitchel also played the tenant class card in announcing that:

> of all the classes of men with whom he wished to form a union were the Orange farmers of Ulster, for he knew them well, and knew they could be depended upon [...] when he asked Orangemen to join the Confederation, he did not mean the Orange aristocrats, but the Orange farmers, and in asking them he could tell them that the only mode of preserving their rights as tenants was by doing so.[41]

This proposed alliance was never allowed to be tested as Mitchel was considered a serious threat by a government who had a worried eye on events in Europe, and he (and later Martin) was transported to first Bermuda and then Van Diemen's Land on questionable charges of treason in May 1848.

PROTESTANT PANIC

The removal of Mitchel and Martin from the frame was not enough to ease Protestant fears that a genuine rebellion was imminent. Gavan Duffy and his confederate comrades, although not as radical as Mitchel, remained active while Confederate Clubs, which tended to side with Mitchel's militant principles, thrived in urban centres with over fifty existing in Dublin alone. This activity and the continuing (but unrelated) activity of Ribbonmen in general was enough to spread panic and fear among many of the Ulster gentry who increasingly engaged in widespread correspondence with Dublin Castle. The *Protestant Journal* ominously cautioned:

> let us not deceive ourselves by attributing the conduct of Young Ireland to folly and madness. Rebellion is organized; Ribbon lodges are in full operation; the peasantry of the south and west are well armed; their leaders are appointed; teetotalism has made them sober and determined in their plan; forward they must go; and the pretended moral force of the Old Irelanders neither can, nor will it restrain the movement at a fitting opportunity.[42]

41 *DEP*, 6 April 1848. **42** *BPJ*, 1 April 1848.

This panicked editorial was indicative of the general alarm sweeping through the Protestant upper classes especially. The Young Irelanders had placed special emphasis on the recruitment of the landed gentry hoping to tap in on the discontentment that this particular class felt with the government. Yet it was this very class that reacted most vigorously against them. Many magistrates, most of whom were smaller landowners and who also frequently acted as land agents to larger landlords, wound themselves into a frenzied state. It was they that faced the greatest threat from a possible shake up in the landed status quo. This frantic anxiety was reflected in the bombarding of Dublin Castle with hysterical reports. For instance, in Moneymore, County Londonderry, JP Rowley Miller warned of 'large parties of young men assembling openly and with impunity for the purpose of rifle practice and that very many of them are only waiting their opportunity to attack with effect the loyalists who are without organization and unprepared [...] From what I can learn the manufacture of pikes is going on extensively everywhere'.[43] It was reported in Derry city that arms were being stored in certain houses, while police informant Samuel Dodd stated that he was taken to a house and shown about 80 pikes and about 100 stand of arms.[44] Pomeroy magistrates warned that 'we are in a far more unprotected state than in the year 1798 [...] there are bad characters in the town of Pomeroy selling guns and powder and making pikes, much exciting the people in the large range of mountainous country'.[45] As many magistrates were themselves Orangemen, their hysterics filtered through at ground level. Despite the loss of much of their legal power, magistrates were still heavily influential at local level and remained as pillars of the community. The result of this was that rank-and-file Orangemen still looked to these familiar figures for guidance. Their determination not to align with the Confederates was therefore reflected in the attitudes of most Orangemen. In imitation of, and most likely at the behest of, the magistracy, many lodges also petitioned the government. Castlewellan Orangemen presented a memorial to lord lieutenant Clarendon claiming that 'we are actually surrounded for miles by Ribbonmen and Rebels of all denominations, with the exception of here and there, a few lodges of loyal Orangemen and Protestants, in the ratio of 1 to 50 [...] there cannot be a shadow of doubt that the rebels here are all well armed and ready for the appointed signal for midnight murder'.[46] Already, the petition claimed, a false alarm had resulted in 'thousands of Ribbonmen gathering in the mountains'. A memorial from Antrim town feared that 'a numerous portion of the inhabitants are united with those who have openly arrayed themselves against

43 NAI: Outrage Reports, Co. Londonderry (1848) 40/18. **44** NAI: Outrage Reports, Co. Londonderry (1848) 78/18; Co. Antrim (1848) 101/1. **45** NAI: Outrage Reports, Co. Tyrone (1848) 195/28. **46** NAI: Outrage Reports, Co. Down (1848) 190/8.

the constituted authorities and are ready at any moment to take up arms for the overthrow of the Constitution, and the slaughter of all loyal subjects'.[47] Yet, little government action seemed forthcoming. Other than allowing respectable inhabitants to be sworn in as 'Special Constables' in Belfast and providing them with batons, no provision of extra manpower was offered by Dublin Castle. The presiding fear among Protestants was that in the seeming absence of government mobilization against this perceived threat, they would have to defend themselves. The problem in their view, however, was that they did not possess sufficient armoury to defend themselves even though many former members of the now-defunct yeomanry had not turned in their weapons. The Antrim memorial called on Clarendon to provide arms for 1,000 men, while H. Ellis of Belfast also presented a memorial seeking to raise a company of 100 men in the parish of Ballymartin[?] near Carrickfergus as he claimed that many of the Protestant inhabitants 'possess no arms whatever to defend their lives and properties'.[48] At a meeting in Downpatrick called to form a volunteer company, it was resolved to ask the lord lieutenant to supply the company with arms and that should he decline they would purchase arms at their own expense.[49] Magistrate Joseph Douglas of Cookstown viewed 'with feelings of alarm the present state of things [...] yet [there was] no appearance of Her Majesty's government putting a stop to it'. Writing to the lord lieutenant, Douglas pleaded, 'if your Excellency would be most graciously pleased to give arms to such as would be willing to swear allegiance to our most Gracious Queen, we, the loyal Protestants of this district would use them in maintaining and supporting the dignity of the law and in the protection of our lives and property'.[50] These calls were repeated throughout the province as a daily flow of panicked memorials and petitions from grand juries, magistrates and Orange lodges were sent to Dublin Castle. A County Down declaration of loyalty to Clarendon contained 33,000 signatures, while 3,665 of Farnham's tenants, including 200 Catholics, signed a similar declaration.[51] Although the Whig government was considered an enemy of Orangeism, there was no shortage of support offered by the Order. The out-of-touch Dunmore Lang had written to prime minister Russell expressing his confidence that Orangemen would not rise against Repealers and had considered any idea of them taking up arms 'preposterous'.[52] But Lodge no. 184 from Armagh summed up the feelings of many with its declaration that:

47 NAI: Outrage Reports, Co. Antrim (1848) 110/1. **48** NAI: Outrage Reports, Co. Antrim (1848) 32/1. **49** NAI: Outrage Reports, Co. Down (1848) 99/8. **50** NAI: Outrage Reports, Co. Tyrone (1848) 119/28. **51** *AC*, 21 April 1848. **52** Dunmore Lang, 'Repeal or revolution'.

> In every county of Ulster, in Dublin, and other parts of Ireland are numbers of Orangemen closely united together for the sole purpose of preserving the British constitution in church and state, without interfering or intending to interfere with the full enjoyment of liberty by their fellow subjects of every creed. Of these men 'good and true' could be formed an army of which any nation might be proud – an army strong, faithful and compact, with loyalty in their hearts, and vigour in their hands. At a few days' notice a force of upwards of 100,000 men could be mustered who, if trained, and supplied with arms would, with the assistance of the God of their fathers, repel any foe foreign or domestic daring to attack their country. It is for your lordship and other members of Her Majesty's government to decide whether it would not be well to at once organize a body of such men who *could be relied on in the hour of danger*, and who – like their fathers of yore – would peril their fortunes and lives to beat down the common enemies of the empire, and to death stand by the banner of truth and freedom.[53]

As Roden put it, 'It is of little consequence to us now what political party is in power – perhaps the least danger is to be apprehended from those who are at the present ministers of the Crown – but, I am sure, it is our duty as loyal Orangemen to give every support in our power to the earl of Clarendon's government'.[54] Although 'nationalist leaders were extremely reluctant to admit that the unionism of the landed gentry was much stronger than their current alienation from the Whig government', judging from the torrent of petitions received by the lord lieutenant it is clearly obvious that there was never any possibility of any form of support coming from this upper-class Protestant stratum.[55]

A UNITED ORANGE FRONT?

On the other hand, the hard line of Roden may not have been reflective of all Orangemen if Mitchel's short-lived *United Irishman* newspaper was to be believed. One 'John McCarter' from Banbridge claimed to speak for 'some three hundred loyal Orangemen' who complained that they were not consulted in any manner regarding an address sent to the lord lieutenant in their name. He added, 'let it not be thought that the feelings of the Orangemen are contained in those addresses; they are *not*. We ought to know you well, and so we do; and when the

53 *NG*, 15 March 1848. **54** *FJ*, 11 July 1848. **55** James S. Donnelly Jr, 'A famine in Irish politics' in W.E. Vaughan (ed.), *A new history of Ireland*, v: *Ireland under the Union, 1801–70* (Oxford, 1989), pp 357–71.

fighting comes, if come it does, we have only to tell you that we *won't* desert the land that nourishes us and "we keep our powder dry"'.[56] Similarly, 'an Orangeman of the Annahoe district' poured cold water on the declaration of loyalty signed by district master Anketell Moutray, and countered that 'neither the masters or men of our district were ever consulted on the subject, nor would they, had they been consulted, permit Master Moutray to palm any such false trashery [*sic*] on the representative of our Queen – so far from it, sir, our views and objects at present are in direct opposition to what this address would imply'. It was explained that 'our loyalty to the Queen is beyond question, but to state that we are delighted with Lord Clarendon's administration, when it is known to every man of us, that during his administration an artificial famine has been created, by which, at least, a million of our fellow countrymen have been consigned to their shallow graves *like dogs*, is an audacious falsity that cannot be too severely deprecated'.[57] Yet, such letters need to be treated with caution. In particular, the blame attached to Clarendon over the Famine deaths smacks of Mitchel's later absolute belief of a genocidal action by the government and would suggest that he himself may have authored the letter. More damaging was a letter from David Allen, secretary to the Moneymore district, dismissing the authenticity of a letter written by 'William McAlister'. Allen knew no-one of that name and added that 'it would appear that some person or persons are practicing on your credulity, by sending you such letters [...] the writer, it appears has taken a lesson from the worthy Mr McCarter, of Banbridge, and like him, proves to be a man of straw; at any rate, he is not an Orangeman'.[58] The letters do appear too well written to have come from 'average' Orangemen but it *is* highly likely that lower-class Orangemen were not consulted or included in the addresses sent to Clarendon. In Mitchel's defence, he had previously dismissed as fabricated a letter of support from 'an Orangeman of the Enniskillen lodge', and surely would have been aware that his publication would have been discredited by incredulous insertions.[59] Given the general discontent regarding tenant right and the Famine, it is quite possible that rank-and-file Orangemen, whose loyalty was after all conditional, may well have had serious misgivings regarding such addresses to the lord lieutenant. It is possible that the mass mobilization of Orangemen promised by the upper classes may not have materialized quite as expected in the event of a rebellion. It must be remembered that at this stage the Grand Lodge of Ulster was still the main representative of ordinary Orangemen. Unfortunately, one can only speculate; the offers of assistance continued to flow to Dublin Castle, unhindered by any concerted dissent from those who were being offered as the latest defenders of the crown and its government.

56 *UI*, 15 April 1848. **57** *UI*, 15 April 1848. **58** *UI*, 22 April 1848. **59** *UI*, 8 April 1848.

REACTION OF THE LORD LIEUTENANT

Clarendon publicly was dismissive of such offers of help. Answering the Downpatrick Orangemen, he 'passed on his appreciation but did not feel he could comply with this request as the measures already taken were sufficient in his opinion'.[60] The Castlewellan Orangemen, meanwhile, were told that 'His Excellency would not feel justified in arming any body which was not aligned with the sanction of Her Majesty'.[61] The lord lieutenant was placed in a difficult situation, a situation summed up by prime minister Lord John Russell. Russell wrote in his correspondence to Clarendon that 'a nice point will be determined how far you will avail yourself of the offers of the Orangemen to arm and form Volunteer Corps – the spirit of religious hatred is very bad – but you cannot let your throats be cut to avoid religious animosity [...] it is for you to decide'.[62] Nevertheless, he did caution Clarendon 'in extremis not to rebuff offers of help from Orange associations, and to envisage arming the Protestants'.[63] But, while naturally extremely distrustful of Catholics, Clarendon did have to weigh up the probability that arming and mobilizing Orangemen would enflame an already agitated Catholic population. On the other hand, it is generally recognized that Clarendon was a 'known alarmist'; he had already moved his family back to England and had increased his Dublin garrison to 10,000 troops.[64] Therefore, despite the apparent snub delivered to Orangemen by the government, behind the scenes moves were made to bring them on board if the worst case scenario of a rebellion should arise. Government emissaries Captain J.P. Kennedy, Major Turner and Colonel R.W. Phaire held clandestine talks with senior Orangemen regarding arming and organization should a full-scale rising break out. At a meeting of Dublin Orangemen held at Whitefriar's Hall on 13 March 1848, Colonel Phaire, a reputed Wexford Orange grand master, appeared and asked those present to spy on the rebels on behalf of the government. He also demanded they withdraw a potentially damaging address condemning Clarendon that had been drawn up by the Orangemen. Phaire was assisted by Turner who 'intimated to the Orangemen that the Irish Government placed much reliance on their courage and loyalty, that in the event of an insurrectionary outbreak, posts of great moment would be confided to their keeping, and that detachments of the military should be so ordered, as to act in concert with them'.[65] This representation of Phaire and Turner was confirmed by Clarendon's secretary

60 NAI: Outrage Reports, Co. Down (1848) 99/8. **61** NAI: Outrage Reports, Co. Down (1848) 190/8. **62** John Saville, *1848: The British state and the Chartist movement* (Cambridge, 1990), p. 157. **63** Christine Kinealy, *The Great Irish Famine: impact, ideology and rebellion* (New York, 2001), p. 199. **64** Bridget Hourican, 'George William Frederick Villiers', *Dictionary of Irish biography*, online edition, accessed 14 November 2019. **65** PRONI, Printed volumes containing reports of the Grand Lodge of

Correy Connellan, and was further backed up by Enniskillen who later claimed to have 'had a conversation with the Master of the Horse for the time being, Major Turner'. According to Enniskillen £5,000–6,000 was given to him by Phaire and arms were procured in Birmingham. Difficulties in landing the arms in Dublin were overcome by Colonel Brown, head of the police, who allowed them through to Dublin Castle. This was later denied by Clarendon, but as Enniskillen pointed out, 'I cannot say what was done at the Castle with the arms, because it was denied by the lord lieutenant. Lord Clarendon told me he would not give the arms; but we received money from his Master of the Horse, and we leave it for the public to say where it came from'.[66] The evidence would seem to leave little ground for doubt that the government was, despite its later denials, secretly prepared to use the Order to supplement the military in crushing any possible insurrection.

ORANGE STRENGTH AND THE RETURN OF THE ELITES

The approach of the Twelfth of July of 1848 saw a feverish renewal of vigour in Orange activities in response to the actions of the Confederates. While the previous year had seen much debate over the propriety of marching in the midst of Famine, the feeling of impending rebellion and the subsequent need to stage a show of strength ensured no such comment or appeals for restraint on this occasion. In the spirit of hysteria, the desire of Protestants in Cavan to demonstrate loyalty was such that it was reported, 'the demand for orange ribbons and sashes was so extensive, for the last week as to induce some of the shopkeepers to send specially to Dublin, for a further supply'.[67] This frenzied behaviour was mirrored throughout Ulster. An estimated 10,000 marchers paraded through Omagh and 'presented a display, which has not been equalled in our town since the great Orange demonstration about fourteen years ago'.[68] A reported crowd of 17,000 marched in Ballymena, while processions were also held at Monaghan, Belfast, Carrickfergus, Randalstown, Lisburn, Banbridge, Lurgan-Portadown, Newtownards and Comber, Armagh, Newry, Ballyward, Cavan, Coleraine, Bushmills, Ballymoney, Newtown-Limavady, Ahoghill, Rasharkin, Desertmartin, Enniskillen, Kesh, Tempo and Raphoe.[69] The numbers involved in these displays presented a clear message to the government and indeed to those considering a rebellion. The *Dublin Herald* claimed that over 120,000 Orangemen had marched in Ulster and in doing so 'presented a

Ireland, D2966/16/1. **66** *Report of the commissioners of inquiry into the origin and character of the riots in Belfast, in July and September 1857*, HC 1857 (2309), xxvi.1, p. 180. **67** *NW*, 15 July 1848. **68** *LJ*, 18 July 1848. **69** *LJ*, 19 July 1848. **70** *NG*, 15 July 1848.

machinery by means of which, at one week's notice, if needs be, the entire mass may be arrayed at Her Majesty's summons as an efficient regular army'.[70] In addition to the numbers of 'ordinary' Orangemen involved, the return of the elites to the arena of public demonstration was obvious. It was reported that among a crowd of 10,000 in Newtownhamilton, 'many respectable persons having jaunting cars and others riding horses mingled with the procession'.[71] Following a county demonstration in Monaghan, a number of prominent men including Sir George Forster (MP 1852–65 for Monaghan), Charles Leslie Powell (MP 1843–71 for Monaghan), James Hamilton, Henry Mitchell and John Johnson were initiated into the Order.[72] The following week the *Monaghan Standard* reported that 'thirteen members of the Monaghan grand jury, and five clergymen of the Established Church, were initiated into the Orange Society of this county; and we have since learned, that a great number of the gentry and clergy have signified their desire to become members. This is as it should be. God speed the good work'.[73] The Grand Lodge of Antrim was later able to report that 'your committee have much great pleasure in being able to state, that there has been a great increase in the number of Brethren within the last twelve months. In the district of Belfast, alone, the ranks are augmented nearly two-fold, amongst whom are many of the most respectable and influential members of the community'.[74] The swelling of membership was also evident in Dublin where, 'in consequence of the great increase in the number of lodges in the city and county', it was recognized that the city and county required division into districts.[75] The Grand Lodge of Ireland's financial statement for November of 1848 showed a healthy balance of £143 4*s.* 1*d.*, the highest figure since re-organization.[76] The increase in popularity and elite membership was further evidenced as nine lodges from Gortin met with eight from Ardstraw, and assembled at the demesne of A.W. Cole Hamilton. At Annahoe (rather diluting the previous claims published in the *United Irishman*), thirty-one lodges gathered on a large hill adjoining Favor-Royal, the seat of J.C. Moutray.[77] In Ballinahinch, between 1,400 and 1,500 Orangemen assembled at Saintfield House, the home of J.B. Price, while at Ballyhaise Castle, several thousand Orangemen gathered where they were addressed by Farnham who told them that 'there was never a period when their loyalty was not more needed; and were they not disposed, heart and soul, to evince and prove it? Yes, that glorious display of loyalty was sufficient to overcome any sedition or rebellion that might appear (great applause)'.[78] Many of

71 NAI: Outrage Reports, Co. Armagh (1848) 168/2. **72** Aiken McClelland, 'Orangeism in County Monaghan', *Clogher Record*, 19:3 (1978), pp 384–404. Hamilton, Johnston and Mitchell were all magistrates. **73** *BN*, 25 July 1848. **74** Grand Orange Lodge of Ireland, Proceedings of the Grand Lodge of Antrim, 25 October 1848. **75** Grand Orange Lodge of Ireland, Proceedings of the Grand Lodge of Ireland, 15–16 May 1849. **76** Ibid. **77** *LJ*, 19 July 1848. **78** *AC*, 14 July 1848.

these better classes included government officials such as magistrates and grand jury members who, exasperated at the lack of government action, took it upon themselves to organize local defence. The return of the elites was also demonstrated at the *soirée* held in the Rotunda in Dublin by members of the Orange Institution. It was reported that of the 800–1,000 members in attendance, at least half 'were ladies in their gayest attire' and that 'as a spectacle, it may be ranked among the most splendid celebrations ever witnessed in the same building [...] The Round Room, where the entertainment took place, was brilliantly lighted and decorated with banners and emblems indicating the various lodges in the city'.[79] The high turnout of the better classes was warmly welcomed by the *Dublin Evening Mail*, and it would appear that with rebellion seemingly on the horizon those among the elites who previously had backed away from public demonstration now felt comfortable to make their allegiances evident.[80] For those not yet convinced of the merits of Orangeism, the Lisburn sermon of the Revd Hartley Hodson starkly highlighted the urgent need to join. Hodson reminded the 'Protestant landlords of Ireland' that 'your property is in danger; you have been shot down by the dozen like dogs' and appealed to them to 'join the Orange Institution. We are no democrat mob. We acknowledge the rights of property, and are men who will die to defend them. We will respect your persons – attend to your counsel – your interests are ours'. The sermon also told the 'Protestant noblemen of Ireland' that:

> greedy eyes are on your land and titles; you are renounced as intolerable tyrants, men who should not be suffered to live. Take refuge in our Orange ark. What honour could be greater or sweeter than the affection of our loyal hearts? Does it not ennoble the nobleman thus to stand among his trusty dependents? Does it not ennoble the nobleman to make common cause with such men – to cheer them with his honoured presence – to rejoice in their happy smiles – to feel strong in their loyal strength?[81]

It is difficult to assess whether such appeals were successful in bringing some of the more ambivalent members of the elites on board the 'Orange ark' but it is evident many were already doing so with or without the prompting of Hodson.

REPUBLICAN FAILURE IN ULSTER

The return of the elites helped ensure that the July demonstrations were the biggest held since dissolution in 1836. The *Newsletter* had no doubt as to the

79 *NG*, 15 July 1848. **80** *DEM*, 14 July 1849. **81** *PW*, 21 July 1848.

reasons for this explaining, 'It is manifest that, of late, the Orangemen, so far from having their ranks thinned or their loyalty deadened, by the recent monster growth of republicanism and disaffection, have been spurred on by it to renewed activity and more enthusiastic ardour'.[82] The *Londonderry Journal* was of a similar opinion, noting that 'the celebrations have been more numerous, and on a greater scale, than on any previous anniversary of the like kind. Indeed, it cannot fail to be observed that the spirit of party in the North was never so intense as it is now'.[83] The anti-Orange *Northern Whig* was scathing of the Repeal movement as 'they have given a new impulse to Orangeism, which was long a source of bitter evil in the country; and they have done much to place the party in a popular position, by enabling them to assume the attitude of genuine supporters of law, property, and order, in opposition to the enemies of all three'. The paper also dismissed any notion that Orangemen had been swayed by Repeal approaches pointing out that:

> Whatever it may please the Repealers to say, they must now very sensibly feel, that their sinister coquettings [*sic*] with the Orangemen have been very unsuccessful, and that their boasts of having made great way in seducing that party to join their treasonable ranks were utter falsehoods. The manner in which they attempted to fawn upon and delude the Orangemen was alike contemptible and disgusting; and now they see how their advances are met.[84]

The *Constitution* similarly opined that 'the revolution-mongers, who have been labouring to cram the public with their conviction that their pike-and-rifle doctrines meet with sympathizers amongst the Ulster Orangemen, have had their foul falsehoods practically refuted and cast in their teeth by the determined manifestation of unbending loyalty, which the stalwart men of the north have exhibited'.[85] Clearly, as far as many Protestants were concerned, events had moved way past any flirtation with Repealers whether of the Young Ireland or 'Old Ireland' variety. Matters had reached a crisis point and it seemed as if their loyalty could be put to the test at any given moment. The *Newsletter* joined the increasing hysteria:

> As we have said already, rebellion is *imminent* – on the eve of practical organized outbreak. This can hardly be doubted, when we find that the city of Dublin has been mapped out into districts for the mustering of the clubs, and the throwing up of barricades – that cart loads of pike handles

82 *BN*, 14 July 1848. **83** *LJ*, 19 July 1848. **84** *NW*, 15 July 1848. **85** *TC*, 14 July 1848.

> are openly cut and carried from the plantations of the gentry – that twenty thousand stand of arms have been purchased in London for the insurgents, and are on their way to their destination – that 'vans' of muskets and other arms are daily drawn through the streets of the metropolis for distribution – in short, that every symptom of daring, defiant, and stubborn determination to bring the affair to a crisis, is exultingly manifested.[86]

On the other hand, the *Irish Examiner* contended cynically that:

> The display of the Twelfth may be attributed to Castle manoeuvring. All the old machinery, by which Irishmen were arrayed against Irishmen, was brought into play. A demonstration of numbers and arms, and marching, was necessary for the ends of the Government. Declarations of Orange loyalty and undying adhesiveness to Church, State, British bayonets, and starvation rule, were required in order that LORD CLARENDON should make a shew [*sic*] of some counter check to the repeal opinion of the country. Thus are the Orangemen made tools by successive administrations. SIR R. PEEL called them 'vagabonds', and LORD CLARENDON pats them on the back![87]

Although the *Newsletter* greatly overestimated the strength of Young Ireland mobilization, it is true that rebellion was indeed imminent. However, the strength of this rebellion was weak at best. The reason for Clarendon's reluctance to arm and mobilize Orangemen was that he knew full well of the poor military state of the confederates. The movement was riddled with government spies and had little or no rural public support from a populace devastated by the continuing famine. Granted, the arrest and transportation of Mitchel had pushed Gavan Duffy and Meagher to a more extreme position and had moved many of the confederates to drill with pikes. But the idea of purchasing arms from London and distributing them daily throughout Dublin was implausible in the extreme. Nevertheless, Smith O'Brien did tour southern Ireland in a bid to establish Confederate Clubs and his lieutenants actively encouraged armament. By now, even the moderate Duffy had moved to a position of support for a rebellion in the event of repeal being refused. Clarendon became especially anxious following failed attempts to gain French aid (the French were unwilling to jeopardize relations with Britain). Therefore, the government did take action by arresting Duffy, Meagher, Michael Doheny and Thomas D'Arcy McGee, and on 22 July suspended *habeas corpus*. Under this statute, suspected membership of

86 *BN*, 25 July 1848. **87** *FJ*, 18 July 1848.

any confederate club became an arrestable offence, which resulted in many members being imprisoned. In desperation, those who remained at liberty decided to press on with the rebellion invoking the spirit and idealism of 1798.

REBELLION

Although a reported 50,000 people had attended a demonstration on 16 July at Slivenamon in Tipperary, mustering support from a famine-ravaged populace for an armed insurrection was a different matter entirely. It had been hoped to wait until the crop had been harvested but increased government repression forced the Young Irelanders to strike earlier than was practical. Leadership of the rebellion was passed on to a reluctant Smith O'Brien who was unable to overcome the poor planning and organization of a decimated group. The climax of what little activity occurred was carried out in Tipperary during an encounter with armed police at the widow McCormack's house on 29 July. Although easily defeated, Smith O'Brien, Doheny (who had been released from prison by then) and John O'Mahoney remained at large for the remainder of the summer months. Rumours that insurrectionary movements were renewing their activities abounded in the national and provincial press. It was reported that 4,000 rebels were encamped on Aheny Hill in Tipperary, while O'Mahoney had supposedly led an attack on the marquis of Waterford's residence at Curraghmore. There were unconfirmed accounts of a skirmish at Portlaw in which lives were reportedly lost on both sides.[88] These rumours, no doubt, kept the Protestant population on edge but they had, in fact, little substance. In any case, by this stage 35,000 British troops were stationed throughout the country. Of the remaining leaders, some escaped to the Continent, others including Smith O'Brien were soon captured, sentenced to death but instead transported to Van Diemen's Land. Thus ended a campaign for repeal that had been waged since 1840 and which had passed through various transformations culminating in an armed rebellion seeking outright independence for Ireland.

The ease with which the rebellion had been stamped out ensured that the government did not need the help offered by the Orange Order; in fact, the regular army had not even been needed. The arrest of Smith O'Brien saw the lighting of tar barrels in Armagh city and an outbreak of joy, replicated throughout Protestant Ulster.[89] The delight felt by most Protestants at the failure of the rebellion was added to by the report of the *Newsletter*, which cheerily recounted that:

88 *BN*, 15 September 1848. **89** *BN*, 18 August 1848.

> In our last [edition] we alluded to rumours which had been circulated of the re-appearance of the potato disease of 1845–6 in various parts of Ireland. We have the utmost satisfaction in recording our conviction that there is not the slightest ground for apprehension. Against the few isolated reports of partially discoloured leaves, and tainted tubers, we are to place the cheering and encouraging accounts received from a number of localities, in which no trace of the blight has manifested itself.[90]

A crushed rebellion and the promise of a good crop provided grounds for high optimism as 1849 loomed. In such spirit, *The Protestant Watchman* giddily predicted that:

> Orangeism promises to be more prosperous now than ever. The highest in the land enlist themselves beneath its banners, and every day the best and most pious of the Protestant clergy flock to its proud standard. This must be gratifying to the lay members, and should particularly stimulate the humbler classes of Protestants in coming forward at this highly critical juncture.[91]

What the *Watchman* conveniently ignored was the fact that 'the humbler classes of Protestants' had already come forward; many, in fact, had never withdrawn from the Order.

EFFECTS OF THE REBELLION ON ORANGEMEN

The lead up to, and the eventual rebellion, did have the effect of bringing a closer alignment between rank-and-file Orangemen and the Grand Lodge of Ireland. The rumours of pike-making, drilling and target practice surely must have caused apprehension among the ranks of the Protestant lower classes. With a similar scenario to 1798 seemingly imminent, the defensive and militaristic nature of Orangemen once again came to the fore. In 1848, the Protestant elites called on Orangemen to mobilize and be prepared for military action. This was what many Orangemen had long craved. Previous campaigns against Catholic mobilization had sought to remain peaceful and therefore were deemed pointless by lower-class Protestants. This time, sanction for military action had been provided by the Protestant elites. At a meeting held in Armagh in May, the Grand Lodge of Ireland called for unity, and pleaded with Orangemen to 'put down rebellion,

90 *BN*, 21 July 1848. **91** *PW*, 10 November 1848.

and, in accordance with their obligation, to defend the Majesty of England against every enemy whether "foreign foe or domestic traitor"'.[92] It surely must have appeared, at long last, that the shackles had been removed from ordinary Orangemen. This, naturally, would have had the effect of bringing a new unity within the Orange circle. Almost immediately, the hitherto-independent Dublin Protestant Operative Society merged with the Order.[93] The likes of Enniskillen and Roden, with their promises of military action, could now be considered on the same side as the lower-class majority Order membership. With this in mind, it was surely inevitable that the Grand Lodge of Ireland would now take overall control as the governing body of Ireland's Orangemen.

In August of 1848 the Grand Lodge of Ulster, under the leadership of Fredrick Woods Mant, rector of Armoy, met in Newtown-Limivady 'for the purpose of considering the question of an amalgamation with the Grand Lodge of Ireland'.[94] At a meeting of the Grand Lodge of Ireland in November 1848, it was decided to open new talks with the Ulster faction.[95] Following the winter months, in Coleraine on 27 February 1849, the Grand Lodge of Ulster resolved to accept the proposals of the Grand Lodge of Ireland and amalgamate with the national body. This union was forthcoming in May, allowing the Grand Lodge of Ireland to take full control as the central authoritative body of the Orange Order in Ireland, albeit with the Ulster leaders incorporated. Unfortunately, the secrecy of these meetings, and the lack of surviving records, do not allow for an in-depth examination of negotiations between Ulster and Dublin. But by May 1849, the Grand Lodge of Ireland was back in full control of the Orange Order for the first time in thirteen years. Some four years after the idea had been first mooted, the Orange Order was once again a united institution under the control of one central body.

* * *

Appeals from O'Connell Loyalists and from the Young Irelanders for Orangemen to join with them in the campaign for repeal were drastic failures. These appeals merely had the effect of re-igniting Orange distrust towards Catholics while heightening the division that already existed between extremists on both sides. As pointed out by Kinealy, 'after 1848, therefore, the non-sectarian ideals of Young Ireland were replaced by more polarized divisions between Catholics and Protestants, especially in the north-east of the country'.[96] Also evident was the

92 *The Warder*, 20 May 1848. **93** *BPJ*, 13 May 1848. **94** Edward Rogers, *Memorials of Orangeism*, i, ii, iii. **95** Mattison, '"From Dolly's Brae to Westminster"', p. 37. **96** Kinealy, *Repeal and revolution: 1848 in Ireland*, p. 229.

return of many from within the elites who had hitherto remained cautious and non-committal towards joining or re-joining the Order. The failed rebellion, roundly blamed on Catholics, provided complete vindication for those who had brought about the revival of the Orange Order. In retrospect, the timing of the Orange revival could scarcely have been any better. The failed actions of Young Ireland allowed the Orange Order to dramatically swell in size, while also gaining a reserved approval from the government. At this juncture, surely it appeared that little could now prevent the Order from increasing further in size and regaining its previous influence. To many observers, it certainly must have seemed that the recovery of the Orange Order, in a shorter period of time than ever could have been imagined, was complete.

CHAPTER FIVE

Dolly's Brae and its fallout

PROBABLY BECAUSE OF THE miserable nature of the rebellion, few great expressions of joy or victory were forthcoming from the Protestant population of Ireland, or indeed from the Orange Order in its aftermath. A general relief was the order of the day, which was coupled with a quantity of self-praise from within the Orange leadership. That the government did not publicly acknowledge the assistance offered by the Orangemen festered among some but most members were content in the knowledge that they had been ready should they have been called upon. From this position of relative strength with the 'Catholic' enemy cowed, this promised to be a period of continued expansion for the Order. It was a position that could never allow the Order full government acceptance but it did allow for a secure future, free from government interference or even suppression. Yet a mere twelve months after the failure of the rebellion, the Orange Order once more would find itself under fierce attack from the very government it believed it had defended during its time of crisis in Ireland.

PROTESTANT REACTION TO THE REBELLION

Government reaction to the Young Ireland rebellion was measured. The relief felt by Protestants at the quashing of the rebellion soon turned to apprehension as it was feared by Orangemen that any government reactionary ban of large associations such as the Repeal Association might also include the Orange Order. This was exactly what had happened in 1825 with the Unlawful Societies Act. This fear prompted a call from the Dublin Grand Lodge to Irish MPs to ensure that 'a clause of exemption be inserted [in any such Act] relative to the Orange Institution', a call that was unnecessary in any case as the government took no such action.[1] The non-appliance of any repressive act was typical of the government's overall calm response to the rebellion. In fact, the rising was generally dismissed and minimalized publicly by an exceedingly careful government anxious not to lend credibility or create public sympathy during this time of wider European revolution. There was no knee-jerk reaction or creation

1 PRONI, Minute book of Hardcourt, Dublin and Grand Lodge of Ireland 1844–48, MIC 201/2.

of martyrs in the way that there would be later with the failed rebellion of 1916. As summed up by Donnelly, 'presented with the gift of a ridiculous rebellion, the government was not disposed to throw this away through an excess of repressive zeal'.[2] The leaders were tried, some including Smith O'Brien were sentenced to death, but the sentences were soon commuted to transportation. Indeed, some Protestants had been instrumental in pressing for leniency. Among these was Donegal lawyer Isaac Butt, hitherto an Orangeman, who had been editor of the *Dublin University Magazine* during his study period at Trinity College Dublin. Described as 'a journal which attempted to promote a patriotism that constituted loyalty to the union with a love of Gaelic culture and enthusiasm for Irish antiquity', the *DUM* did echo some parallel sentiments of Davis in particular and represented a more youthful and energetic strand of unionism.[3] Coming from a position of moderate unionism, Butt had then been badly shaken by the horrors of the Famine and the inadequate government reaction to it. During this period, he underwent somewhat of a political transformation. He would later, in the 1870s, found the initial Home Rule party, which sought to bring parliament back to Dublin while remaining within the Union. Part of this transformation saw him defend Smith O'Brien in court. Many Orangemen, who it must be noted had not undergone Butt's political metamorphosis, considered that Smith O'Brien, as a Protestant gentleman and a former MP, had been duped by the Catholic clergy and was being used as a scapegoat by the government. But, in fact, most of the clergy had remained loyal to O'Connell's principles and had not supported Young Ireland, the fear of bloodshed and the unlawful toppling of the establishment being considered ungodly in their opinion. The small numbers that were involved had eventually withdrawn their support at the demand of the Catholic hierarchy following the shooting dead of the archbishop of Paris while negotiating at the city's barricades. Despite this, their early involvement was damning in the eyes of many Protestants. The real culprits were, in their opinion, Derry's Bishop Maginn and more specifically priests such as Fr John Keynon from Tipperary who had been actively involved prior to the rebellion. This perception was crisply pointed out by Revd Daniel Bell, Glenavy, who at the opening of a new Orange hall in November at Inch, County Down, 'censured the government for screening the Roman Catholic bishops and priests, with respect to their conduct in instigating the recent rebellion'.[4] Yet, little condemnation was forthcoming for the actual participants of the rebellion. At 'a numerous meeting of Dublin Orangemen', a memorial 'praying for a mitigation of sentence' was agreed to.[5] The memorial was not well received by Clarendon who considered

2 Donnelly, 'A famine in Irish politics', pp 357–71. 3 Bartlett, *Ireland: a history*, p. 304. 4 *BN*, 14 November 1848. 5 *BN*, 20 October 1848.

that outside interference with the court of law was unwelcome. The memorial was dismissed as 'a groundless imputation upon the impartial administration of justice by the Executive Government'.[6] Countering Clarendon's displeasure, Charles M. Fluery, an Order grand chaplain, explained that 'we feel ourselves only performing a Christian duty in renewing our humble and respectful, but earnest and anxious request that the life of Smith O'Brien may be spared'.[7] Standardized petitions from Enniskillen, Lurgan, Newry, Ballymena and Armagh pleaded that 'their lives should not be wasted in painful exile or protracted imprisonment'.[8] It might be wondered why Orangemen did not seek the full sanction of the law on rebels who could be considered their arch enemy. The fact that little or no bloodshed occurred and that the action, if it could be called this, was limited to rural Tipperary far removed from Protestant population centres, probably explains this. The battleground was much different to that of 1798 where thousands of people perished over a period of some months and the general population bore witness to, and indeed were subjected to, atrocities of the vilest kind. 'Ordinary' Protestants had not needed to get involved this time nor did they suffer any loss of life or damage to property. The polarization and the level of hatred invoked fifty years previously quite simply was not a factor as the rebellion of 1848 was quashed almost before it even began. A large number of Orangemen therefore played their part by signing petitions in favour of the prisoners, petitions that were eventually heeded by the government.[9] Although the *Newsletter* bemoaned 'that too much of a joke has been made of the insurrection at Ballingarry', the leading Young Irelanders were granted a measure of mercy as few Protestants, or indeed Orangemen, called for serious retribution.[10]

INCREASE IN MEMBERSHIP

This did not mean that those seeking to maintain the union rested on their laurels. The extremist *Constitution and Church Sentinel* fearfully warned that 'the snake would appear to be only scotched, not killed'.[11] With such thoughts in mind, new members continued to flock to the Order. The *Sligo Champion* claimed that Orange lodges 'were in active play' in Collooney, Templehouse, Cooper's Hill, Riverstown and Carney.[12] Sandy Row gentleman Richard Curry related that:

6 *BN*, 24 October 1848. **7** Ibid. **8** PRONI, Files of reports relating to Orange processions, MIC 371. **9** *The Spectator*, 21 October 1848. **10** *BN*, 3 November 1848. **11** *CCS*, 15 September 1848. **12** *Sligo Champion*, 3 February 1849.

> Our friends are joining our ranks – the noble and the good are patronizing our institution – our members are rapidly increasing – our enemies are cowering in the distance, not a little disappointed at our recent resuscitation, crestfallen that their hell-born mechanizations for the destruction of the Protestant faith have so signally failed, and that Orangeism is prospering in the land.[13]

The Protestant Watchman happily reported that:

> In Dublin, as we said before, the good work goes bravely on. Last week witnessed wonders. Hundreds were enrolled in different lodges, and three new lodges have been established with all the usual ceremonies. A deputation from the Grand Lodge attended at each to install the respective masters and officers, and the following lodges were added to our glorious Organization – 1755, Melanchton Lodge (revived), 1855, Salim Lodge, and the Salem Lodge 1857.

Material expansion was thus needed with the Grand Lodge of Dublin taking 'the noble house, no. 3, Stephen's Green North, for the use of the institution, their former rooms being found entirely too narrow for the increasing numbers', while Belfast district felt the need to rent a hall for the lodges under its jurisdiction rather than have them meet in private residences as before.[14] On the lower scale, Blacker had previously admitted that 'the majority are obliged, through necessity, to meet in taverns and public houses'.[15] This continuing dearth of official Orange halls was considered problematic as lodges had continued to meet in public houses in their absence. This fact, of course, facilitated the abuse of alcohol and increased the possibility of trouble, which had to be countered as far as the better classes were concerned. The plan for a new Orange hall in Newry was indicative first of the growth of the organization but also of the desire to eradicate the use of alcohol, the consumption of which was in any case counter to the rules of the Order. This model hall was to be:

> A plain, commodious, substantial edifice, two stories high. The principal door will be of oak, neatly ornamented. On the ground floor, in front, there will be two rooms – one of which is intended for a library, the other for a news-room. In the rear, on the floor, there will be comfortable apartments for the keeper of the Hall; and the kitchen will be furnished

13 *BPJ*, 23 December 1848. **14** *PW*, 4 September 1848; *BPJ*, 23 December 1848. **15** *First report on Orange lodges*, p. 113. **16** *BPJ*, 16 June 1849.

> with an extensive range, capable of cooking for as many as the Assembly-room will accommodate. The second floor will mainly consist of one room, which will be capacious, lofty, and handsomely furnished. Behind it will be the committee-rooms, which on the occasion of an assembly, can be used as retiring rooms. It will thus be seen that the accommodations will be complete, and that the Orangemen of this district are actuated by a laudable desire to be removed from the pernicious influence of public houses, and to obtain facilities for the improvement of the mind. In both respects their conduct furnishes an example for the imitation of their brethren throughout the country.[16]

The hall was to be funded by private donation and subscription from lodge members. If newly found respectability was to be maintained, such buildings that advanced the education and awareness of the core membership were key to the overall health of the Order.

Meanwhile, at the top level, elite Order members, the marquis of Downshire and the earl of Erne, were part of a delegation that presented to Clarendon a 'Declaration against the repeal of the Union between Great Britain and Ireland', which was signed by 80,000 people.[17] In the wake of this, a new 'Belfast Protestant Association for promoting the doctrines of the British Reformation, and for maintaining the legislative Union between Great Britain and Ireland' was formed in October with the patronization of Verner and Roden. This association of the Belfast upper classes promised that 'the loyal and Protestant spirit which was evoked in Ulster during the progress of that revolutionary mania which was imbibed by the disaffected in Ireland from the doctrines promulgated on the continent, is not about to evaporate into "thin air"'.[18] Similarly, the Grand Lodge considered it vital that the Order remained on alert warning that:

> it may be urged now, that the bubble has burst, there is no further occasion for the services of these men, and that the organization of their society should cease. But what guarantee have the Protestants that there will not be another attempt at insurrection (perhaps more successful than the last) in which their properties would be destroyed, and their lives not worth one day's purchase?[19]

While the threat of a rebellion had disappeared for the time being, the attempt by O'Connell's son John (although rather politically inept) to revive the tattered Repeal Association was enough to keep the general Protestant population on the

17 *BN*, 15 September 1848. **18** *BN*, 10 October 1848. **19** Rogers, *Memorials of Orangeism*, ii.

alert. Remaining especially alert were indeed the Orangemen, many of whom agreed with the scepticism of William Keown Esq., high sheriff of County Down, who 'spoke of Orangeism as preferable to all the other Protestant Associations. All others, which had ever risen, had vanished like snow off the sunny side of a hill, while Orangeism alone had stood its ground'.[20] The Grand Lodge wholeheartedly agreed, declaring that 'late events have done great service to the cause of Orangeism; the idea of Protestants remaining lukewarm, or "halting between two opinions" is altogether exploded; Whig, and Radical, must give place to the only principle which can eventually secure to us victory in the contest, and that is UNCOMPROMISING ORANGEISM'.[21] These sentiments may well have had some substance; the many Protestant associations that had sprang up over the previous twenty years to counter Catholic progression and government favour had in effect achieved little. Following this latest perceived Catholic uprising it really did appear as if the Orange Order was the only Protestant body capable of providing the long-term coherence and unity necessary for the protection of Protestantism in Ireland.

BASKING IN THE GLORY

Thus, while the rebellion may have been farcical, Orange leaders were not slow in claiming credit for their offer and willingness to fight. Indeed, the part played by Orangemen 'quickly became part of Protestant mythology'.[22] At the *soirée* and opening of the new Inch Orange hall, Revd Mr Gault proudly claimed that, 'now Orangemen were considered the safeguards of Ireland. The Repealers were more afraid of the Orangemen than of the soldiers'.[23] Verner would later remind the government that because of Orange mobilization, 'the whole of the troops in the province of Ulster were withdrawn except two depots. In whose hands, then, remained the preservation of the peace of the province? In those of the Protestants'.[24] The new vigour instilled in the Order ensured that celebrations on 5 November greatly surpassed those of previous years. It was reported, for instance, that St Thomas's Church in Dublin 'was crowded to excess – pews, aisles, and passages – both morning and evening, and many were obliged to go away unable to obtain entrance'.[25] The *Newsletter* glowed with pride at:

> The men whose noble determination which threatened the throne of Sovereign, and the safety of their country – paralysed rebellion in its earliest

20 *BN*, 24 July 1849. **21** *BN*, 10 September 1848. **22** Kinealy, *Repeal and revolution: 1848 in Ireland*, p. 283. **23** *BN*, 14 November 1848. **24** *Hansard, HC debate, 26 July 1849, vol. 107, cc 1004–16.* **25** *CCS*,

> stage, and, by inspiring an ungrateful government with confidence, rendered it an easy matter for a handful of police to crush the monster before it had begun to emerge from the caverns of conspiracy into the light of day.[26]

The paper also angrily responded to the condemnation of November's great Protestant meeting in Belfast by what it termed the 'utensils' of the Whig government, the *Dublin Evening Post* and *The Times*. These papers described the Orangemen as 'agitators' because of the continuance of their activities much to the fury of the *Newsletter*, which asked:

> What, if, at the same moment [as the rebellion], Lamartine had sent over a hoard of republican volunteers to help the Irish traitors, as he sent them into Belgium? What, if the Romish priests had openly joined the insurrection, and from altar, platform, and barricade, preached a bloody crusade against British rule? What, if Feargus O'Connell and his Chartists, instead of crouching, panic-stricken, under the batons of the special constables of London, had displayed the energy and ferocity of the *canaille* of Paris, or the burghers of Germany? How acceptable – how necessary – would the stalwart arms, the trusty hearts, the cool and determined bravery of the loyal volunteers of Ulster [then be]?[27]

These liberal papers, and seemingly the government by connection, now considered these 'agitators' as 'equally guilty with those against whom their moral and physical strength was recently employed'. These sentiments correlated with the general feeling that a lack of appreciation had been forthcoming from the government and that it was now reverting back to its old position of anti-Orangeism. Almost as a response, and to remind the government of services rendered, the celebrations the following Twelfth of July were marked by speeches from the platform highlighting the military importance of the Order. In Belfast, the Revd Dr Thomas Drew, later to come to prominence as a fiery street preacher, questioned the loyalty of Catholic servicemen in the army and asked the prime minister if he was:

> Sure of the police in the South? They certainly did a very gallant act in Ballingarry, and more strength to them when they had the heroes of the cabbage garden to deal with (Laughter). I ask you where is England's strength to be found? You are 15,000 registered men (Cheers). You are not

10 November 1848. **26** *BN*, 3 November 1848. **27** *BN*, 14 November 1848. Lamartine, a French poet, was installed as foreign minister of the Second Republic.

> the paid lifeguards of a master. We are the unpaid lifeguards – (Loud cheers) – and, as long as the Queen is a Protestant, and will only let us love her, we will still be the unpaid guards of the empire.[28]

At a meeting in Antrim, Mr Price reminded his audience that 'this time last year, the Orangemen of Ireland were, under God, the means of rescuing their country from carnage and the dreadful effects of a bloody civil war', while in addressing 1,000 Orangemen in Cootehill, Theophilus L. Clements of Rathkenny House was happy to state that 'they were assembled there today in very different circumstances than on the last anniversary – rebellion was now crushed, the reign of terror was over'.[29] The parades of July 1849 were reported in the press as being 'on a more imposing scale than on most former occasions'.[30] An estimated attendance of between 40,000 and 60,000 was present in Antrim town at the demesne of Lord Massareene. Such large attendances were greatly supplemented by the elites who now felt confident that the government could not possibly take any action against them in the aftermath of the rebellion. Present in Antrim town were 200 of the upper classes, including many ladies, who sat in a platform on the top of a hill.[31] A 'great many of the local gentry' were present at Brookdale House in Lisburn where a crowd of 8,000 had assembled. Here, the press reported that 'the class of men who walked in procession seemed superior to any we have seen for some years; they were much better dressed – more respectable looking as a whole; and what is better, there was an evident improvement in habit'.[32] Freed from the shackles of government disapproval and possible sanction, many better-class Protestants now felt confident enough to openly display their Orange leanings. In addition to this, the line of thought that the Orange Order was indeed the only form of defence against Catholic rebellion drew a new vigour and energy from those of previous questionable enthusiasm.

LOGISTICS OF MOBILIZATION

The assemblage in Antrim town allows an insight into the mechanics of mobilizing such a large group of people, and shows the strength of organization that the Order now possessed. Under the instruction of the Belfast district, forty lodges assembled at the city's Linen Hall at 8.30 a.m. It was reported that 'the members of the lodges were, as usual, arrayed in the various badges and insignia of their rank, and in front of each a gay and, in most instances, a very rich and

28 *BN*, 13 July 1849. **29** *BN*, 13 July 1849; *AC*, 20 July 1849. **30** *LJ*, 11 July 1849. **31** *NG*, 18 July 1849. **32** *NG*, 18 July 1849.

costly banner floated in the breeze – those of the Belfast heroes, Lodge 1033, the Bakers' Lodge, and one or two more being pre-eminently tasteful'.[33] Each lodge was accompanied by a drum and fife, while an Orange band in military uniform was also in attendance. With the band leading, the lodges moved in file to the station of the Belfast and Ballymena railway. The coming of railways to Ulster played an important role in the transportation of Orangemen to venues around eastern Ulster, especially as the 1840s came to an end. Although a mere sixty-five mile network of rail had been laid by 1845, intense speculation of capital led to a short-lived boom in railway expansion.[34] By the end of the decade, Ballymena, Hollywood, Newtownards and Armagh had also been linked with Belfast. The coming of railways was one aspect of the changing face of a modernizing society. In this instance, such modernization was beneficial to the Orangemen. A special train consisting of thirty-eight carriages left the station and the cheering crowds at 10.30 a.m. and began its eighteen-mile journey heavily overcrowded with Orangemen. On arriving at Antrim station, it was noted that another 'monster train' carrying brethren from the Ballymena district had travelled the twenty-mile route from Ballymena, bringing with it a reported 2,800 Orangemen. Upon alighting, both districts were met by men from the Antrim district who were led on horseback by attorney William James Gwynne esquire through Antrim town to the demesne of Lord Massareene. The lodges marched to the erected platform passing the castle of their host 'which was crowded with fashionable spectators' on their route.[35] It was reported that 'the number of banners counted 180, indicating the number of the lodges, but great numbers of these had not reached the front of the platform until the meeting had been dismissed'. Upon the break-up of the meeting, the Belfast Orangemen followed the instruction of Gwynne, who 'intreated [*sic*] the assemblage to go quietly home', and made their way back to Antrim station.[36] At 3.30 p.m. they were picked up, arriving in Belfast at 5 p.m. Such were the numbers returning that another train had to transport remaining Orangemen back to the city at 5.50 p.m. Here ended a forty-mile round trip for thousands of Orangemen who could retire to their home lodges by early evening – a trip that could not have been facilitated without the use of a new mode of transport brought about by the industrial revolution. The assembly in Antrim town was one of the first in which Orangemen took advantage of this new mode of travel. It enabled Orangemen to meet and interact with brethren from far off areas, previously out of reach due to distance considerations, thereby further fostering the solidarity felt within the association.

33 *BN*, 13 July 1849. **34** W.A. McCutcheon, 'Transport, 1820–1914' in Liam Kennedy and Phillip Ollerenshaw (eds), *An economic history of Ulster, 1820–1939* (Manchester, 1985), pp 109–36. **35** *BN*, 13 July 1849. **36** *BN*, 13 July 1849.

DISSENTING VOICES

There were, of course, those within the circle of Protestantism who could not countenance supporting the Order. The increased size of processions occurred despite the wishes of the new bishop of Down and Connor, Robert Knox, who had asked for a peaceful and quiet celebration. Knox had only been consecrated in early May. But his following of Whig principles, coupled with his acceptance that the disestablishment of the Established Church was inevitable, ensured much scepticism within this sector of his flock. In a newspaper address, the bishop reminded his brethren that:

> In a few days that period will arrive when it has been the custom of some of you to walk in procession, with party badges and music; innocent as such demonstrations may be in themselves, yet they cease to be so when they are looked upon by a large and influential portion of our fellow-citizens and neighbours as a triumph of party, calculated to renew old and by-gone feuds, and to keep alive in our breasts anger, wrath, and malice, instead of love, joy and peace towards those with whom we should live in harmony and goodwill; for says Christ – 'By this shall all men know that ye are my disciples, if ye have love one to another'.[37]

However, the bishop's plea was predictably not well received in some quarters. It was reported that 'in the Dioceses of Down and Connor, some of the clergy in deference to the Bishop resolved not to appear in the processions but some of the Belfast clergy felt constrained to come to a different conclusion'.[38] Speaking from the platform in Antrim, Mr Price stated that:

> The Lord Bishop of Down and Connor, and Dromore, has though proper to issue an address to the members of this Church, denouncing the Orange Institution, and calling upon the members of the Church to refrain from meetings and processions on this day, as calculated to make those attending them forget that Christian feeling of brotherly love which ought always to animate our breasts and influence our lives. I wish to speak of the Bishop with all due respect. I give him every credit for his desire to promote the spiritual welfare of the people committed to his clergy; but as one of the members of the Church addressed by him, I do deny that anything is to be found in the laws of the Orange Institution, or in any one of its meetings,

37 *LJ*, 11 July 1849. **38** PRONI, Letters to Beresford about Twelfth of July Orange processions, D32279/C/31/1.

> which is at all calculated to make us forget that Christian love which we feel towards all our countrymen.[39]

Lord Massareene (who claimed to have disarmed all Orangemen who entered the field) rightly pointed out that 'if your lordship's most Christian letter had been addressed exclusively to the clergy over whom, by Divine permission, you have been so happily called to preside, the effect of your "earnest and affectionate language of admonition, warning and advice" would have been greatly enhanced. The clergy appear to be the chief promoters of the Orange demonstrations'.[40] Bishop Knox was also condemned from the many platforms erected around the province. At Massareene, the Revd Thomas Knox Magee Morrow, although not an Orangeman, was invited onto the platform by John Jellet, the Ballymena district master. However, Morrow was largely shunned by the Orange dignitaries alongside him. The reason for this was Morrow's, and indeed Knox's, perceived support for the government's educational reform which continually sought to introduce a non-denominational model of education. Such support was totally unacceptable to hardliners of both sides of the religious divide. Morrow was less than impressed by the speeches from the platform and complained that 'with the *attempted* sermon, or rather harangue, of the vicar of Belfast, and the *mob-speech* of the clerk of Christ's Church, every right-minded Protestant must find fault'.[41] If the government was to be condemned, it was the opinion of Morrow that Queen Victoria as the supreme head of the government was also subject to this condemnation. The liberal-minded Victoria made her position clear the following year by refusing to visit the premises of the Ulster Society for the Education of the Deaf and Dumb during her visit to Belfast as it was open only to Protestants and it openly opposed non-denominational education.[42] As patron of Muckamore national school, Morrow was also included by connection in the condemnation from the platform, condemnation that was particularly forthcoming from the Revds Drew and Millar. To some Protestants such as Morrow, it seemed as if the Order was moving away from its Christian principles because of its vigorous denunciation of Church leaders such as Knox, the Crown, and its government. For this section of Protestants of a more liberal mindset, the further entrenchment of the Orange position following the rebellion offered little to entice them into joining.

The issue of education had also reared its head within the Belfast Protestant Association because of its criticism of what it considered to be contemplated Presbyterian acceptance of the government proposals. The BPA quickly attacked

39 *BN*, 13 July 1849. **40** *LJ*, 18 July 1849. **41** *NW*, 15 July 1849. **42** Kinealy and McAtasney, *Hidden famine: hunger, poverty and sectarianism in Belfast*, p. 184.

the Presbyterian Church 'for its connexion with the National Board'. This attack was swiftly repudiated by the *Londonderry Standard*, which defended the National Board 'because it treats all religious parties alike, and denies to the Established Church its old legal monopoly over the education of the people'.[43] Once more, the frosty relationship between the mainstream Protestant churches came to the surface. The dominant position enjoyed by the Established Church became yet again a sore point for Presbyterians just as it was over the issues of tenant right and the existing cartel of Church of Ireland landlords. Efforts by Revds Drew and Campbell to entice Presbyterians to the Episcopalian Church were met fiercely by the *Standard*, which condemned the attempt 'to entrap the Presbyterian laity and more especially the Presbyterian Orangemen into a confederacy against their own church and clergymen, under pretence of advancing exclusively Protestant objects'.[44] The *Banner of Ulster* considered the BPA to be blatantly anti-Presbyterian and demanded that Presbyterian educational societies 'be left alone'.[45] It reminded Presbyterians of a hesitant mind that, 'whilst loyal to your Queen, you must neither be traitors to your God nor turncoats to your Church'.[46] The paper published an address from fifty-nine Presbyterian members of the BPA declaring their withdrawal as 'that Association has been perverted by its leaders into a hotbed for sectarian scandal and prolatic [*sic*] intolerance'. The *Standard* hoped that any Presbyterian Orangemen who had 'been tricked' into joining would now withdraw as 'under pretence of putting down Popery, they are, in reality, to be employed in drawing the "sword of Gideon" against their Presbyterian neighbours'.[47] It may have seemed to some Presbyterians that the BPA was a mere cover association for the 'conversion' of Presbyterians and it must be remembered that while the major Protestant denominations battled for the souls of 'heathen' Catholics, the conversion of members of the various Protestant splinter groups was also part of their agenda. Thus, as evidenced with the issue of tenant right, the issue of educational instruction had the potential to cause a schism within the overall Protestant family. By association, it was possible that such division could occur within the Orange Order. The BPA countered that 'within the Lodge, no man is Episcopalian, Presbyterian, or Wesleyan – all are Protestants', a line that was followed by the Ballynahinch district, which seemed to adopt a neutral stance.[48] The district stressed that it would not be divided over the issue and declared that 'consequently we cannot reconcile ourselves with, nor consequently identify ourselves with, the writings and disputation at present carried out between the clergy of the Established and Presbyterian churches, otherwise than respectfully to

43 *BOU*, 3 November 1848. **44** *LS*, 5 January 1849. **45** *BOU*, 16 January 1849. **46** Ibid. **47** *LS*, 5 January 1849. **48** *BPJ*, 3 February 1849.

recommend them to have their differences reconciled in the quickest and best manner possible'.[49] While the issue of tenant right did have the potential to have a very real impact on the lives of rank-and-file Orangemen, the issue of education was of much lesser importance. Consequently, it could be ignored to a large degree while the educated classes fought out their doctrinal battles.

CATHOLIC AMBIGUITY

In any event, it seemed as if the bishop's anxieties of sectarian disturbance were unfounded, at least in some areas, as it would appear that many Catholics were happy to observe and even join in with the Orange festivities. Although sectarian differences had worsened over the previous thirty years due to the activities of evangelical societies and subsequent counter-Catholic resistance, relations remained amicable in many areas when it came to the issue of official parading. The *Armagh Guardian* had previously offered a rather cynical explanation for this tolerance with its assertion that 'the Roman Catholics have been so much benefitted by the circulation of money in the various preparations for this day, that they are unanimous that such an annual demonstration is not only harmless, but beneficial to all'.[50] Whatever their reasoning, commercial or otherwise, many Catholics did not shy away from Orange processions. This was evident in Lisburn where, 'among the crowd of lookers-on there were large numbers of Roman Catholics, and others no less opposed to the principles of Orangeism; yet not a word of taunting exultation from one party, or stern defiance from another, was heard amid all the bustle and excitement which so generally prevailed'.[51] A similar scene was evident in Cavan, where 'it was most gratifying to witness the good feeling which was evinced between the Orangemen and their Roman Catholic brethren, all seemed anxious to oblige and promote good fellowship. At many Roman Catholic houses along the road, the Orangemen were gratuitously supplied with plenty of milk which was most acceptable as the day was excessively hot'.[52] Such affable relations were a continuation from the previous year which had seen 15 lodges march to Billyhill, outside of Cootehill, where 'their Roman Catholic brethren, although differing in Church discipline, evinced the most cordial feeling imaginable towards them, and seemed to enjoy their music, as there were no offensive party tunes played'.[53] With the quashing of the rebellion, and with the ongoing famine still an issue, a greater togetherness seemed to prevail between Catholic and Protestant, at least in more rural areas. Most

49 *BOU*, 27 February 1849. **50** *CC*, 18 July 1846. **51** *NG*, 18 July 1849. **52** *AC*, 20 July 1849. **53** *AC*, 14 July 1848.

Catholics had disapproved of the rebellion; indeed, many such as Ballymena parish priest John Lynch had attended meetings and signed petitions of loyalty to the government.[54] In certain rural areas, the commonality of famine suffering had overridden religious difference as witnessed in Clogher when Orangemen marched in formation to the house of the parish priest, the Revd James MacDonnell, to thank him for his help during the crisis.[55] Lowering their flag, they 'gave him a vote of thanks for his labours on behalf of the community during the previous winter'.[56] Such respect was also in evidence during the 1845 parade at Donaghmore, which had passed the priest's house but had remained silent as he was ill.[57] Similar understanding was noticeable at the funeral of John Miller, the district master of Benburb. It gave the *Armagh Guardian* 'great pleasure to state that almost all the respectable RCs of the neighbourhood, to show their love for the deceased, accompanied his remains to the place of interment'.[58] The funeral of Mr James Watt, in Clough, was accompanied by eleven lodges but also by 'a number of respectable persons of all religious persuasions'.[59] In Markethill, many Catholics joined with the 450 Orangemen in attendance at the funeral of Thomas McWhirter where:

> the remarkable good conduct of the men called forth the warmest expression of admiration of all present, Roman Catholics as well as Protestants – furnishing an evident proof that Romanists are inclined to live in harmony with their Protestant neighbours [...] out of the three public houses in Mountnorris, two of them are occupied by Roman Catholics – now those two houses were thronged exceedingly on this occasion, and every accommodation afforded, whilst in the Protestant house only a very few were in attendance.[60]

Such respect and intermingling was relatively common in rural Ulster where everyday relations between Catholics and Protestants were much more cordial than in Belfast. In Bailieborough, the field had been provided by a Catholic, Mr P. Fitzsimmons, and 500 Catholics had mingled with the crowd to hear Revd Mr Winder, rector of Killkare, who spoke 'of the calamity of the times, and exhorted them to deeds of charity, and told those who were distressed to be comforted in the Lord – that sudden death was sudden glory'.[61] These parades were held as famine, which admittedly had passed its worst period, nonetheless continued to take its toll in Ulster. The *Newsletter* glumly reported that 'it is with sincere regret

54 NAI: CSORP, OR: 32 1 1848. **55** Dewar, Brown and Long, *Orangeism, a new historical appreciation*, p. 135. **56** Jack Johnston, *Orangeism in the Clogher Valley, 1795–1995* (Clogher, 1995), p. 13. **57** *DEM*, 14 July 1845. **58** *AG*, 22 June 1847. **59** *Downpatrick Recorder*, 11 April 1848. **60** *AG*, 5 May 1846. **61** *AC*, 20 July 1849.

that we have to announce no better news today as to the cholera statistics of the town [Belfast]. The characteristic of the present aggravated increase of the epidemic is, that it has invaded the more affluent class, among whom it has numbered many victims'.[62] In the midst of continued affliction, religious polarization, at least in some rural areas, would seem to have had a much more blurred line in place than in an urban context.

RATE-IN-AID

As the government continued to distance itself from the sufferings in Ireland, it had already suspended soup kitchen relief, now it introduced a rate-in-aid tax, which was to be paid by Poor Law unions to supplement the other unions that were in most dire need. The payment of this tax was not popular in Ulster as the notion persisted among the better classes that the province was not affected as badly by the Famine as areas in the south and west were. The Revd Andrew Breaky of Killyleagh put it that, 'they, in Ulster, needed not a rate-in-aid, and why? Because it was Protestant Ulster; because they, the Orangemen, had self-respect, and self-esteem, and self-exertion, all induced by their principles; therefore, they had no need of a rate-in-aid'.[63] Nor was it popular with Poor Law guardians, who mounted a vigorous campaign against its introduction. At a meeting of the Lurgan Poor Law guardians, chaired by William Blacker, it was resolved 'to hold a meeting in protest with the view of signing a petition against taxing Ulster and Leinster for the support of idleness and improvidence elsewhere'.[64] Placards erected around the town condemned the government 'for forcing the farmers of Ulster to support the paupers of the south and west!!!' Continuing in the vein of supposed Ulster superiority, the notice queried 'do you think yourselves able to support the poor of Mayo and Galway?'[65] Some Orangemen, such as those belonging to the Moneymore Loyal Independent Hanoverian Lodge, also adopted petitions to be sent to the houses of parliament in protest.[66] The failure of these, and of subsequent protest meetings, was further evidence that the burden of the Famine was being placed by the government back onto Irish landlords such as Roden and Farnham, who had been expected to take more responsibility to ease the suffering. Despite this, the cholera epidemic continued through the summer of 1849. Against this backdrop, the Twelfth, although joyous for many relieved Protestants, did not turn into the antagonistic occasion that it might have done in other years. There were minor skirmishes in

62 *BN*, 20 July 1849. **63** *BPJ*, 28 July 1849. **64** *BN*, 27 February 1849. **65** NAI: Outrage Reports, Co. Antrim (1849) 51/2. **66** *BN*, 17 April 1849.

Carnew, County Wexford (described as 'the great seat of Orangeism and party bigotry in Leinster' by the *Freeman's Journal*), but little else to report from around the country in the way of trouble, apart from the death of one Catholic following clashes at Ballymacarrett.[67] Glowing in the aftermath of its part played in securing the country, and back to its previous position of ambiguous government favour (although somewhat covert), the Order had no desire to fall foul of Dublin Castle.

DOLLY'S BRAE

This position was soon to drastically change as news filtered through from Castlewellan, County Down, the stronghold of Lord Roden. The previous year Roden had invited Orangemen to his demesne to celebrate the Twelfth. The traditional route was a narrow mountain pass known as Dolly's Brae. While taking this route, Orangemen found their way blocked by hundreds of armed Ribbonmen leaving them with no option but to proceed via an alternative course. For this climb down, Orangemen were taunted and humiliated locally for the following twelve months. According to Walter Berwick, QC, 'very gross and insulting songs were printed and sang publicly in the market towns to celebrate this victory. One of these songs was called the "Dolly's Brae song"'.[68] This ongoing humiliation was further added to the following February when an Orangeman, David McDowell, was murdered by Ribbonmen in the area. On St Patrick's Day, another Orangeman, named McAnnity, was shot and killed by Ribbonmen near Rathfriland. The funerals of both men saw a huge Orange turnout with processions, which included heavily armed Orangemen, stretching a reported three miles. Following the funeral of McDowell, a number of Orangemen attacked and destroyed several Catholic homes as frustration spilled over.[69] The owner of one of the attacked houses was 'considered influential among the Ribbonmen of that neighbourhood' according to the police.[70] This would indicate a lack of secrecy within this so-called secret society and once more highlights the level of familiarity that existed between the communities. The *Newsletter* reported that 'the country is in an awful state of excitement […] the parties in the neighbourhood are nearly equally divided, and it is needless to say, that party spirit runs high, and the worst consequences may be apprehended, if further collisions take place, which it is to be hoped the police and military will use their best exertions in preventing'.[71] A similar situation existed in

67 *FJ*, 25 July 1849. **68** *Dolly's Brae inquiry*, p. 5. **69** *Dolly's Brae inquiry*, p. 5. **70** PRONI, files relating to Orange processions, MIC 371. **71** *BN*, 16 February 1849.

Newtownhamilton, County Armagh, following the death of a Catholic named McElherron in 1846 during an affray with Orangemen. Police explained that 'since that period a deep revengeful feeling prevails and when these people meet, they receive each other in the same light that two hostile armies would [...] the country around Newtownhamilton is mountainous – the people are independent and fierce in their disposition. They are divided into two hostile factions – Orange and Catholic – they are mostly all armed and I am informed mostly carry arms about them'.[72] It was generally the case that sectarian tensions spiked in many areas during marching season and subsequently lessened for the remainder of the year, provided that no loss of life or perceived humiliation had occurred. The build-up of tension in Rathfriland was set to explode in July 1849.

The prediction of the *Newsletter* was to prove far-sighted during the summer marching season as the local Orangemen were determined that no backing down would occur on this occasion. As the Party Processions Act had not been renewed in 1845, government hands were rather tied as it deliberated over a course of action to take. With recent events in mind, trouble was anticipated but no law was now actually in existence to ban the procession. Therefore, the decision was taken to provide a heavy police and magisterial presence in order to keep the parties apart. The Orangemen, this time heavily armed and prepared, proceeded through Dolly's Brae and on to Roden's demesne despite a heavy Ribbon presence on the hillside. At Tollymore, they were greeted and addressed by Roden who called on them to 'show to those who disapprove of your organization that you are not a faction, driven by party violence to commit unlawful acts'.[73] However, the words of Roden were not enough, and the fragile peace maintained by the police and magistrates was not held on the return journey. Despite their best efforts, an accidental shot sparked a flurry of shooting during which the Orange faction routed the Ribbonmen. The aftermath of the incident uncovered possibly as many as six Catholics killed and dozens wounded. While local Orangemen wildly celebrated their victory and the restoration of their 'honour', it was the last thing the newly returned upper echelons of society wanted to hear. Although County Down grand master William Beers, who had been present at Tollymore, called the incident a 'little blot, if blot he could call it', a furious government acted quickly to hold a commission of inquiry.[74] The *Anglo-Celt* summed up the feelings of many in hoping that the 'government will profit this fatal lesson, to pass an act putting down party processions of all kinds and hues'.[75] Even the

72 NAI: Outrage Reports, Co. Armagh (1847) 303/2. **73** *Dolly's Brae inquiry*, p. 45. **74** *BN*, 24 July 1849. **75** *AC*, 24 July 1849.

partisan *Newsletter* condemned a subsequent parade of 14 lodges that took place in Newbliss, County Monaghan, on 1 August and questioned the 'propriety of a procedure of holding a procession at any time without the sanction of the Society, but particularly while a government investigation was pending into the melancholy consequences of the affray at Castlewellan'.[76] The Order was now once more placed on the defensive and under the hostile glare of a Westminster microscope.

GOVERNMENT CENSURE

This government inquiry placed the blame squarely at the feet of the Orange party, Beers and Roden, both of whom, along with Beers' brother Francis, were removed from the magistracy. It concluded that Beers 'never did himself make the slightest attempt to influence the Orange body to go home by the new road, but, on the contrary, advised them to return by the same way by which they had came [*sic*]'. In response, Roden and many Orangemen rather irrationally placed the blame on the government for having not prohibited processions, and again Clarendon, already widely despised for denying that he sought Orange help in 1848, came in for heavy criticism. The reaction of the government appeared to be in marked contrast to its lukewarm reaction in punishing the leaders of the Young Ireland rebellion. Beers defiantly pointed out that:

> It may be said that the Queen's troops were more than sufficient to have saved the country, but it was a well known boast amongst the rebellious party that so many of them were tainted with disaffection that they would have joined the rebel banner and fought against the Queen and government, a course of conduct not at all unlikely after the loyal preaching of Fathers Kenyon, O'Malley and Meehan, Bermingham, Hughes and company, into whose conduct upon that occasion there was no Mr Walter Berwick, of 'Offenses Bill' notoriety, fed handsomely by the government to hold a public 'investigation'.[77]

Letters of support for Roden streamed in from around the country and indeed from mainland Britain, a good number of which bemoaned the apparent treachery of the Whig government. A large number of magistrates resigned their government commissions in support of their comrade. 'The Protestants of Bandon' spoke for many in their summation that 'in their hour of need, the

76 *BN*, 7 August 1849. **77** *DD*, 20 October 1849.

government have relied upon the Protestants of Ireland for support; let that time pass and they are neglected and insulted'.[78] Despite such shows of support, Roden, with little room left to politically manoeuvre, rather withdrew from the entire episode. In reply to a letter of support from the Norwich Protestant Association, he responded that 'I have felt it my duty to avoid all reference to any topics which might be calculated to excite or inflame the minds of those who have my honour and my interest so much at heart'.[79] Former Derry MP, George Dawson, once an Orangeman but now arch enemy of the Order, gloated that it was:

> Strange to say Lord Roden has lost all his popularity among the Orangemen; they think he showed the white feather in not defending himself and them more manfully and they speak with the utmost contempt of him. Such is the fate of all agitators who will not go the full length with their blind and bigoted followers; they say at Tollymore, his own place, that he is so much annoyed with these manifestations of unpopularity that he intends to absent himself for two years.[80]

For the likes of Dawson and other enemies of the Order, Dolly's Brae was a godsend as it presented the perfect legitimization to resume the attack on the Orange body after a somewhat dormant period.

ON THE DEFENSIVE

Fighting a desperate rear-guard action, the Grand Lodge of Ireland felt the need to scotch rumours claiming some Orangemen had considered joining rebel ranks. It was alleged that, due to their dissatisfaction at the government prior to the rebellion, 'the Orangemen of Ireland, disgusted by the conduct of partial rulers, were disposed, if not to swell the ranks of the rebel party, to stand, at least, neuter in the struggle between the disaffected and the government'.[81] The level of general Orange unhappiness towards the government was admitted by Fermanagh MP Mervyn Archdall, as he told parliament 'it was not pretended that the Orangemen were not dissatisfied, for they had many reasons to be dissatisfied [...] but there was a wide distinction between dissatisfaction and disaffection'.[82] Although Archdall went on to re-affirm Orange loyalty, such claims continued because the Order had sought proof of the government's

78 *DEM*, 5 November 1849. **79** *DEM*, 9 January 1850. **80** PRONI, Rt Hon. George Dawson at Dublin to Sir William Fremantle, T2603/19. **81** PRONI, Printed volumes containing reports of the Grand Lodge of Ireland, D2966/16/1; *NW*, 4 December 1849. **82** *Hansard, HC debate, 10 April 1848,*

sincerity by asking for arms when Phaire approached them. This led a Grand Lodge investigation to conclude that 'they have been blamed for their presumption in daring to suspect the pure intention of the Irish Government, and for their falsehood in asserting, or their simplicity in believing, that the Government could countenance them or their institution to such a degree as would be implied by supplying them with arms'. The investigation found no fault in this line of thinking and maintained that its members 'sought no personal aggrandisement or advantage for themselves; they asked no more than proof that they were not to be betrayed; they desired to be trusted, and to be put in a condition to defend their country and rights'.[83] The notion of spying for the government had been thoroughly rejected but the fact that a bribe was allegedly offered by Phaire to one Orangeman, who would be released from debt if he agreed, was highlighted by the investigation as further proof of the underhand tactics of the government. That the government denied supplying them with arms came as no surprise to the Orange commission. It considered that Captain Kennedy, who allegedly forwarded a £600 cheque to a Dublin lodge master, had been made a scapegoat by Clarendon and that his intervention 'was resorted to as affording a facility of renouncing the alliance when the storm passed by'. The report summed up Orange distaste for the government by concluding that 'it was not likely to come to pass that friendly relations could ever be maintained by a Whig government with the Orange body, no matter how loyal and brave, and constitutional they might be'.[84] But with the Order under the microscope yet again and the government toleration gained in 1848 now well and truly lost, it became apparent to the Order's leadership that a new line of legitimacy was now required. It was decided that political representation would be the new way forward.[85]

Little in the line of defence had been offered in parliament by those MPs that belonged to the Orange Order. This irked leading Orangemen who decided that greater political involvement was needed. Yet another 'new' respectability was needed following the public relations disaster of Dolly's Brae – political involvement was considered the best answer to both of these issues.[86] Hoppen considers that the new Central Conservative Society founded in 1853 had its origins in a special electoral sub-committee set up by the Grand Lodge in 1851.[87] The elections of 1852 saw Orangeism play an influential role, especially in the defeat of Sharman Crawford in County Down, and saw the return to parliament of Orangemen Verner, Knox, Brooke, Leslie, Bernard and Lord Claude Hamilton. What Hoppen terms 'polished Orangeism which could still produce

vol. 98, cc 73–125. **83** *NW*, 4 December 1849. **84** *Report of the special committee of the Grand Lodge of Ireland appointed November, 1849* (Dublin, 1849), p. 21. **85** Mattison, '"From Dolly's Brae to Westminster"', p. 66. **86** Ibid. **87** Hoppen, *Elections, politics and society in Ireland, 1832–1885*, p. 323.

support but without the tribal savagery of the unvarnished article' was gladly welcomed by Conservatives.[88] But once again, Orange leaders found a core membership not entirely in keeping with such ideals. Lisburn Orangemen did not back the 'chosen' candidate Mr Jonathan Richardson and thus handed the seat to the Liberals. Such lack of deference ensured that 'polished Orangeism' was not destined to last despite the best efforts of leaders such as Enniskillen. The riots of 1857, 1860 and 1864 brought back the negative face of Orangeism that its leaders tried to eliminate. Popular Orangeism found its champion in Johnston of Ballykilbeg during the 1860s, while 'the *official* "moderation" of post-Famine Orangeism so infuriated sections of the movement that some even made curious overtures to the Liberals'.[89] The planned for 'new' voice in parliament had little impact; in any case most of the Orangemen elected in 1852 had been MPs in 1849 and continued to contribute little in the way of defence throughout the 1850s. It must be thus considered that the new post-Dolly's Brae policy of the Grand Lodge that hoped to present respectable Orangeism was a marked failure, as popular Orangeism looked to the confrontational Johnston as its flag bearer.

GROUND-LEVEL REACTION

While many districts and counties such as the Fermanagh Grand Lodge offered letters of support to Roden and Beers, at ground level a small number of lodges took an altogether different line and wound themselves up in disgust at the actions of their fellow Orangemen.[90] It was considered by some brethren that the activities of these Orangemen and the resulting violence were quite simply not in keeping with the Christian principles that were a cornerstone of the organization. James Murphy, district master of Moneymore, was 'of opinion that the present organization was not in accordance with the spirit of the age', therefore he and his fellow members deemed 'it our duty, as members of the state and as Christians, to dissolve our connexion with that organization'.[91] For others, the inevitable re-introduction of the Party Processions Act on 12 March 1850 signalled the ending of their Orange activities. Roden calmly greeted the Act by announcing that 'of the present measure he had nothing to complain, and he felt sure that the Orangemen would be the first to give it effect, by refraining from those processions which they had so much enjoyed and so frequently indulged in'.[92]

88 Ibid., p. 324. **89** Ibid., p. 325. **90** PRONI, Minute book of the County Fermanagh Loyal Grand Orange Lodge, D1402/1/1. Wright, *Two lands on one soil*, p. 156. **91** *AC*, 21 June 1850. **92** *Hansard, HL debate, 28 February 1850, vol. 109, cc 126–33.*

But the idea of a cessation of parading was too much for some members who felt, once more, betrayed by the government. The *Banner of Ulster* reported that the masters of the Stewartstown district, 'in consequence of a bill having been lately passed against party processions', gathered in the town 'when a bonfire was made in the Market-Square, and fifteen or sixteen warrants belonging to the district were burned, and it was agreed that the members of the district should henceforth live in peace with their Roman Catholic countrymen'.[93] The masters of the Fintona district burnt their warrants declaring 'that they no longer feel bound, in any emergency, to support the present government'.[94] The brethren of Blundell's Grange Orange Lodge pledged to dissolve, assemble and 'proudly' burn their emblems and banners, while Derryscallog and Loughgall Lodges resolved to symbolically burn their paraphernalia at the Diamond.[95] Mattison explains that the reason for such symbolic burning was sheer frustration and anger at the government.[96] The conditional loyalty provided to the Queen's government was no longer binding in the eyes of these Orangemen hence the burning of their warrants. On declaring their intention to dissolve, Moneymore Orangemen proposed a novel replacement indicative of an era which increasingly recognized the value of education:

> We would humbly tender our advice to the various lodges, instead of assembling for political purposes, as heretofore, to establish reading societies throughout the length and breadth of the land, and devote their money to the diffusion of knowledge, which, in a short time, with the blessing of God, would raise them to a higher degree in the scale of public opinion than ever they had attained under the 'old regime', always remembering that 'knowledge is power'.[97]

Not all Orangemen chose this route of self-improvement however; the grand master of Londonderry furiously 'repudiated the Moneymore people, as contumacious and disobedient to all rule and authority, and did not recognize them as Orangemen, nor is he aware that they have ever since then been received into fellowship by the County Grand Lodge'.[98] Larne district, while not as animated, unanimously expressed its deep regret at the fact that lodges 948 (Portadown) and 118 (Loughgall) had felt compelled to burn their warrants and other Orange emblems but strongly expressed its own desire to continue.[99] To actually burn warrants, which were considered to be almost sacred, was a highly divisive measure. Such activity compelled the *Tyrone Constitution* to fear that the

93 *FJ*, 15 April 1850. **94** *LJ*, 15 May 1850. **95** *DEP*, 21 May 1850. **96** Mattison, '"From Dolly's Brae to Westminster"', p. 63. **97** *LJ*, 19 June 1850. **98** *BN*, 21 June 1850. **99** *BN*, 21 June 1850.

Orange Order was 'falling into fragments' but these concerns proved to be without foundation.[100] Indeed, a revival in Drogheda was reported by the *Dundalk Democrat* where, 'within the last few months a strenuous effort has been made by the descendants of the old "true blues" to establish one [a new lodge] on the banks of the Boyne'.[101] A revival of sorts was also evident in Cork as 'some former members of the Orange Society, who had retired from that institution on its break up in 1837', met to discuss 'the propriety of again starting their old warrant which had been "boxed up" for the past twelve years'. The reason put forward for this revival 'was the conduct pursued towards their own friends and patrons, Lord Roden and Messrs Beers'.[102] Clearly, as far as many Protestants were concerned, the government had over-reacted to the events at Dolly's Brae, and with their sanctioning of Roden and the Beers brothers. Rather than see a collapse of the Order as the government may have hoped for, 'Clarendon has given it a helping hand, never calculated on'. Therefore, by May the Grand Lodge of Ireland was able to report that only eighteen of the 1,900 lodges in existence had wound themselves up, and also that rumours of Portadown's withdrawal were untrue as they had in fact been circulated by a disaffected ex-officer.[103] Verner pledged that the Order would not dissolve again and reminded brethren that the Order 'was not founded for purposes of parade or display'; it was, in fact, a defensive organization that was still needed as far as he was concerned.[104] Although it was soon reported that the Killen district had dissolved itself (falsely as it transpired) following a meeting in Castlederg, the advice of Verner was largely heeded by the many Orangemen who remained and began a period of quiet membership. This is in keeping with Bardon's assessment that, in contrast to the ever-expanding Belfast, 'rural Ulster was remarkably quiet in these years'.[105] For thousands of Orangemen political matters played only a small part of their reason for membership. Granted, they did rally to the political causes of the day but the grand processions and protest meetings that drew tens of thousands to central urban venues were the exception rather than the norm in the lives of 'ordinary' Orangemen. More relevant were day-to-day occurrences that passed beneath the interest of the landed elites or newspaper correspondents. These aspects of the Order continued unabated in marked contrast to the large-scale parades and processions, which were no longer deemed acceptable. Thus, while Clarendon predicted 'the extinction of Orangeism' in the wake of the Dolly's Brae fallout, his prophecy did not consider the importance of the local bonds and camaraderie that Orangeism facilitated and that these would never allow the

100 *TC*, 10 May 1850. **101** *DD*, 23 February 1850. **102** *NG*, 20 October 1849. **103** *BN*, 21 May 1850. **104** *LJ*, 22 May 1850. **105** *LJ*, 12 July 1850; Bardon, *A history of Ulster*, p. 307.

Order to die.[106] A typical example of the localized fraternal activity of the Order was reported in the *Tyrone Constitution* which noted that:

> On Saturday last, a large body of Orangemen proceeded to the lands of Mr Abraham Wylie, situated in Gowerstown, Culrevog, and Broghadooey, and cut down some fifty acres of prime oats, as a mark of respect for the owner. They then returned to the house of Mr Wylie, accompanied with banners, music, and various loyal insignia, and headed by their district master, Mr J. Gilmour. A substantial dinner was prepared for them, to which ample justice was done.[107]

In addition to such displays of deference, other issues such as death and burial, for instance, remained important events in the local social calendar. The funeral of thirty-eight-year-old James Mitchell of Seskanore, County Tyrone, was characteristic of such an occasion. This funeral:

> was attended by upwards of six hundred persons, all the men wearing white hat scarfs, which gave an exceedingly picturesque appearance to the solemn scene. There were nine beautiful flags; which, with the hearse, were placed in the front, the drums being muffled, the masters of lodges marched close to the flags, and the Orangemen marched behind the masters and before the hearse, and the Augharonan Lodge, of which the deceased was deputy-master, brought up the rear. On arriving at the graveyard the body was committed to the dust, with the secret rites and ceremonies pertaining to the interment of a member of the Orange association.[108]

The colour, choreography and pageantry on display were symptomatic of such local events far removed from wider view. The funeral ritual allowed for 'many good and desirable results among the brethren, presenting as it does, a fit opportunity for religious thoughts and serious reflection'.[109] Burial rites were of extreme importance especially to members of Black institutions who according to Mattison 'rigidly looked to the Israelite exodus from Egypt' as the perceived parallels between the exodus of Protestants and the Israelites were played out to the full.[110] The religious aspect of the Order remained of paramount importance albeit an importance often overshadowed, unfairly as far as many members were concerned, by sectarian conflict. Critics simply did not see nor care for the familial side of Orangeism. The erection of a headstone in Enniskillen by

106 Kinealy, *Hidden Famine: hunger, poverty and sectarianism in Belfast*, p. 176. **107** *BN*, 25 September 1849. **108** *TC*, 31 July 1846. **109** *ECEP*, 30 September 1847. **110** Mattison, '"From Dolly's Brae to Westminster"', p. 177.

members of the McKinley Orange Lodge, no. 1539, 'over the remains and to the memory of two of the deceased brethren, William and Osborne Elliott, the latter of whom was accidently drowned in our lake on the 27th of August 1847' attracted little interest other than from those directly involved.[111] Also of little interest, other than of a local nature, was the farewell supper held by Coleraine Lodge no. 2 at which lodge master John Elliott was presented with 'a handsome silver watch' prior to his departure to Sydney. Nor did the fete attended by 200 brethren to honour Mr Reilly of Hollywood, master of the Loyal Sentinel Orange Lodge, no. 672, before he too left for a new life in Australia, cause any stir outside of its immediate area.[112] An Orange band drawn from general operatives and trained by Mr Brown, clerk at St Anne's, entertained a numerous attendance of the working classes in the Music Hall in Belfast but was again largely ignored by the elites.[113] These instances provided little in the way of news and were not noted in the corridors of power but they were typical of the spirit and solidarity engendered by membership of the Order. A strong case could be made that membership was not exclusively a simple reaction to fear, suspicion and mistrust of the 'other' community. Nor did membership necessarily serve as a protest against a government in London which surely felt part of another world, a world of which a lower-class Protestant weaver or an inner city factory worker had little real knowledge or even less direct contact. While these were probably secondary reasons for joining, it is also quite likely that being a part of an organization that provided a social outlet and a support mechanism was the main reason that many Protestant males enrolled in the Order.

AFTERMATH

Of course, sectarianism and the defence of territory remained a preoccupation for many, especially in the contested streets of Belfast, which were not quite so tranquil. As previously mentioned, serious party rioting occurred on a regular basis, most notably in 1857, 1864 and 1872. But the general calm within Orangeism lasted until the successful campaign of Johnston of Ballykilbeg to have the Party Processions Act removed over twenty years after its passing. Indeed, the summer of 1850 was marked by acceptance and a resulting dullness within Orange membership. The visit of Queen Victoria to Belfast the previous August was notable for its lack of Orange fanfare in the wake of Dolly's Brae. Roden, in his address to the crowd at Tollymore, had looked forward to the Queen's visit and imagined 'how her eyes would sparkle at such a sight now

111 *BN*, 13 February 1849. **112** *BPJ*, 26 May 1849; *BN*, 23 July 1850. **113** *BN*, 27 June 1849.

before me in the assembling of that multitude of loyal men, ready to lay down their lives in defence of her crown and her rights!'[114] This vision was not to be fulfilled. Although Roden was chosen by his fellow landlords to officially welcome the Queen, and while Verner and Enniskillen were present among the dignitaries, the Order had no role to play. Instead, Victoria was greeted not by Orange or purple flags but by largely neutral banners, many reading 'céad míle fáilte' as Catholics and some Belfast Protestants instead chose to emphasize their Irish heritage.[115] Again, a low-key profile was evident the following November during celebrations to mark the gunpowder plot. For instance, Ballybay Orangemen had planned a procession to their church but owing to advice from Roden did not turn out.[116] Fearing trouble, Clarendon had flooded Ulster with extra troops but the Protestant press scorned that 'the Orangemen were better advised than to fall into the trap laid for them'.[117] The activities of those who did assemble were haphazard at best. The *Dundalk Democrat* mocked the Orangemen of Collon, County Louth, drolly reporting that:

> On Monday last a motley group of ragamuffins assembled about 3 o'clock, at the Orange Lodge rooms in the immediate vicinity of the Church, for the purpose of outraging the feelings of the Roman Catholics of Collon. A large Orange flag flaunted across the road, and an effigy supposed to represent either Guy Faux [*sic*] or Lord Clarendon was hung up and burned. The pockets of the dress in which the figure was encased, were filled with gunpowder, but several ineffectual attempts were made to cause it to explode, thus showing that the Orangemen of Collon do not 'keep their powder dry'. In the evening, the gang assembled in the Lodge room to drink, and the next morning several of them were to be seen endeavouring to stagger to their homes. In the course of the evening the police several times visited the Lodge room to warn them against any breach of the peace. The Catholics of Collon treated the whole scene with the contempt it deserved.[118]

In the face of such shambolic occurrences, other than the prevention of a small sham fight outside Newry, Clarendon's troops were largely rendered redundant.[119] The funeral of a Protestant who had died after lingering for months as a result of injuries sustained at Dolly's Brae was well attended but notable for the absence of weaponry among the mainly Orange congregation. A muted atmosphere

114 *Dolly's Brae enquiry*, p. 45. **115** James Loughlin, 'Allegiance and illusion: Queen Victoria's Irish visit of 1849', *History*, 87:288 (2002), pp 491–513. **116** NAI: Outrage Reports, Co. Monaghan (1849) 163/23. **117** *BN*, 8 November 1849. **118** *DD*, 10 November 1849. **119** *DEM*, 7 November 1849.

prevailed as July of 1850 saw none of the pomp and procession of previous years as most Orangemen followed the advice of the vicar of Belfast T.F. Miller not to parade:

> Whatever political changes have come over the minds of others – however Government may have vacillated, recognizing you in their day of peril, casting you off when peace was restored; however friends have frowned upon and deserted you, and the taunt, and invective, and calumny were directed against you – still, amid these discouragements, you possess in your trials the magnanimity of a true patriotic spirit, which passing unscathed through every fiery ordeal, comes forth the more refined, and joins the more fervently in united feeling and effort for future good.[120]

To be sure, both Miller and Henry Cooke listened to the advice of magistrates and the police and cancelled sermons that they had planned to preach in Belfast.[121] Although two Orange youths were injured in clashes with the police at the Malone turnpike in Belfast on the Eleventh night, and the police barracks at Bradbury Place was subsequently attacked by angry Orangemen, there was no disturbance in the city the following day as members by and large met and dined privately in their own lodges.[122] The *Newsletter* reported that 'a large number of the military was present in Banbridge but 'you would scarcely have seen an Orange lily during the day', while little or no activity was reported throughout the province.[123] An increase in military force was noticeable throughout Ulster as the government feared a repeat of the trouble of 1849 but it was not needed. Although the 39th Regiment was ordered in advance to Portadown, 'obedience to the law seemed the order of the day'.[124] Sporadic incidents did occur such as at Tartaraghan, County Armagh, where a small police force who tried to disperse an Orange assembly was attacked but such episodes, directed against the police rather than against Catholics, were scarce.[125] Tensions had remained high in Rathfriland since Dolly's Brae; the police had prevented an Orange sham fight the previous November, while apprehensions expressed by the parish priest and magistrates over a Ribbon assembly on St Patrick's Day had proved unfounded due to a large military presence.[126] By July, however, the area was considered to be 'perfectly quiet'.[127] In Lisburn, previously an Orange stronghold, 'the streets presented a bustling appearance, without any excitement or tumult, or even an

120 *BN*, 12 July 1850. **121** NAI: Outrage Reports, Co. Antrim (1850) 126/1. **122** Daragh Curran, '"The path in front of their barrack was literally covered with a pile of stones" – the attack on Bradbury police station 11 July 1850', Academia.edu, accessed 11 November 2019. **123** *BN*, 16 July 1850. **124** *DEM*, 15 July 1850. **125** NAI: Outrage Reports, Co. Armagh (1850) 253/2. **126** NAI: Outrage Reports, Co. Down (1849) 486/8, (1850) 113/8, (1850) 125–6/8. **127** NAI: Outrage Reports, Co.

approach to disturbance'.[128] Most Orangemen, such as those in Rasharkin, chose to celebrate the day quietly in their lodge rooms. The lodges of Coleraine dined together 'and pledged themselves to be more firmly united than ever in the bonds of brotherhood, and to live in peace and goodwill with all denominations of men'.[129] Roden had not opposed the Party Processions Act and had expressed confidence that the Orangemen 'would be the first to give it effect, by refraining from those processions which they had so much enjoyed and so frequently indulged in'.[130] This confidence had been well placed. The *Coleraine Chronicle* proclaimed that 'the loyalty of the people has shown itself in an implicit and universal obedience to the laws', while the *Newry Telegraph* praised the Orangemen who 'have, on the confession of even their bitterest enemies, entitled themselves to the highest credit for their scrupulous abstinence from everything, in act or appearance, tending to excite party feeling'.[131] Overall, the *Freeman's Journal* was relieved (and possibly disappointed given its overall agenda) to report that 'the anniversary of national disaster has passed away with an order and repose unknown to former days'.[132] As a body, the Order, of course, continued to exist, it had not been banned by the government. At its half-yearly meeting held in Dublin in December 1850, Enniskillen, who remained as grand master, proudly claimed that:

> Our reputation has remained unsullied – the districts in which our society prevails have been marked by their uniform tranquillity and order, and notwithstanding the insidious and persevering efforts to divide and weaken us, the necessity of close and effectual union has become more sensibly felt by all our brethren, and the strength of the Orange Society has known no abatement.[133]

Nevertheless, the re-implementation of the Party Processions Act had seriously damaged the Orange Order by taking away the right to march held so dearly by many of its members. In later years the Act was breached and serious riots did occur, especially in Belfast as evangelical preachers such as Drew and Hugh Hanna whipped up sectarian tensions. But the introduction of the Party Emblems Act in 1860, following riots at Derrymacash, further hurt core membership and it was not until the future campaigns of Johnston that the Order was returned to some semblance of its old popularity, at least amongst the lower classes who regained something of their previous militant spirit. It would take the threat of Home Rule, which began to rear its head in the 1880s, to bring

Down (1850) 357/8. **128** *BN*, 16 July 1850. **129** *DEM*, 15 July 1850. **130** *LJ*, 6 March 1850. **131** *DD*, 20 July 1850. **132** *FJ*, 16 July 1850. **133** *BN*, 3 December 1850.

the upper classes back to their previous leadership positions. It is entirely possible that the widespread Protestant protest with its military overtones evidenced following the passing of the third Home Rule bill in 1912 could have been preceded by similar reaction had repeal been seriously considered by the government in the 1840s. However, this possibility was never allowed to materialize as by 1850 the worst years of the Famine had passed and the threat of repeal and the flames of republicanism had been extinguished. In addition to this was a return of a good degree of economic prosperity over the next decade, easing the economic competition that had taken on a sectarian face. With such factors in play, it is safe to conclude that the short-lived revival of the Orange Order, which had gained such momentum in such a narrow time frame, was well and truly over.

* * *

Dolly's Brae was surely a disaster for the upper tiers of Orange leadership. From a position of covert government acceptance, leadership now found itself fighting several different defensive fronts. From within the rank and file some discontent was also apparent as a small number of lodges burnt their warrants in anger. But the lower classes, to a much greater degree than the upper classes, contributed greatly to ensuring that the Order fought through the fallout of Dolly's Brae by continuing the everyday activities so central to their otherwise humdrum existence. Indeed, a somewhat lukewarm relationship between the Grand Lodge and many ordinary Orangemen continued to exist in areas of mid-Ulster. Disregard for official rules saw the Grand Lodge suspending the warrants of Lodges 61, 253, 306, 1241 and 1244 of the Tanderagee district 'for having refused to hold meetings or pay the county dues'.[134] Although unity and obedience could be achieved in the face of a larger adversity, bitterness and antagonism over the status of non-sanctioned degrees clearly remained, especially in Armagh. Official instruction simply was not a prerequisite for the continuation of Orange activity among the lower classes. It was this sector of popular Protestantism that allowed Orangeism to continue to function until the next great cementing threat, the threat of Home Rule, emerged almost forty years after Dolly's Brae.

134 PRONI, Proceedings of the Grand Lodge of Ireland, 1849–60, D2966/16/1.

Conclusion

In a time of great uncertainty for the Protestants of Ireland, the return of the Orange Order surely was inevitable. Economic recession, the increase in Catholic campaigning (both peaceful and violent), and the continuation of prime minister Peel's perceived generosity to the Catholic Church were reason enough for the revival of such a popular Protestant association. By 1845, the ground was ripe for this revival. Such was the popularity of this association, among the lower classes especially, that initial internal dispute and mistrust were overcome, while the national disaster that was the Famine merely held up but failed to halt its progress. While the Famine may not have been as serious in Ulster as in other areas of the country, it did have a major impact on the province affecting Protestants on much the same scale as Catholics. In spite of the ever-worsening effects of the Famine, especially through 1847 and 1848, the lower classes in particular continued with their Orange activities whether in public procession or even amid the misery of the workhouse. In the midst of death and disease, the feeling of belonging and the expression of identity took on a greater importance. This resolution to continue was greatly strengthened by continuing repeal agitation and the eventual uprising of the Young Ireland movement.

This is not to say that all Protestants or even Orangemen were certain where they stood on the key issues that arose during this period. A small number did briefly flirt with repeal organizations, such was the dislike and distrust of the London government; a good many others seeking security on the land paid substantial attention to the tenant right movement and followed the campaign of McKnight and Sharman Crawford. Although the Order was eventually controlled by a central national body, it is evident that it was not a consistent national organization. The very landscape of Protestant settlement meant a sharp division between urban and rural, especially in Ulster, which ensured localism continued to be of central importance within the wider overall picture of Orangeism. A different dynamic can be seen in the rural context especially with the emergence of the tenant right question, which naturally did not affect city or larger town dwellers. A much greater acceptance of Catholics prevailed in rural areas that were not affected to any great degree by the spatial issues leading to sectarian clashes being fought out in the contested streets of Belfast in particular. A different type of Orange Order can be seen in rural areas, one whose members generally interacted with Catholics on a greater scale despite the ever-present suspicion that remained since 1641. Bigotry and sectarianism undoubtedly were ever present, fuelled in no small way by evangelical zeal, but to many Orangemen local issues whether involving death, burial, camaraderie and friendship often overrode the ongoing national religious or even political campaigns of the day. Away from the bigger issues such as repeal and rebellion, Orangeism remained very much localized in it make up, which was most likely the reason that it had survived post-1836 in the first place.

Thus, it could be said that the Orange Order mirrored Protestant society in that it was by no means a fluid entity. Conflict between the Established Church and the mainstream Presbyterian Church can also be traced through the Order, which allowed occasion for frequent disharmony. The tenant right campaign, in particular, was an important issue especially to Presbyterians and the coming on board of Orangemen seems to indicate that some at least were willing to go against the instruction of their Orange leadership when it came to matters of personal importance. Although most Orangemen did eventually succumb to the age-old 'Popish plot' rhetoric of their leaders, the fact that an alliance with Catholics was considered at all would indicate that this was a time of confusion for many members and that national issues were not as clear cut as they may previously had been. Upper-class instruction that had manifested and solidified itself through the Order had been part of the cement that held Protestant society together following the ending of the European wars in 1815 as landlords strove to re-establish the traditional ties of deference that had been somewhat eroded in the previous century. The abandonment of the Order by most of this class in 1836 denied grass-root membership the leadership it had been used to and could well have been the catalyst for the loosening of the ties that had been rather tenuously re-established. In the urban context of Dublin for example, this vacuum paved the way for the extremism of Tresham Gregg. Had the majority of the upper classes returned to the Order sooner, or indeed not abandoned it to begin with, then perhaps this confusion could have been avoided. But the return of the better classes to the fold was a sluggish process, a process that was not helped by factional dispute and by the government public censure of the likes of magistrate James Watson. Running the risk of government sanction was a step too far for some of this class and it was not until 1848 and the run up to rebellion that many felt it 'safe' to join and remind the core membership where its loyalty should lie. Calls for re-organization from the elites were eventually heeded and the traditional leadership role of the better classes was re-established. The imminent rebellion was a period that re-focussed the Protestant mind and saw a general re-awakening of the notion that Orangeism served as the best defence against any attack on the Crown whether from Republicans or Catholics. Although not as smooth as previously had been the case, the relationship of deference between the Protestant classes held firm despite occasional bouts of inter-church conflict.

The immediate period that followed the failed rebellion saw a reluctant government approval, marking the highest point of official Orange Order acceptance since the early part of the century. It was not to last. The clash at Dolly's Brae was a hollow victory for the Orangemen; in the cold light of day it could be considered a disaster. With Catholics in general somewhat cowed with the fading of repeal agitation following the rebellion and still suffering in any case from the worst ravages of the Famine, and the Order basking in the glory of its expressions of loyalty to the government, Orangeism was in a position it had not enjoyed for over thirty years in that it could again claim the moral high ground. The outcry that followed Dolly's Brae put an abrupt end to this second honeymoon. The lack of elite protest was no great surprise given their previous reactions to government disapproval; what was a surprise was the fact that some lodges and their lower-class members outwardly displayed their frustration at the government and burnt their warrants in protest. For the majority that remained, the next thirty years would see a change in the dynamic of leadership as William Johnson emerged from the unlikely position of mere moderate social standing to become the champion of Orangeism. However, not until the Home Rule crisis on the eve of the First World War would the leadership previously applied by the elite classes return to the Orange Order.

The 1840s revival of the Orange Order was short lived. Its renewal did not come about in isolation, it was the result of a number of factors and events all of which could justifiably have been considered a threat to Protestantism, or which possibly could have even caused the destruction of Protestantism in Ireland as a whole. Within a mere four years of reconstitution its peak popularity had been reached, albeit still not to its 1835 strength, but nonetheless to a position of extreme strength. This renewal had proved successful and the association moved from being little more than a rump organization for the lower classes during its lowest ebb to one frequented and accepted by the elites once more – a considerable achievement given the trauma of this period. Guarded government appreciation had been regained, restrictive legislation eased, the worst ravages of famine and disease overcome, initial internal dispute solved, and the threat of rebellion had been staved off. Never again would the Order be banned or forced to disband by the government. Yet from this position of apparent strength the Order imploded. It was not to be the critical social and political issues of the late 1840s that stalled the revival of the Orange Order – it was to be, perversely, the 'victory' at Dolly's Brae.

Bibliography

MANUSCRIPT SOURCES

National Archives of Ireland

Chief Secretary's Office Registered Papers, Outrage Reports: County Tyrone, County Londonderry, County Down, County Antrim, County Armagh, County Fermanagh

National Library of Ireland

The Farnham papers, letters from Marcus Beresford to the earl of Farnham, MS 18,608

Public Record Office of Northern Ireland

Account book of Glenawly Orange Lodge, County Fermanagh, D1433/1

Copy of letter from E. Lucas, Dublin Castle, D714/7/3

County of Tyrone grand warrant for Lent assizes 1836 (Omagh, 1836), p. 228, TYR 4/1/48

Dublin minute books, October 1846, MIC 201/2

Files of reports relating to Orange processions, MIC 371/4

Letter book for Earl Annesley's affairs, D1854/6/3

Letters to Beresford about Twelfth of July Orange processions, D32279/C/31/1

Minute book of Hardcourt Orange Lodge, Dublin and Grand Lodge of Ireland, 1844–9, MIC 201/1

Minute book of the County Fermanagh Loyal Grand Orange Lodge, D1402/1/1

Poor Law minute books, BG/4/A/2

Poor Law minute books, BG/A/5

Printed volumes containing reports of the Grand Lodge of Ireland, D2966/16/1

Rt Hon. George R. Dawson at Dublin to Sir William Fremantle, T2603/19

Grand Orange Lodge of Ireland

Half-yearly proceedings of the Grand Lodge of Ireland, 1846–50

Half-yearly proceedings of the Grand Lodge of Ulster, 1847

Proceedings of the Grand Lodge of Antrim, 25 October 1848

Proceedings of the Grand Lodge of Ireland, 15–16 May 1849

Edward Rogers, *Memorials of Orangeism*, i, ii, iii, box 49, shelf E

Hansard Parliamentary debates

HC debate, 4 July 1837, vol. 38, cc 1790–7

HC debate, 1 May 1838, vol. 42, cc 755–95

HC debate, 11 March 1839, vol. 46, cc 308–21
HC debate, 29 January 1840, vol. 51, cc 737–835
HC debate, 9 August 1843, vol. 71, cc 426–70
HC debate, 1 July 1844, vol. 76, cc 136–7
HL debate, 16 July 1844, vol. 76, cc 876–8
HL debate, 18 July 1845, vol. 82, cc 651–6
HC debate, 17 April 1846, vol. 85, cc 703–86
HC debate, 19 February 1847, vol. 90, cc 251–93
HC debate, 10 April 1848, vol. 98, cc 73–125
HC debate, 26 July 1849, vol. 107, cc 1004–16
HL debate, 28 February 1850, vol. 109, cc 126–33

PRINTED PRIMARY SOURCES

Day, Angelique, and Patrick McWilliams (eds), *Ordnance Survey memoirs, parishes of County Down I, 1834–6, south Down* (Belfast, 1990).

Day, Angelique, and Patrick McWilliams (eds), *Ordnance Survey memoirs, parishes of Fermanagh I, Enniskillen and Upper Lough Erne* (Belfast, 1990),

Day, Angelique, and Patrick McWilliams (eds), *OSM, parishes of Fermanagh II, Lower Lough Erne* (Belfast, 1992).

Killen, John (ed.), 'Famine in Ulster', *The Famine decade, contemporary accounts 1841–51* (Belfast, 1995), pp 60–1.

Lewis, Samuel, *A topographical dictionary of Ireland* (Dublin, 1837).

Parliamentary papers

Minutes of evidence taken before the select committee of the House of Lords, appointed to inquire into the state of Ireland, more particularly with reference to the circumstances which may have led to disturbances in that part of the United Kingdom, 24 March–22 June 1825, HL 1825 (521).

[First] report from the select committee appointed to inquire into the nature, character, extent and tendency of Orange lodges, associations or societies in Ireland, HC 1835 (377), xv.

[Second] report from the select committee appointed to inquire into the nature, character, extent and tendency of Orange lodges, associations or societies in Ireland, HC 1835 (475) (476), xv, xvi.

[Third] report from the select committee appointed to inquire into the nature, character, extent and tendency of Orange lodges, associations or societies in Ireland, HC 1835.

Orange lodges. Copies of addresses to the king from Orange lodges in Ireland; with the answers returned thereto, HC 1835 (30), xlv.453.

Orange Societies. Addresses from the Brotherhood Club, and Orange Stradbally Lodge; with the answers thereto, HC 1835 (84), xlv.449.

Royal commission of state of religious and other public instruction in Ireland. First report, appendix, second report, HC 1835 (45) (46) (47) xxxiii.1, 829, xxxiv.1.

Third report from the select committee on fictitious votes, Ireland; with the minutes of evidence, appendix and index, HC 1837–8 (643), xiii.ii.1.

Report from the select committee of the House of Lords, appointed to enquire into the state of Ireland in respect of crime, and to report thereupon to the House; with the minutes of evidence taken before the committee, and an appendix and index. Part 1. Report, and evidence 22 April to 16 May 1839, HL 1839 (486), xi.1, xii.1.

Hand-loom weavers. Return to an address of the Honourable the House of Commons, dated 15 February 1839: – for, copies of certain reports of the assistant hand-loom weavers' commissioners, HC 1840 (43–11), xxiii.367.

Report of Her Majesty's commissioners of enquiry into the state of law and practice in respect to the occupation of law in Ireland, HC 1845 (606), xix.

Papers relating to an investigation held at Castlewellan into the occurrences at Dolly's Brae, on the 12th July, 1849, HC 1850 (1143) LI331.

Report of the commissioners of inquiry into the origin and character of the riots in Belfast, in July and September 1857, HC 1857–8 (2309) xxvi.1.

Contemporary newspapers

Anglo-Celt
Armagh Guardian
Banner of Ulster
Belfast Commercial Chronicle
Belfast Newsletter
Belfast Protestant Journal
Coleraine Chronicle
Constitution and Church Sentinel
Cork Constitution
Cork Examiner
Downpatrick Recorder
Dublin Evening Mail
Dublin Evening Packet
Dublin Journal
Dundalk Democrat
Drogheda Conservative Journal
Enniskillen Chronicle and Erne Packet
Freeman's Journal
Kilkenny Independent
Londonderry Journal
Londonderry Sentinel
Londonderry Standard
Nenagh Guardian
Newry Examiner and Louth Advertiser
Northern Standard
Northern Whig
Sligo Champion
The Nation
The Protestant Watchman
The Statesman
The Spectator
The Vindicator
The Warder
Tyrone Constitution
United Irishman
Wexford Conservative

Contemporary pamphlets

The charge of the Hon. William Fletcher to the grand jury of the county of Wexford at the summer assizes in 1814 (Dublin, 1814).

The Anti-Jacobin Review, and True Churchman's Magazine, Jan.–June 1815, vol. xlviii (London, 1815).

Some observations upon the present state of Ireland (London, 1837).

Dublin University Magazine, vol. ix, January–June (Dublin, 1837).

Refusal of the Orangemen of Dublin to fraternise with Repealers, or to join in the present revolutionary movement (Dublin, 1848).

Repeal or revolution; or, A glimpse of the Irish future: in a letter to the Right Honourable Lord John Russell (Dublin, 1848).

Report of the special committee of the Grand Lodge of Ireland appointed November, 1849 (Dublin, 1849).

Trade directories

Pigot's Directory of Ireland (Dublin, 1824).

Biography directories

Farrell, Stephen, 'Mervyn Archdall', https://www. historyofparliamentonline.org [accessed 5 September 2019].

Hourican, Bridget, 'Robert Jocelyn', *Dictionary of Irish biography*, https://dib-cambridge-org.elib.tcd.ie [accessed 5 September 2019].

Hourican, Bridget, 'George William Frederick Villiers', *Dictionary of Irish biography*, https://dib-cambridgeorg.elib.tcd.ie [accessed 14 November 2019].

Jupp, Peter, 'The history of parliament', https://www.historyof parliamentonline. org/ volume/1820–1832/constituencies/co-fermanagh [accessed 9 September 2019].

SECONDARY SOURCES

Bardon, Jonathan, *A history of Ulster* (Belfast, 1992).

Bartlett, Thomas, *Ireland: a history* (Cambridge, 2010).

Begley, Anthony, and Sionbhe Lally, 'The Famine in County Donegal' in Christine Kinealy and Trevor Parkhill (eds), *The Famine in Ulster, the regional impact* (Belfast, 1995), pp 77–98.

Bew, Paul, and Frank Wright, 'The agrarian opposition in Ulster politics, 1848–87' in Clark and Donnelly Jr (eds), *Irish peasants*, pp 192–229.

Blackstock, Allan, *An ascendancy army* (Dublin, 1998).

Blackstock, Allan, *Loyalism in Ireland, 1789–1829* (Woodbridge, 2007).

Blackstock, Allan, 'Tommy Downshire's Boys: popular protest, social change and political manipulation in mid-Ulster, 1829–47', *Past and Present*, 196 (August, 2007), pp 125–72.

Blackstock, Allan, and Frank O'Gorman (eds), *Loyalism and the formation of the British world, 1775–1914* (Belfast, 2014).

Blackstock, Allan, 'The trajectories of loyalty and loyalism in Ireland, 1783–1849' in Blackstock and O'Gorman (eds), *Loyalism and the formation of the British world*, pp 103–24.

Bowen, Desmond, *The Protestant crusade in Ireland, 1800–1870* (Dublin, 1978).

Bryan, Dominic, *Orange parades, the politics of ritual, tradition and control* (Belfast, 2000).

Cahill, Gilbert, 'The Protestant Association and the anti-Maynooth agitation of 1845', *The Catholic Historical Review*, 43:3 (October, 1957), pp 273–308.

Cahill, Gilbert, 'Some nineteenth-century roots of the Ulster problem, 1829–48', *Irish University Review*, 1 (1970–1), pp 215–37.

Clark, Peter, *British clubs and societies, 1580–1800* (Oxford, 2000).

Clark, Samuel, and James S. Donnelly Jr (eds), *Irish peasants, violence and political unrest, 1780–1914* (Dublin, 1983).

Cottrell, Michael, 'Green and Orange in mid-nineteenth-century Toronto: the Guy Fawkes' Day episode of 1864', *Canadian Journal of Irish Studies*, 19:1 (July, 1993), pp 12–21.

Cousins, Mel, 'Philanthropy and poor relief before the Poor Law, 1801–30' in Laurence M. Geary and Oonagh Walsh (eds), *Philanthropy in nineteenth-century Ireland* (Dublin, 2015), pp 23–37.

Cunningham, John, 'The Famine in County Fermanagh' in Kinealy and Parkhill (eds) *The Famine in Ulster*, pp 129–45.

Curran, Daragh, '"The path in front of their barrack was literally covered with a pile of stones" – the attack on Bradbury police station 11 July 1850', https://www.academia.edu/7476869/_The_path_in_front_of_their_barrack_was_literally_covered_with_a_pile_of_stones_-_The_attack_on_Bradbury_Place_police_station_11_July_1850.

d'Alton, Ian, *Protestant society and politics in Cork, 1812–1844* (Cork, 1980).

d'Alton, Ian, 'From Bandon to … Bandon: sectarian violence in Cork during the nineteenth century' in Kyle Hughes and Donald MacRaild (eds), *Crime, violence, and the Irish in the nineteenth century* (Liverpool, 2017), pp 175–92.

Davis, Richard, *The Young Ireland movement* (Dublin, 1987).

Dewar, M.W., M. Brown and S.E. Long, *Orangeism, a new historical appreciation* (Belfast, 1967).

Donnelly, Jr, James S., 'Pastorini and Captain Rock: millenarianism and sectarianism in the Rockite movement of 1821–24' in Clark and Donnelly, Jr (eds), *Irish peasants*, pp 102–39.

Donnelly Jr, James S., 'A famine in Irish politics' in W.E. Vaughan (ed.), *A new history of Ireland;* v, *Ireland under the Union, 1801–70* (Oxford, 1989), pp 357–71.

Farrell, Sean, *Rituals and riots: sectarian violence and political culture in Ulster, 1784–1886* (Lexington, KY, 2000).

Farrell, Sean, 'Providence, progress and silence: writing the Irish Famine in mid-Victorian Belfast', *Canadian Journal of Irish Studies*, 36:2 (Fall/Autumn, 2010), pp 100–13.

Fitzpatrick, David, *Descendancy: Irish Protestant histories since 1795* (Dublin, 2013).

Gray, Peter, 'National humiliation and the Great Hunger: fast and famine in 1847', *Irish Historical Studies*, 22:126 (November, 2000), pp 193–216.

Guinnane, Timothy W., and Ronald I. Miller, 'Bonds without bondsmen: tenant-right in nineteenth-century Ireland', *Journal of Economic History*, 56:1 (March, 1996), pp 113–42.

Haddick-Flynn, Kevin, *Orangeism, the making of a tradition* (Dublin, 1999).

Hempton, David, and Myrtle Hill, *Evangelical Protestantism in Ulster society, 1740–1890* (London, 1992).

Hill, J.H., 'The Protestant response to repeal: the case of the Dublin working class' in F.S.L. Lyons and R.A.J. Hawkins (eds), *Ireland under the Union, essays in honour of T.W. Moody* (Oxford, 1980), pp 35–68.

Hill, J.H., 'The 1847 general election in Dublin city' in Allan Blackstock and Eoin Magennis (eds), *Political and popular culture in Britain and Ireland, 1750–1850, essays in tribute to Peter Jupp* (Belfast, 2007), pp 41–64.

Hill, J.H., 'National festivals, the state and "Protestant Ascendancy" in Ireland, 1790–1829', *Irish Historical Studies*, 24:93 (May, 1984), pp 30–51.

Hill, J.H., 'Carrying the war into the walks of commerce: exclusive dealing and the southern Protestant middle class during the Catholic emancipation campaign' in F. Lane (ed.), *Politics, society, and the middle class in modern Ireland* (Hampshire, 2010), pp 65–88.

Hill, J.H., 'Loyalty and the monarchy in Ireland' in Blackstock and O'Gorman (eds), *Loyalism and the formation of the British world, 1775–1914*, pp 81–102.

Hill, Myrtle, *The times of the end: millenarian beliefs in Ulster* (Belfast, 2001).

Hirst, Catherine, *Religion, politics, and violence in nineteenth-century Belfast: the Pound and Sandy Row* (Dublin, 2002).

Holmes, Andrew R., 'Millennialism and prophecy in Ulster Presbyterianism' in Crawford Gribben and Timothy C.F. Stunt (eds), *Prisoners of hope? Aspects of evangelical millennialism in Britain and Ireland, 1800–1880* (Milton Keynes, 2004), pp 150–76.

Holmes, Andrew R., *The shaping of Ulster Presbyterian belief and practice, 1770–1840* (Oxford, 2006).

Holmes, Andrew R., 'Covenanter politics: evangelicalism, political liberalism and Ulster Presbyterians', *English Historical Review*, 125:513 (2010), pp 340–69.

Hoppen, K.T., *Elections, politics and society in Ireland, 1832–1885* (Oxford, 1984).

Hoppen, K.T., *Ireland since 1800* (Harlow, 1989).

Jackson, Alvin, *Ireland, 1798–1998* (Oxford, 1999).

Johnston, Jack, *Orangeism in the Clogher Valley, 1795–1995* (Clogher, 1995).

Katsuta, Shunsuke, 'Conciliation, anti-Orange politics and the sectarian scare: Dublin politics of the early 1820s', *Dublin Historical Record*, 64:2 (Autumn, 2011), pp 142–59.

Kelly, James, '"Disappointing the boundless ambition of France": Irish Protestants and the fear of invasion, 1661–1815', *Studia Hibernica*, 37 (2011), pp 27–105.

Kennedy, Liam and Peter M. Solar, 'The rural economy 1780–1914' in Liam Kennedy and Phillip Ollerenshaw (eds), *Ulster since 1600, politics, economy, and society* (Oxford, 2013), pp 160–76.

Kenny, Kevin, *The American Irish, a history* (Harlow, 2000).

Kerr, Donal, 'Peel and the political involvement of the priests', *Archivium Hibernicum*, 36 (1981), pp 16–25.

Kinealy, Christine, and Trevor Parkhill (eds), *The Famine in Ulster, the regional impact* (Belfast, 1995).

Kinealy, Christine, *Hidden Famine: hunger, poverty and sectarianism in Belfast* (London, 2000).

Kinealy, Christine, *The Great Irish Famine: impact, ideology and rebellion* (New York, 2001).

Kinealy, Christine, *Repeal and revolution: 1848 in Ireland* (Manchester, 2009).

Kinealy, Christine, *Charity and the Great Hunger in Ireland: the kindness of strangers* (Manchester, 2013).

Kingon, Suzanne T., 'Ulster opposition to Catholic emancipation, 1828–29', *Irish Historical Studies*, 34:134 (2004), pp 137–56.

Kissane, Noel, *The Irish Famine, a documentary history* (Dublin, 1995).

Loughlin, James, 'Allegiance and illusion: Queen Victoria's Irish visit of 1849', *History*, 87:288 (2002), pp 491–513.

Lyons, F.S.L., *Ireland since the Famine* (London, 1971).

MacDonagh, Oliver, 'Ideas and institutions, 1830–45' in Vaughan (ed.), *A new history of Ireland*, v, pp 193–217.

MacRaild, Donald M., 'Wherever Orange is worn: Orangeism and Irish migration in the 19th and 20th centuries', *Canadian Journal of Irish Studies*, 28/29:1 (Fall, 2002–Spring, 2003), pp 98–117.

McAtamney, Neil, 'The Great Famine in County Fermanagh', *The Clogher Record*, 15:1 (1994), pp 76–89.

McAtasney, Gerard, and Christine Kinealy, 'The Great Hunger in Belfast' in Crowley, Murphy and Smyth (eds), *Atlas of the Great Irish Famine* (Cork, 2012), pp 434–9.

McCavery, Trevor, 'The Famine in County Down' in Kinealy and Parkhill (eds), *The Famine in Ulster*, pp 99–127.

McClelland, Aiken, 'Orangeism in County Monaghan', *Clogher Record*, 19:3 (1978), pp 384–404.

McCutcheon, W.A., 'Transport, 1820–1914' in Liam Kennedy and Phillip Ollerenshaw (eds), *An economic history of Ulster, 1820–1939* (Manchester, 1985), pp 109–36.

McMahon, Richard, 'The madness of party: sectarian homicide in Ireland, 1801–1850', *Crime, History and Societies*, 11:1 (2007), pp 83–112.

Malcomson, Paul, *The forgotten history of the Orange Order – the Institution's historic struggle against the Royal Arch Purple and Black degrees (1798–1925)* (Banbridge, ?)

Miller, David W., 'The Armagh troubles, 1784–95' in Clark and Donnelly Jr (eds), *Irish peasants*, pp 155–91.

Miller, David W., 'Irish Presbyterians and the Great Famine' in J.H. Hill and Colm Lennon (eds), *Luxury and austerity: Historical Studies,* 21 (Dublin, 1999), pp 165–81.

Miller, Kerby A., *Emigrants and exiles* (New York, 1985).

Miller, Kerby A., Bruce D. Boling and Liam Kennedy, 'The Famine scars: William Murphy's Ulster and American odyssey', *Eire-Ireland* (Spring–Summer, 2001), pp 98–123.

Morash, Chris, 'Boys be wicked', *Irish Review*, 29 (2002), pp 10–21.

Niven, Richard, *Orangeism as it was and is* (Belfast, 1899).

Norman, E.R., 'The Maynooth question of 1845', *Irish Historical Studies*, 15:60 (September, 1967), pp 407–37.

Ó Ciosáin, Niall, *Print and popular culture in Ireland, 1750–1850* (Hampshire, 1997).

Ó Gráda, Cormac, *Ireland before and after the Famine: explorations in economic history, 1800–1925* (Manchester, 1993).

Ó Luain, Kerron, '"Calculated to excite the minds of the public": south Ulster and the Young Ireland rebellion 1848' in *The Irish Story Online*, http://www.theirishstory.com/2018/06/21/calculated-to-excite-the-minds-of-the-public-south-ulster-and-the-young-ireland-rebellion–1848/#.XcnZwzP7TIU

Ó Muirí, Reamonn, 'Orangemen, Repealers and the shooting of John Boyle in Armagh, 12 July 1845', *Seanchas Ardmhaca*, 11:2 (1985), pp 435–529.

O'Neill, Thomas P., 'The land question, 1830–1850', *Studies: An Irish Quarterly Review*, 44:175 (Autumn, 1955), pp 325–36.

O'Neill, Thomas P., 'From Famine to near Famine, 1845–79', *Studia Hibernica*, 1 (1961), pp 161–71.

O'Tuathaigh, Gearoid, *Ireland before the Famine, 1798–1848* (Dublin, 1972).

Owens, Gary, '"A moral insurrection": Faction fighters, public demonstrations and the O'Connellite campaign, 1828', *Irish Historical Studies*, 30:20 (November, 1997), pp 513–41.

Gary Owens, 'Nationalism without words: symbolism and ritual behaviour in the repeal "monster meetings" of 1843–5' in J.S. Donnelly, Jr and Kerby A. Miller (eds), *Irish popular culture, 1650–1850* (Dublin, 1999), pp 242–69.

Parkhill, Trevor, 'The Famine in County Londonderry' in Kinealy and Parkhill (eds), *The Famine in Ulster*, pp 147–68.

Rafferty, Oliver P., *Catholicism in Ulster, 1603–1983* (Dublin, 1994).

Saville, John, *1848: the British state and the Chartist movement* (Cambridge, 1990).

Senior, Hereward, *Orangeism in Britain and Ireland* (London, 1966).

Smelser, Neil J., *Social paralysis and social change: British working-class education in the nineteenth century* (Oxford, 1991).

Smyth, Jim, 'The men of no popery: the origins of the Orange Order', *History Ireland*, 3 (Autumn, 1995), pp 48–53.

Solar, Peter M., and Luc Hens, 'Land under pressure: the value of Irish land in a period of rapid population growth, 1730–1844', *Agricultural History Review*, 61:1 (2013), pp 40–62.

Walker, Brian, 'Politics, elections and catastrophe: the general election of 1847', *Irish Political Studies*, 22:1 (2007), pp 1–34.

Whelan, Irene, *The Bible war in Ireland: the 'Second Reformation' and the polarization of Protestant–Catholic relations, 1800–1840* (Dublin, 2005).

Whyte, J.H., 'Daniel O'Connell and the Repeal Party', *Irish Historical Studies*, 11:44 (September, 1959), pp 297–316.

Wilson, James, 'Orangeism in 1798' in Thomas Bartlett, David Dickson, Dáire Keogh and Kevin Whelan (eds) *1798: a bicentenary perspective* (Dublin, 2003), pp 45–62.

Wright, Frank, *Two lands on one soil* (Dublin, 1996).

UNPUBLISHED THESIS

Mattison, Jonathan, '"From Dolly's Brae to Westminster", the loyal Orange Institution in Ireland, *c.*1849–1886' (PhD, Queen's University Belfast, 2005).

Index

Act of Union, 23, 155, 156
Antrim County Grand Lodge, 167
Antrim town, 161, 182–3
Antrim, County, 18, 77, 122, 140, 155
Archdall, Edward, 96, 99
Archdall, Mervyn Edward, 53, 60, 92, 193
Archdall, Mervyn, 92
Armagh city, 93, 183
Armagh County Grand Lodge, 94
Armagh, County, 18, 77, 122
Atthill, Edward, 101, 108, 109
Aughnacloy, Co. Tyrone, 34

Bailieborough, Co. Cavan, 188
Baker, H.R., 29, 70
Ballinahinch District Lodge, 186
Ballinahinch, Co. Down, 167
Ballintra, Co. Donegal, 80
Ballybay and Castleblayney District Lodge, 132
Ballybay, Co. Monaghan, 55, 123, 200
Ballyhaise, Co. Cavan, 108, 167
Ballymacarrett, Co. Down, 117, 190
Ballymena, Co. Antrim, 103, 166, 183
Ballymoney, Co. Antrim, 142
Ballyshannon, Co. Donegal, 140
Banbridge, Co. Down, 117, 139, 201
Bandon, Co. Cork, 69, 87
Bandon, earl of, 68–9
Barton, Hugh, 101, 111
Bateson, Sir Robert, 61, 82
Battle of Garvagh, 45
Battle of the Diamond, 20
Beers, Francis, 192
Beers, William, 111, 134, 191–2, 195, 197
Belfast Protestant Association, 179, 185–6
Belfast, 18, 32, 82, 83, 134, 139, 145, 149, 156, 162, 178, 183, 189, 199, 204
Bell, Revd Daniel, 176
Belmore, earl of, 119
Benburb, Co. Tyrone, 48, 188
Benevolent Orange Institution, 54
Beresford, J.C., 65–6
Beresford, Revd Marcus, 57, 63, 86
Betty, Stewart, 131–2
Blacker, Stewart, 28, 29, 47, 178
Blacker, William, 35, 39, 63, 75, 93, 111, 189
Blakely, Revd Fletcher, 117
Booth, R.B., 98–9
Boyton, Revd Charles, 58–9, 74
Brooke, Sir Arthur, 44, 58, 59, 99, 101, 104, 119, 143, 194
Brunswick Clubs, 54, 55, 59
Butt, Isaac, 176

Caldbeck, William Eaton, 111
Canada, 130–1
Carland, Co. Tyrone, 38, 83
Carlow, County, 22
Carnew, Co. Wexford, 190
Carrickfergus, Co. Antrim, 126, 162

Carrickmacross, Co. Monaghan, 123
Castledawson, Co. Londonderry, 40, 46
Castlewellan, Co. Down, 161, 165, 190, 192
Catholic emancipation, 29, 38, 46, 48, 53–6
Cavan, County, 18, 106, 187
Cavan town, 150
Central Conservative Society, 194
Chartist movement, 159, 181
Clarendon, Lord, 147–8, 161–2, 164, 165–6, 170, 176–7, 179, 192, 194, 197, 200
Clogher, Co. Tyrone, 188
Clones District Lodge, 132
Clones Orange Lodge, 30
Clones, Co. Monaghan, 83
Clough, Co. Antrim, 188
Coleraine Lodge no. 2, 199
Coleraine, Co. Londonderry, 39–40, 84, 91, 111, 145, 158, 173, 202
Collon, Co. Louth, 200
Comber, Co. Down, 117
Confederate Clubs, 156, 160, 170
Cooke, Revd Henry, 68, 123, 155, 201
Cookstown, Co. Tyrone, 123, 162
Cooper, E.J., 69
Cootehill, Co. Cavan, 79, 108, 115, 142, 187
Cork, County, 78, 88, 106, 197
Coulter, Phillip, 150–1
Courtenay Lodge Ballymena, 142
Cumberland, duke of, 26, 73

Dane, W.A., 102, 104, 110
Dartree Orange Lodge, 137
Davis, Thomas, 152, 154, 158, 176
Dawson, George, 193
Defenders, 19
Derry/Londonderry, County, 18, 77, 115
Devenish, Co. Fermanagh, 41
Devon Commission, 117, 121
Dillon, John Blake, 153, 157
Doheny, Michael, 157, 170, 171
Dolling, Robert M., 91, 152
Dolly's Brae, 13, 15, 190–2, 194, 197, 199, 200, 203, 206
Donegal, County, 18, 115
Down, County, 18, 77, 140, 155, 157
Downpatrick, Co. Down, 144, 158, 162, 165
Downshire, Lord, 36, 95
Downshire, marquis of, 126, 179
Drew, Revd Thomas, 181, 185, 186, 202
Dromore, Co. Down, 126
Duffy, Charles Gavan, 152, 154, 160, 170
Dungannon Convention, 20, 123, 156
Dungannon, Co. Tyrone, 67, 83, 123, 125, 126, 149
Dyan, Co. Tyrone, 20

Ecclesiastical Titles Act (1851), 128
Edwards, Hugh Gore, 34
Eldon Lodge Belfast, no. 7, 133
Ely, marquis of, 44, 59, 61, 91, 96
Emmet, Robert, 23
Encumbered Estates Act (1849), 122
Enniskillen, Co. Fermanagh, 41, 44, 59–61, 67, 101, 105, 111, 139, 198–9
Enniskillen, earl of, 44, 58, 63, 65, 97, 99, 101, 102, 106, 108, 111, 120, 152, 166, 173, 195, 200, 202
Erne, earl of, 96, 97, 99, 100, 120, 179

Falls, John, 83
Farnham, earl of, 57, 63, 65, 85, 91, 98–9, 100, 101, 106, 107, 108, 110, 162, 167
Fermanagh, County, 18, 97, 106
Fintona District Lodge, 196
Fintona, Co. Tyrone, 39
Fletcher, William, 27, 45
Fluery, Revd Charles M., 177

Garvagh, Co. Londonderry, 126, 127
Gilford, Co. Down, 157
Glenawly Orange Lodge, 30, 80
Graham, Sir James, 85, 89, 90
Gray, Sam, 25, 55
Gregg, Revd Tresham, 41, 70, 87, 91, 110–11, 145, 205
Gregory, W.H., 145
Grogan, Edward, 145
Gunn Browne, Revd Daniel, 117
Gwynne, William James, 183

Hanna, Revd Hugh, 202
Hayes, Edmund Samuel, 63
Hillsborough, Co. Down, 67, 68
Hodson, Revd Hartley, 135–6, 138, 139, 144, 168
Holmes, Arthur, 96–7

Inch Orange hall, 180
Irish Independent Party, 128–9
Irish Metropolitan Conservative Society, 74, 82
Irish Tenant League, 128–9

Jellet, John, 185
Johnston, Henry G., 85, 101, 135, 137
Johnston, William of Ballykilbeg, 195, 199, 202, 206

Kennedy, J.P., 165, 194
Keown, William, 180
Kesh, Co. Fermanagh, 41
Keynon, Fr John, 176, 192
Killeshandra, Co. Cavan, 98
Killyman, Co. Tyrone, 80–2
Kilrea, Co. Londonderry, 46, 126
Knox, Bishop Robert, 184–5

Lalor, James Fintan, 152
Larne District Lodge, 196
Lawless, John, 55, 149
Lees, Sir Harcourt, 54, 55
Leitrim, County, 77, 78
Lendrum, James, 99, 111
Limerick, County, 77
Lisburn, Co. Antrim, 30–1, 89, 91, 95, 139, 182, 187, 195, 201–2
Litton, Edward, 74
Londonderry, marquis of, 118–19
Longford, County, 77
Loughgall Orange Lodge no. 118, 196
Loughgall, Co. Armagh, 20, 80
Loyal Anti-Repeal Association, 149
Loyal Sentinel Orange Lodge no. 672, 199
Lurgan poorhouse, 115
Lurgan, Co. Armagh, 20, 123, 139, 189
Lurgan, Lord, 116
Luther Orange Lodge, Dublin, 152

Madden, William, 158
Maghery, Co. Armagh, 39, 82
Maginn, Bishop Dr Edward, 123, 176
Maguire, Fr Tom, 41
Malin, Co. Donegal, 40
Manchester, duke of, 64–5, 107
Markethill, Co. Armagh, 188

Martin, Thomas, 153, 154, 159–60
Massareene, Lord, 182–3, 185
Maynooth grant, 88–90, 144
Mayo, County, 78
McGavern, Fr Edward, 77–8
McKinley Orange Lodge no. 1539, 199
McKnight, James, 122–7, 129, 204
Meagher, Thomas Francis, 153, 156, 170
Miller, Revd T.F., 185, 201
Mitchel, John, 151, 154, 157, 158, 160, 163, 164, 170
Monaghan, County, 18, 106, 122, 167
Moneymore District Lodge, 164, 195, 196
Moneymore, Co. Londonderry, 161
Montgomery, Revd Henry, 128
Montreal, Canada, 130
Morrow, Revd Thomas Knox Magee, 185
Mountmellick, Queen's County, 70–1,
Moutray, Anketell, 164

Napier, Joseph, 105
Nevin, William, 132
Newbliss, Co. Monaghan, 192
Newry District Lodge, 136
Newry Orange hall, 178–9
Newtownards, Co. Down, 117, 118, 183
Newtownhamilton, Co. Armagh, 117, 167, 191
Northland, Lord, 83

O'Connell, Daniel, 12, 31, 48, 51, 53–6, 58, 59, 68, 72, 76, 83–4, 86, 87, 88, 114, 128, 148, 154, 156, 159
O'Connell, John, 179
O'Neill, Fr Bernard, 141
Oakboys, 19, 33, 34
Omagh District Lodge, 132
Omagh, Co. Tyrone, 166
Orange Orphan Society, 78

Party Emblems Act 1860, 202
Party Processions Act, 76, 85, 90, 92, 144, 191, 195, 199, 202
Peel, Sir Robert, 45, 67, 88–9, 90, 94, 114, 115, 122, 170, 204
Peep-o-Day Boys, 19, 20
Pettigo, Co. Donegal, 41–4
Phaire, R.W., 165, 194
Philadelphia, United States, 131,
Plunkett, Randall, 69, 75
Pomeroy District Lodge, 83–4
Pomeroy, Co. Tyrone, 161
Portadown Lodge no. 948, 196
Portadown, Co. Armagh, 20
Protestant Association, 86, 89
Protestant colonies, 63–7
Protestant Conservative Society, 58–62, 67, 74
Protestant Operative Association Belfast, 95
Protestant Operative Association Cork, 86
Protestant Operative Association Dublin, 86, 173
Protestant Repeal Association, 150–1

Queen Victoria, 73, 75, 185, 199–200
Queen's County, 77

Ranfurley, earl of, 119
Rathfriland Orange Lodge, 85
Rathfriland, Co. Down, 191, 201

Repeal Association, 83–4, 137, 150, 151, 154, 157, 175, 179
Repeal clubs, 149
Repeal of the Union, 114, 147–53
Reynolds, John, 145
Ribbon Society, 27, 41, 45, 47, 48–9, 57, 76, 78, 84, 98–9, 144, 161, 190, 201
Roden, earl of, 61, 76, 90, 95, 100, 120, 163, 173, 179, 190–3, 195, 197, 199–200
Rogue degrees, 47, 79
Rostrevor, Co. Down, 34
Royal Nassau Lodge, no. 670, 133
Russell, Lord John, 128, 162, 165

Saurin, William, 36–7, 51
Schomberg Lodge Belfast, no. 486, 133
Schomberg Lodge Dublin, 109, 152
Seymour, Sir Horace, 144
Sharman Crawford, William, 121–3, 127, 128, 154, 194, 204
Shiel, Richard, 37
Slievenamon, Co. Tipperary, 171
Sligo, County, 77
Smith O'Brien, William, 153, 154, 155, 156, 170, 171, 176, 177
Somerville bill (1848), 122, 123, 126
Steelboys, 19, 33, 34
Steele, Thomas, 92, 108, 149
Steen, Revd George, 141
Stewartstown District Lodge, 196
Stradbally Orange Lodge, 67
Stronge, Sir James, 120

Tanderagee District Lodge, 203
Tanderagee, Co. Armagh, 64–5
Tenant Right, 114, 120–9, 150, 157, 164, 186, 187, 204, 205
Tommy Downshire's, 34, 35, 38
Toronto, Canada, 130
Trinity College Lodge, 67
Turner, Major, 165–6
Tynan, Co. Armagh, 118
Tyrone, County, 18, 44

Ulster Custom, 121
Ulster Tenant Right Association, 121, 123, 125, 127, 150, 153
United Irishmen, 21, 22
United States, 131

Verner Lodge, no. 853, 133
Verner, Thomas, 22
Verner, William, 28, 46, 48–9, 53, 65, 73, 76, 85, 90, 91, 93, 95–6, 100, 107, 115, 116, 141, 179, 180, 194, 197, 200

Waring, Holt, 26, 52, 91
Watson, James, 91–6, 99, 111, 136, 205
Wexford, County, 22, 70, 77
Wicklow, County, 70
Wylie, Abraham, 198

Yates-Johnston, Samuel, 96, 100, 101, 109, 110, 111, 152
Yeomanry Corps, 21, 22, 23, 27, 45, 62, 89, 132, 162
Youghal, Co. Cork, 87
Young Ireland, 13, 15, 147, 153–60, 169, 171, 173–4, 175–7, 204